Strategies for
Instructional Management

Strategies for Instructional Management

LANORE A. NETZER   GLEN G. EYE

Department of Educational Administration
University of Wisconsin–Madison

DWIGHT M. STEVENS   WAYNE W. BENSON
Deputy State Superintendent   *Director of Secondary Education*
of Public Instruction   *Public Schools*
Madison, Wisconsin   *Neenah, Wisconsin*

ALLYN AND BACON, INC.   Boston • London • Sydney

Library of Congress Cataloging in Publication Data

Includes Bibliographies and index.
1. Classroom management. 2. Interaction analysis in education. 3. Teacher-student relationships. I. Netzer, Lanore A. II. Title.
LB3013.2.S75   371.1'02   78-24433
ISBN 0-205-06448-5

Printed in the United States of America.

Contents

Evaluation of Strategies
Strategies Make the Strategists
Strategized Reading

Foreword

Dr. Glen G. Eye and Dr. Lanore A. Netzer rank among the most productive and creative scholars in educational administration. During professorial careers that span more than four decades, they teamed to generate many significant volumes, influenced greatly the thinking of many students in their university classes, and left indelible impressions on many grateful graduate students who completed Masters' and Doctors' degrees under their guidance. This writer happens to be only one of hundreds who appreciates the products of their dedicated, creative minds. It is, therefore, an honor to prepare a foreword for yet another professional work that includes the names of Eye and Netzer.

It is difficult to talk or write about educational supervision, instructional leadership, and organizing resources to promote learning without encountering the names of Eye and Netzer. They are recognized as leading authorities in these dimensions of school administration. In this and other volumes they generated innovative approaches, described exciting new concepts, and promoted a humanistic philosophy that helped to provide fresh perspectives and new operational strategies in the management of instruction in complex institutions. Readers who have come to expect so much from past writings of this team will not be disappointed with this one. They continue to provide much that will stimulate thinking and action. One interesting difference is that two former students with impressive records as effective and practical administrators in the field, namely, Dr. Wayne W. Benson and Dr. Dwight M. Stevens, join Eye and Netzer in this new work on instructional management. The writing team of distinguished university professors and effective practitioners in the field enhances the balance of thought and perspective needed to come to grips with a demanding set of tasks that face educational administrators.

We now know that it was folly to expect that the great social problems of our times could be stopped at the schoolhouse door. Rather, educational institutions have become primary cultural instruments for the promotion of needed social change. The past two decades have made it clear that schools are expected to do more than simply transmit our cultural heritage. Although the missions of education have become more controversial, nonetheless, the stimulation of learning remains what it is all about. For it is through learning that schools transmit the cultural heritage, enhance the development of human resources, and/or help to resolve the social, political, or economic issues of our times. In other words, the increased expectations, vandalism, conflict, or even violence that may be a part of education should not be allowed to obscure the justifiably high priority that should be granted to the historic instructional leadership role of the administrator, supervisor, or manager.

Learning and instruction are two sides of the same coin, one emphasizing activities of students and the other describing functions of teachers. To repeat, it is with and through the learning and/or the instructional process that schools help to create attitudes essential to ameliorate social injustices, enhance harmonious race/ethnic relations, minimize poverty, increase employability, and in so many ways enable people to cope with or adjust to the rapid pace of technological development.

The writing team of Eye, Netzer, Stevens, and Benson, of course, was not the first to sense the importance of instructional leadership to education. What they accomplish in the chapters that follow is to give to this time honored responsibility a fresh perspective, innovative conceptual frameworks, and meaningful strategies. Instructional leadership may be only one of many factors competing for the time of administrators, but that is no reason for ignoring it or slighting it.

Learning is a social process as well as an individual pursuit. Furthermore, there are teachers, learning specialists, supervisors, and administrators in interaction in large and complex environments called schools and districts. Unifying the varied talents within the instructional process, so that they can take full advantage of the potential within material and fiscal resources available in schools, calls for a skillful and humanistic manager and an effective management system. Throughout this volume, the problem of leadership is viewed as the ability to identify the talents within individuals and groups in the system and to organize and relate to these talents so that they may multiply in effectiveness. The writing team focuses on the managerial system needed to enhance instructional effectiveness, but stresses the human side, or humanistic dimension, of school management. Increasingly in the field of education the term *management* is being accepted as a synonym for the long-used term *administrator*. This volume reflects this growing trend and management is used in its warmest and best sense. The humanistic side of school management is stressed as, to use the writers' terms, a "facilitator of desirable accomplishment rather than a thwarting influence over individual opportunity and ingenuity."

Eye, Netzer, Stevens, and Benson prefer to address the specific operational demands for instructional leadership, educational change, and accountability over the sweeping generalizations and rhetoric that leave one wondering what to do next. The writing style is crisp.

The sentences are relatively short. Theories, models, and matrices for viewing instructional leadership and management strategies are described in concise ways. I was intrigued by the sophisticated concepts, criteria, and arguments used to probe the critical questions encountered by those concerned with the improvement of the most basic of educational responsibilities, namely, that of learning. This volume is characteristic of others that include the name of Eye and Netzer, namely, a tremendous number of ideas and pragmatic strategies are packed into a volume of relatively modest size. It isn't often that one finds so much said so well on problems of such importance to educational institutions and their administrators.

Whether judged by its intriguing writing style, the new perspectives it gives to the challenges of instructional management in today's complex work, or the practical orientation attached to management strategies that translate instructional leadership tasks into operational behaviors, this new volume deserves to be on every supervisor's and school administrator's reading list with careful study by all professionals.

Stephen J. Knezevich, Dean
School of Education
University of Southern California

Preface

The word *management* over the decades has stimulated reactions of various types. Some people see in it the identification or image of a control system. Others see management as a means by which people can work together for common or separate purposes in the interest of achieving greater freedom. In short, management has served as either an idea to resist or a facilitator of rewarding action.

The human element in any management system must never be ignored. Perhaps the resistance to management in many enterprises has arisen because management became a technique of operation without considering the human beings manipulated or supported through its facilities. The drive in recent years to increase participation of all people involved in organized action has brought about the opportunity for the application of the unique expertise that each person can bring to a program of action. This recognition of the appropriateness of participation and the recognition that participation provides for the application of individual expertise has stimulated the concept of mutuality between all persons involved in group activities.

An open system of interpersonal relationships and organizational design can establish the human prerogatives that make management a facilitator of desirable accomplishment rather than a thwarting influence over individual opportunity and ingenuity. Talent must grow. Talent exists in every group. The job of leadership is to find talent and to find an opportunity for its application. Talent can be used on the many items requiring decision. The talent possessed by individuals in a group must be related to decision, policy, and the strategies of various types of individual and group activity. Talent becomes the substance of concern here as we talk about the management of instruction.

Applying talent to the selected targets in a group enterprise gives talent a chance to grow. If management is to maintain the human perspectives, work sharing must be accepted with respect. Work sharing is not a matter of disposing of one's undesirable and routine obligations in order to gain ego satisfaction in the more visible and spectacular types of operation. Delegation itself is a process by which talent can be brought into contact with those targets where its uniqueness can be helpful in achieving the goals set. Work sharing must include the concept of empowerment. That is, when a work assignment is made or self-assigned, the worker must be able to control the variables that are essential to accomplish the purpose of the assignment. In this sense, delegation is a leadership process in which all persons can find the opportunity to put their own unique specialities to work. Management, then, must synchronize the talent of the people in the operational group with the many small targets of accomplishment that meld into the major outcomes of the organization.

Coordination is a management of resources. Resources include the personnel involved in the organizational activities. Beyond personnel are the various facilities and other support elements as well as the environmental acceptance and stimulation that is required to establish coordination in a work-sharing activity. Coordination, then, means that the getting-ready-to-act requires a careful analysis of all resources and also of all barriers that might be encountered among both the human and the material resources. Analysis and inventory of resources and barriers plus plans constitute the getting ready for the accomplishment of coordination. As the analysis and inventory and planning are done, inventorying and planning have begun. An increasing dependence on self-management in all assignments of the organization should develop naturally.

Professional efforts and instructional outcomes constitute the major targets of the strategies of management in developing a strong instructional program with its chosen acceptable goals. This means that the concept of accountability becomes one of testing not whether a person should be continued in or dismissed from position but rather whether the professional effort has been appropriately supported and applied so that the outcomes selected for the total program are being achieved. Self-esteem is a part of the concept of self-management and thus also is a resource in the total operation. Self-analysis and evaluation become the surest way to maintain the self-esteem and to establish the accountability of the individual and group involved in the operation.

The chapters in this book present many aspects of the concerns expressed here. The examples of strategies following many sections in the book are intended to bring the general discussion into sharp focus so that action has an acceptable payoff both for those instituting the action and for the recipients of the action. Work attitudes become resources that must involve the strategies for action. The nonroutine orientation of the illustrative strategies must become a leadership target.

The writing and organizational style of a book should seek first to establish a communication facility and, second, to maintain an accepted pattern of composition. We have sought to achieve both, but the message is our dominant interest. For this reason, the first two chapters seek to humanize management concepts with the goals of *Management Acceptability* and the openness of *Impact and Response*.

The writing style uses frequent cross-referencing to various parts of the book in order to maintain continuity of strategy development and an interrelationship of human characteristics with management requisites.

Lanore A. Netzer
Glen G. Eye
Dwight M. Stevens
Wayne W. Benson

Strategies for
Instructional Management

Management Acceptability

The classical concept of education is that education results from the one-to-one relationship between the teacher and pupil. This kind of education does not occur very often in today's so-called practical, modern age. The truth is that the pupil probably does the best learning when engaged in individual effort. Undoubtedly, a teacher with a responsibility of tutoring one pupil conceivably could do better than a teacher who is responsible for twenty or thirty pupils. Schools, however, are primarily group enterprises. The school is not a place in which a person can choose to be an isolate. Not being isolated leads to the thought and conclusion that a group enterprise operates by certain rules, commitments, and understandings. Even though people sometimes may want to be alone, people generally like to be with other people. The people that a person usually wants to be with are of the person's own choice.

Most people like to work with others. The teacher works with the pupils, with other teachers, with service and management staff, and with parents and other laymen in the community. This does not mean that selfishness is necessarily eliminated simply because people like to be with other people. Selfishness primarily is self-centeredness. That is, each individual is inclined to seek the satisfaction of personal wishes above those sought for others. Other people might be enjoying the same kind of satisfactions, but each individual wants the other people's satisfaction to occur without any impingement on the personal one. People generally want to control other people. The controls that give freedom to the individual may not be seen as personal constraints. The people who are controlled, however, may react as though the constraints are offensive.

The self-perception of self-need affects the kinds of controls that one exercises over people in the immediate environment. The self-perception of self-needs, then, is highly related to the self-role in the management scene. This chapter will explore some aspects of management and will extract a rationale that can help all people to work in and with management with a high degree of acceptability of the need for management.

DIFFERING CONCEPTS OF MANAGEMENT

Concepts, in large part, are all-encompassing mental images. The images in the individual's mind often involve a highly complex array and relationship of variables of many types. The concept seems to be a simple way of reducing all the complexity in one's environment to something clear and acceptable. Concepts often are held over long periods of time and are seldom analyzed as such. Analyzing a concept requires making the image less simple so that the complexities of what is perceived and analyzed can be described and placed into an acceptably workable order.

Concepts, whether analyzed or not, often condition how the individual reacts to others, to situations, and to self. What is seen is often merely a reflection of the concept that reduces the complexity of the scene to the simple image held in one's mind. Thus, concepts of management often are an over-simplification of the purposes of management as being what is needed in order to accomplish the individual and group purposes that have been selected.

Management as organization. Organization in this sense could mean an ordering of the relationships of the individuals involved in an enterprise. Organization is a differentiation of task assignments and task acceptances. Organization is a way that people can gain their own freedom by accepting the rules of action by all people involved. Organization often is over-simplified as being a hierarchy or bureaucracy. Such things may occur in an organization, but organization itself is the orderliness that can come into the interrelationships between people and between people, tasks, and goals to be accomplished.

Management as control. This is probably the more common simplified concept of management. Management is the control that often is called constraints or restraints. Control is how the limits of action may be defined. Control often is the action required in keeping the effort related to the goal or goals.

Management as direction.   Direction in this sense is somewhat less constraining than the concept of management as control. Direction is pointing the way—either the way to a selected goal or the way to behave—so that the goal can be achieved. Direction often is seen as much more reinforcing than the control concept, which is seen as constraining.

Management as resource.   Management is a resource in the sense that it keeps all other people related to the individual so that constraints are not imposed by peers or by others. Management as a resource means providing the space and material that are required for the accomplishment of the individual task. Management as a resource can be advisory in nature. It can be analytical in type. Also, it can be the security that each individual seeks in pursuing individualized tasks in a group enterprise.

Management as satisfaction.   In this sense, it is highly related to management as a resource. Each individual wants to have a sense of membership and success as well as a recognition of achievement. Management can help individuals relate to each other in mutually reinforcing ways. Such reinforcement can improve the self-image and self-respect. The sense of satisfaction grows as the self-image improves. This is one of the great contributions of management.

Management as coordination.   Much coordination is required in any group enterprise. With differentiated tasks and individuals with differing concepts of personal needs-satisfaction, all people must learn how to operate in a parallel manner rather than at cross purposes. Operating in parallel does not mean that people are pursuing different and unrelated goals. They might be pursuing the same goal with differing intermediate objectives, but each objective when achieved constitues a unique contribution to the common goal. This is the essence of coordination.

Management as efficiency.   Efficiency is the assurance that each individual and each item of material is used to its best purpose, which is related to the overall goal of the institution or organization. Perhaps most important is that management can be seen as human interaction. When management is accepted, the interaction among human beings can be much more rewarding and self-satisfying. It also can be the basis for the best achievement of the organizational goals and purposes.

RELATIONSHIPS OF
CONCEPT TO ACCOUNTABILITY

The concept of management almost invariably involves some aspects of being answerable to somebody with respect to the tasks assigned or accepted. The term *accountability* has been used increasingly in recent years. It is not necessary here to examine the social pressures that have brought about increased concern for accountability. The concept of management, nonetheless, soon raises questions about accountability. These questions relate to accountable to whom, by whom, and for what.

Substantial variability occurs in the concepts of management as they relate to accountability. It usually is assumed that the hierarchy or bureaucracy is the straight line of accountability. In other words, the teacher is accountable to the principal, the principal to the superintendent, the superintendent to the board, and the board to the people. Probably the concept of accountability has been damaged materially by making it so closely related to a hierarchy of control. The accountability that many people experience may be self-imposed. Self-imposed accountability is perhaps the most effective because it is accepted much more readily.

The subject matter of accountability for the teacher involves the learning of the pupil, developing learning materials, and interpreting the purposes and processes of instruction to people who have had less opportunity to study them. The subject matter of accountability for the principal involves scheduling staff time, providing support material and equipment, and identifying resource assistance for staff members. The subject matter of the superintendent involves identifying and acquiring staff expertise, planning for budgetary distribution, and maintaining supportive environmental influences on the school. Accountabiltiy must be closely related to such role perceptions. The role perception suggested here is the one held by the individuals who make contributions of unique expertise to the instructional programs. Wanting to maintain a position and to earn opportunities by fulfilling the expectations of others in the organization and in the environment are important, but such narrow perceptions are not worthy of an accomplished professional educator. A better self-role perception is that of a personal satisfaction in being able to fulfill the expectations both of the organization and of the self.

The role perception that sees accountability and management as resources will be more apparent in people who have accepted the role that was assigned or was sought. The acceptance of being a teacher of a particular grade level or subject is most likely to represent the individual's choice of task arrays. In such a case, the acceptance of role makes the concepts of management and accountability much more favorable than for people who have a role that they tend to reject. In this case, the role is not accepted and any impact of management and accountability can be extremely distasteful.

The individual whose perception and acceptance of role is highly positive most likely will develop a high degree of self-confidence. The individual is confident that, whatever the role assignment, it will be performed in a way that will be pleasing from the standpoint of accountability regardless of how the accountability may have been imposed. Self-confidence is evidence of acceptance of the role of management and of accountability. Many individuals, the conflict seekers, however, have a peculiar perception of their roles as they relate to assigned or assumed tasks. It probably is true that some people develop a desire for a great deal of individualization, but perceive themselves as weak if they have the approval and agreement of others. For these people, satisfaction comes from their attempts to gain freedom from any assigned role, any management control, and any accountability plan. This, however, usually constitutes a rather small percentage of any people involved in a group action such as a school organization.

People were not drafted into school work; they sought the opportunity to do that kind of work. In this sense, most individuals are compliance satisfiers. That is, these individuals see achievement within their own accepted roles as being more probably and readily realized if there is a good management plan. People who find satisfaction by complying perhaps can differentiate between the behaviors of control concepts of management and resource concepts of management. Control is seen performing the individualized task so that the common goal can be achieved and so that an individual's action will not thwart the actions of other individuals working toward the same goal and in the same organization. Those with the dominant concept of management as a resource will see management as an opportunity to have materials provided that make accountability almost inevitably positive. In this sense, management is accountable because the teachers in the organization have been supported well in the activities of instructing youth. Individuals who are not conflict seekers will redefine the essence of coordination and mutual support within the staff and will be able to adapt the concepts of management that they brought to the organization. They also will be able to make adaptions that will make accountability a process that is rewarding in the sense of an awareness of self-achievement.

POWERS OF MANAGEMENT (NOT MANAGERS)

The ideas and concepts of power often are related to the people who hold a post of control and the privilege of invoking sanctions, rather than seeing power as a result of the process of management itself. Basically, power is the potent force in management that stimulates people in an organization to exercise their unique skills and insights in achieving chosen organizational goals. The powers of management can be identified in certain ways as something achieved even by a group rather than by an individual or a group of individuals who possess the title and position usually associated with the exercise of power.

One power that comes from the effects of management is *freedom from disruption*. People often see management as an interrupter because it imposes the will of others on the will of self. This is not one of the more rewarding ways of perceiving the results of management as a power source. Most people who have experienced a high degree of disruption at the hands of others seek controls over those others that will give individuals the freedom to go about their own tasks without interference and disruption. Management has the power of accomplishing this. As mentioned earlier, the concept of management might be that of a resource. The availability of needed time, space, and material certainly is a resource that can result from management acts. In this sense, a power of management is to provide to the individual worker the things needed in order to have the sense and the evidence of achievement of declared goals.

Another power of management is that of *establishing norms*. In this sense, management attempts to define the limits of controls that would be imposed on any individual. At the same time it is important that the limits of freedom can be established in the form of agreements between those who work in the same organization or those who manage within that organization. Defining the limits of freedom and of constraints is an accomplishment of a norm that hopefully all have participated in establishing and that provides the guidelines by which work can progress with great efficiency.

Orderliness for the individual is not limited to the controls over one's self and one's immediate working situation. Orderliness results from the use of management power to hold all situational variables in a relationship that is supportive to the working situation. The control variables inferred are those such as the control of noise, disruptions, humidity, or heat and cold, as well as the people in the environment, many of whom have special interest with respect to the school activities. One power of management can be that of neutralizing the disrupting effects that come from the environment. One way to control the environment is to see that proper interpretations are made to all people in an environment so that disruption is seen as wasteful for all concerned and that reinforcement is seen as a way of getting more for the effort and money spent in the educational enterprise. Management can bring about a balance of effort on the part of the related and unrelated individuals in the school and in the community. Differentiating tasks within the school staff itself can be disruptive if the tasks have been selected or assigned without a common view of the goal. Specialization in almost every human endeavor is a characteristic of efficiency. Management can bring about the relationship of varied individual expertise so that each individual effort is made easier and more effective as well as more satisfying.

One of the greatest powers of management is the *guarantee of security* to the individuals involved in the organizational activity. A current popular notion is that there is no room for failure in any aspect of the school operation. Teachers are confronted with this notion when what they teach does not measure up to the visions held by some who are not directly responsible for the teaching-learning achievement. Management can offer the power of security by seeing that unreasonable demands are not placed on teachers. When experimental work is advisable as a means of resolving some problems, management should give assurance that an analyzed failure is not the signal for the dismissal or destruction of a teacher or teaching group. Security, then, can be guaranteed by management with and through the control of many variables and many environmental influences that continuously play on the classroom situation.

Management has power of stimulation, along with the power of *sanction,* through the use of commendation. The art of commendation has been lost in great part. Many people think that commendation will induce relaxation and weakness. People who have been commended, however, probably would testify that it is stimulating; it sends one back to work with more vigor and with more sense of accomplishment and security. Management has a power of commendation that can perform miracles in the teaching life of many professionals.

Management has the power of rewards, which often are accounted for only in terms of dollars. The so-called merit increase has been one item identified as being a reward for recognized efficiency. The merit system has certain faults in that the system used for determining the merit award has not always been sound and acceptable. Another kind of reward that can represent the power of management is giving the individual the opportunity to do some experimental work, to extend into specialized areas, and sometimes to shift into a different type of responsibility within the school organization and activity.

One of the greatest powers of *management is* providing continuity. Continuity is treasured by the individual who seeks to work with the minimum of disruption and without a continuous threat of being separated from the opportunity to work in the organization. Continuity in this sense is closely related to the opportunities of extension that were alluded to above on powers of rewards. Continuity is not only directed toward the future but it is also one way of describing the extension of the kind of work that one wants to do and to feel that progress in both the manner and outcome will be realized.

POWERS OF ACCEPTANCE

Just as management has powers that can be considered reinforcing or thwarting, so the individual has certain powers over the activities of the instructional assignment by accepting the management activities. An acceptance that orderliness grows out of the concepts and activities of management evolves into the belief that goal security becomes one positive benefit of acceptance. Some characteristics and benefits of acceptance will be discussed here.

Goal security is the assurance that an individual will not be evaluated in terms of one goal one day and another goal another day. This vacillation often has been defined as shifting criteria and can be used as a way of imposing a specialized-interest will on an individual or a group in the school by changing the purpose of the school activities that had been formerly accepted. At times of crisis in society, the goals of the school often do shift and sometimes not with the knowledge and assistance of the educators working in the schools. In an economic crisis, the demands will be made that the schools teach better how the economic life of the people can be made secure and desirable. In times of unemployment, specialized interest can say that the goal of school is to prepare people to hold jobs. As is being experienced now, the high level of automation has changed markedly the kind of expectations that have been placed on the school. Now, people have begun to rediscover that a basic skill expectation was placed on the school and that it has been pushed into the background and subdued by other specialized demands imposed on the school. Thus, teachers have not had the security of goals that they are entitled to have.

Another power of acceptance is an *expansion from the minimum of expectations placed on the school* thus resulting in much personal satisfaction for the individual professional. The minimum, of course, is one way that controlling agents such as legislators, city councils, and boards of education have of imposing their will on the school activities. They hope to insure at least that they are getting their money's worth. Accepting a goal seldom leaves the individual teacher satisfied with the minimum as defined by law or regulation.

Acceptance of management provides the *power to the individual to explore alternative ways of doing things.* Undoubtedly, too often the accountability thrust has been in terms of evaluating the processes rather than evaluating the outcomes. Individual teachers should be free to explore alternative ways of accomplishing the teaching and learning expectations. Without the acceptance of management, the freedom to explore alternatives is seldom experienced. Another result of acceptance and, therefore, a social power is the objectivity regarding failures when certain alternatives have been explored. Objectivity in relation to how to achieve selected goals would put the emphasis not on the processes or the alternative ways of doing things but on the accomplishment of the goals established.

Acceptance of management provides the power that comes from *sharing successes.* People like to interact with their peers and with all interested people who express concerns about the educational process and purpose.

Acceptance of management *provides the individual with the opportunity to project or extend the horizons.* In other words, people may dream of better ways of doing things and of better things to do. Acceptance of management provides some of the power that makes this possible. Another result of the acceptance of management is the *power of respect for self and from others.* People want to respect themselves and their ability to do things, but they also want the respect of others who recognize that they can do and have done worthwhile things.

The acceptance of management provides the *power of managing the pressure* that can grow within the self and that can come from associates in the organization or from people in the community environment. Acceptance of management also provides the power of the sense of belonging. The sense of belonging is an invigorating experience; it provides the opportunity to share and also to secure many resources that can come from the school associates and environment.

RESOURCES OF COMPROMISE

The powers of management and the powers of acceptance of management benefit from the capacity of people to compromise. Compromise is a mutually evolved plan or agreement that minimizes the probabilities of disruptions and conflicts. Acceptance of the need for management and agreements on the procedures by which management takes place made it possible for people to modify their own concepts and perceptions in order to arrive at a mutually agreed on point.

Some popular notions about compromise or the meaning of compromise are obvious distortions. Many people feel that compromise is a sign of weakness in determining the individual postures involved in the compromise. Others feel that yielding a point held is a sign that the point must have been wrong in the first place, else it would not have come into conflict and become the object of compromise.

These are distortions of the true meaning of compromise. More accurately, compromise is an indication of strength on the part of each person involved. It is a sign of strength because people are able to see the mutually determined goals as being a better posture than holding blindly and stubbornly to one's long-held goals. The potentiality of strength in compromise comes from the fact that people are bold enough to be able to expose their own points of view and to seek modifications that accommodate more than one point of view. Hence, the sifting and winnowing of the compromise process results in an agreement that emerges from the process.

The potentiality of weakness in compromise occurs because people might get in the habit of not holding to their own points of view until those points of view have been subjected to analysis and judgment. The basic purpose of compromise is to move group action along in a positive way. Compromise should reduce conflict between the opposing or cooperating parties. The purpose of compromise is to strengthen the total action of an organization through the refinement of the individual points of view into a combination of those within the organization. One resource of compromise is that analysis of issues and points of view is essential to the act of compromise. Analysis often will not reveal the weaknesses that characterize a point of view or a way of doing, but it may reveal the strengths of such points of view or ways of doing.

Analysis invariably leads to the identification of alternatives. The identification of alternatives leads to an analysis of each different way of going about the action and is likely to result in a selection of the strongest possibility. Once the alternatives have been identified, analyzed, and judged, the resources of compromise come into play in the planning procedures. People need to plan with some thoughts about the contributions that each individual can make to the total action. Planning is a resource in the sense that it identifies the expertise of different members of a staff and finds ways of coordinating the areas of expertise. Once the planning procedures have been accomplished, a pilot project is an appropriate way to test out the alternative rather than putting the plan into total operation without having some idea as to its effect and outcomes.

The pilot application assumes that there will be continuing assessment. One basic requisite of successful compromise is to set the time limit for making a review and a judgment on whether the alternative has been effective. In this way, those who use a point of view or modify a point of view know that eventually there will be an opportunity to review the action based on the compromise and to return to original points of views or alternatives if it seems advisable. Such "sunset" agreements, as they are now called, give every person the assurance that can be regained through the process of continuing assessment and objective judgment.

STRATEGIES OF COMPROMISE

The preceding section presented a number of approaches to compromise that were called *resources for action.* It now is important to give more specific thought to the strategies by which compromise can be brought about successfully.

Strategies are ways of doing things. They need to be selected carefully in order to lead to a successful choice of alternatives in resolving differing points of view. It should be recognized at the outset that there are different ways of doing things, which means that there can be differing points of view about strategies. The successful choice of strategy may require a compromise in choosing the ways of doing. Thus, the strategy of a compromise involves the very thing for which the strategies are designed.

One early action in strategy development should be identifying all people involved in the action. Some people may feel that they have performed successfully and, if this is true, there need be no change. On the other hand, if one looks at rigidities objectively and in terms of the alternatives, there may be an opportunity to merge the past actions into some future action. The future may appear as a state of uncertainty. Before a pilot test has been run, the best plan can be envisioned as problematic. Many past rigidities and future uncertainties can be made easier to solve by careful problem definition. That is, the nature of the differing points of views of conflicts should be looked at frankly and described in writing. All people should try their own hand at problem definition and seek compromise on the best definition that can be developed. In the process of this approach to strategy for initiating compromise, there also is the need to list the agreements that all involved parties can identify. This is just as important as listing the differences. A list of agreements provides an opportunity to talk to the issue rather than to talk against each other.

The list of agreements and the list of differences make it possible to set about differentiating between facts and assumptions. Many people have lived with their own assumptions so long that the assumptions are accepted as facts or principles. A strategy of compromise seeks to differentiate between fact and assumption. As facts and assumptions are identified, the strategy then leads directly to active speculations—speculating about the position held by others and speculating about what the outcomes would be if that position were adopted by all involved. There also is the need to speculate about one's own position and to differentiate between fact and assumption.

Then, there can be some self-analysis about the positions held that conflict with the position of someone else.

A third-party evaluation often can facilitate the compromise. A good strategy is to call in someone who will be new to the thinking of the particular task at hand. The third party can look at the lists of differences and agreements. A third party also can look at the analyses of facts and assumptions and can offer an informed opinion about which is the better position or what kind of adaptations can be made. In each strategy of compromise is the possibility of adapting when the position of another seems best or of adapting when two positions are in different status and modifications can be made in each. There also is the possibility of creating a new way of doing that abandons each position that has come into conflict.

An important part of strategy, as indicated in the previous section, is that of the *time-trial agreements*. When a compromise has been achieved at this point in the management process, it is well to set a date for review and to make judgments. The compromise can be continued or it can be modified and again set into some time-trial agreement.

The criteria for judging whether the outcome of compromising is good should be declared when the time is set for a review. It is not enough to wait until that time comes and then to establish the criteria. The setting of criteria is part of the strategy of establishing the compromise itself. These criteria then will be a part of the compromise and will be more useful in the final judgment. Further discussion on compromise can be found in chapter 4.

INITIATORS OF STRATEGY

The kinds of benefits that can come from compromise have been discussed at length. The previous section emphasized the development of strategy by which compromise could be initiated, directed, and completed. Much depends on a mutual understanding by the involved parties. The capacity is needed to analyze one's self and to analyze issues that have come into conflict as a result of different points of view held by different persons. At least, the first mutual understanding should be the common desire to eliminate the conflict. The desire for mutual understanding can find common ground in the desire to resolve the conflict.

Objectively viewing facts, as indicated earlier, is one way to achieve mutual understanding. This becomes one of the first acts in the development of a strategy that leads to an acceptable type of management. The desire to accommodate, not only other people but the requirements of a position assignment, becomes an initiator of strategy development. If the people involved have no capacity or desire to accommodate two differing points of view or to accommodate the wishes of other people, there is little hope that a strategy of compromise and management can be developed. The desire thus becomes one of the initiators of strategy.

Leader expectations long have been prime initiators of action. This action can be the development of strategy for the on-going tasks of an agreed-upon goal to be sought as well as the processes by which the goal will be achieved. Client demands often stimulate the development of a strategy of compromise and management. In the school, the clients are the students and people of the community who want to see educational services performed at a high level for the benefit of all. Legislative bodies such as the state legislature, city council, board of education, and influential special interest groups originate many visions of the future that people think are a desirable end for the educational mission. All people who have legislative impact on the schools are initiators of strategy.

Interaction among people stimulates the initiation of strategy development. People can enjoy working cooperatively or working competitively. Being associated with others reassures the individual that others do not reject either the person or the contribution to action. When the association with others involves a commonly recognized goal and work process, the reassurance to self is even stronger.

The most potent initiator is the *internalized recognition of a need*. It is not enough to be told that a need exists. People must feel that the need is there and that they have some responsibility for developing a strategy that will fulfill that need. Strategy development is a popular goal for group action and for the application of individual insights. The desire to develop strategies of management through the process of compromise constitutes a proper goal for people who would initiate the smooth operation of group action.

INTERNAL-EXTERNAL
EVIDENCE OF COMPATIBILITY

People who seek to become parties to a compromise and who accept the management that grows out of the compromise have achieved the first benchmark of group compatibility. Compatibility may be seen by many as nonessential to successful individual action. But this chapter has emphasized that a school operation is a group enterprise and that the individual activities must fit into the group pattern. Compatibility itself is accepting the conditions under which the work is being done. Management in this sense has become acceptable to the individual as a necessary way of coordinating the differentiated tasks and activities of all members of the teaching staff.

Differentiation of staff does not indicate that the staff members do not have a common goal. Common goal is an institutional or organizational type of direction, and each individual has a certain amount of freedom to contribute to achieving that goal without being forced into unusual constraints in the ways of doing. One essential to compatibility, however, is the respect that each person holds for the role performance and expectations of all others in the organization. This respect for the role of others becomes one of the vehicles for achieving successful compromises and, therefore, management becomes acceptable.

People can develop a tolerance for diverse points of view. This tolerance sets the stage for exploring the first points of view and maintains the respect for the role of others in relating the diversity in the points of view. Compatibility is a relationship among people in which there is an absence of scuttling or destructive activity. It is also the absence of subtle avoidance of those with whom a person may differ. Compatibility does not have room for such antagonistic dispositions and actions among people.

One important evidence of compatibility and of acceptability is observing oneself and others *volunteering assistance* to those who may need help in achieving their own contribution to the common goal. Volunteering assistance is evidence of goodwill and should be nurtured in any group action.

Other evidences of compatibility are the *enthusiasm and vigor* by which each member of a group goes about the individual task assigned and accepted. The enthusiasm and vigor are evidence of confidence in and value of the action that is being taken. The final evidence of compatibility and of acceptability is that people develop continuity in the state of mind that values interacting experiences. Isolation is eliminated and people have achieved a tolerance for each others' differing points of view. They have been able to accept management that provides for coordinated group action even though composed of diverse individuals.

INHERENT REWARDS
OF MANAGEMENT ACCEPTANCE

This chapter started with a thought that management acceptance or acceptability is essential for the successful organization of the school's main enterprises—teaching and learning. The rewards to the individual include a feeling of group membership and valuing that one can become a part of a total group with common goals but respecting the differing ways that individuals contribute to those goals. A reward of management acceptance is the reduction of annoyance. It can be nurtured over long periods of time simply by not giving any attention or effort to the reduction of differences and points of view in ways of doing.

Another reward of management acceptance is to be able to take advantage of the control provided by management actions over the environmental variables that often constitute a negative influence on the teaching activities. The reduction of environmental noises and other annoyances allows individuals to go about their own work without a hardship that they cannot control.

A reward of management acceptance is understanding the constraint patterns that are essential in order that each individual in the activity will not tend to thwart the activities of others. This understanding of the necessity for the boundaries of freedom and constraint is one result and reward of an acceptance of management.

Management acceptance makes it easy for each individual to report needs and concerns to others. If the teacher has some concerns about the teaching-learning program or materials, it ought to be easy for that person to report the existing deficiencies to an administrative officer in order to gain the help that management acceptance can provide. The knowledge of freedom boundaries is the other side of the coin toward the understanding of constraint patterns. People cannot demand freedom to do anything they please regardless of whether it contributes to the common goal. The common goal is an essential. When management acceptance is mutual, all contributors to the total action are confident in themselves, in others, and in the purpose of their work activity.

Work productivity is one of the great rewards of management acceptance. Being able to do what one can do and to know that it is a substantial contribution to the total purpose of the school is a reward. Achievement satisfaction is available to all who have found personal rewards and who can identify the benefits from the procedures of management. Thus, management acceptance has been achieved.

EXAMPLES OF STRATEGIES

The title of this book, *Strategies For Instructional Management,* reveals the authors' intent to focus on the strategies of instructional management. This subject matter will be organized according to various aspects of management and there will be continuous relating of strategies to the many aspects of management.

The following chapters present many examples of strategy. These are intended to be examples rather than a manual of strategy. The authors believe that each school system should develop its own set of strategies. Hopefully, some of the examples can be adapted to the needs of each local system. The examples, then, can serve as stimulators and directional resources. They have been designed for that purpose and will be keyed to the actions of management in the instructional program.

SOME OTHER VIEWS ON MANAGEMENT

Hamilton, Norman K. *New Techniques for Effective School Administration.* West Nyaak, New York: Parker Publishing Company, 1975.

Wadio, Manech S. *Management and the Behavioral Sciences.* Boston: Allyn & Bacon, 1968.

Wilson, John A. *Banneker: A Case Study of Educational Change.* Homewood, Illinois: ETC Publications, 1973.

Instructional Impact— Response Areas

The previous chapter dealt with the concept of management acceptability. It indicated some conditions that might encourage an acceptance of management as essential to the progress and efficiency of both individual and group action. Chapter 1 discussed what encourages acceptability and some advantages of the acceptance of management.

This chapter focuses on the impact and response of operational interaction. In other words, it deals with the contact that one makes with another person and the response that is engendered by that *impact* or contact. Management acceptance facilitates a response in and among individuals as well as within groups. It should be recognized that management and acceptability are not generalizations. Management is specific action and usually consists of a series of behaviors, agreements, and procedures. Management should have a purpose and usually does. The case was made in the previous chapter that management is more acceptable and, therefore, more effective if it is accomplished with a high degree of participation of all people involved. This thought leads to a more detailed consideration of the impact and response interaction among people in an organization who have a common purpose, with individual purposes that are relevant to the common purpose.

Management must have a purpose. That purpose must be accepted by those who will be influenced in a rewarding manner by management. That is, management must have a target. The target can be material or ideational, but most likely will be a personal thing between and among people. The intellectual response to an impact must come from people. Target and impact, then, usually are directed to individuals and to groups. The impact is not relevant to management unless the response is in harmony with the purpose of the impact. This purpose constitutes the target for the effort involved in initiating an interaction with others.

An impact's effect is related to how it was made. The person in a management position whose behavior emphasizes a sense of authority with little consideration for those who are affected by the action or impact probably will alienate those who are receiving the impact. In this case, the impact is not properly directed and the anticipated response may not be forthcoming. The effect of the response to the negative impact received, on the other hand, engenders rejection on the part of the initiator. As indicated in the previous chapter, management acceptability in which the purpose is to make the management impact in a manner that will stimulate a rewarding response is preferred. These effects of the response may alter how management impacts are made.

The concern in this chapter is that the impact and response be such that acceptability is developed and maintained. Hopefully, the relationship between management and those affected by it will be maintained in a wholesome and progressive manner.

INSTRUCTION WITHOUT LEARNING

Teachers sometimes experience a teaching situation in which a mood of futility seems to prevail. The most probable cause of this lackadaisical manner in the classroom is either that the instruction does not stimulate the learner or that the learner is resisting learning. Futility is the best description of instruction without learning.

Management without response is comparable to the observation about instruction without learning. Management can exercise tremendous effort and may get the rewarding response of achieving the target for which the management was designed. On the other hand, the same kind of skill sometimes seems to be applied but without response from those whom it is necessary to influence with a management impact if the institutional purposes are to be achieved. It is not to be assumed here that management has discharged the responsibility simply by behaving in a managing manner. Management probably can stimulate response, as has been indicated many times.

The individuals who are affected by management may resist the coordination that management represents. Perhaps communication, mannerism, purpose, and other elements of the management process fail to achieve an impact-response situation that makes the management and the response relevant in achieving a known purpose. Many people have experienced situations in which the management or co-ordinating behaviors are performed merely by rote. In other words, management may not have a target. A classroom instructor may have many teaching skills, but if they are devoted to obstructing the target, little learning will be achieved. Instruction without a target does not produce an educative experience for the students.

Many factors may interrupt the relevant responses to impact whether it be instruction or management. There are competing diversions. One common competing diversion is conflict of purpose. Therefore, if the impact and response are to be rewarding, a commonality of purpose must be established before the impact-response situation is instituted. Many people may not have the skills to pursue a purpose even when it is known. This becomes a diversion for some people involved in the interacting relationships.

A study of the management impact and response process must assess the kinds of diversions that may thwart the response. Once these diversions have been identified, a program of intervention control can be established. This program should be part of management responsibility as well as staff responsibility. In other words, the impact and response must be an interacting relationship and will not be interaction at all if it is left for one person to work alone.

Teachers are responsible for developing a relationship with students that leads to learning. As indicated above, one of the first ways to achieve that is to make certain that everybody has a common purpose. A teacher, then, has a responsibility in the learning situation of helping the student to know why learning effort is worthwhile. The same thing must be said about management responsibility. There are many ways that management might go on about its business without assessing the kind of responses generated. The responsibility of management becomes most important. Similarly, the student must accept some responsibility for the learning situation. Too often there is the attitude, "Well here I am, teach me"; but it is also true that a staff member might say, "Here I am, influence me." This probably will not happen.

Examples of Strategy

1. Hold a series of small group discussions on "The purpose of management and the purpose of instruction." List and analyze specific examples of conflict.

2. List several intervention methods that can be used by management and by staff to overcome conflicts of purpose in order to arrive at a common purpose and direction.

3. *Select six teachers known to be influential in the district and converse with them on a one-to-one basis about tasks in which mutual responsibility may be necessary to accommodate operational success.*

4. *Ask your secretary to help audit your activities for one week to determine the percent of time devoted to various facets of your job. Compare the results of the audit with a previously identified list of major management responsibilities listed in order of importance and by percent of your job that you believe should be devoted to each. Compare your weekly performance with the plan to determine which competitors are obstructing the fulfillment of your mission.*

INSTRUCTION WITH LEARNING

Most of the interactions between the teacher and the learner result in appropriate outcomes regardless of the periodic criticisms of lack of learning in the school. Long ago, the idea of a Mark Hopkins on one end of the log and the student on the other portrayed the most expeditious way of bringing about an effective teaching-learning situation. The idea of two people, each on one end of the log, suggests that teaching and learning is a one-to-one relationship.

Probably it is more appropriate to interpret the two people on the log as being a two-way communication situation rather than a limitation on the ratio of teacher to student. The teacher must be able to tell the student the kinds of things that will give direction to proper learning, but the pupil also must be a listener. The reverse also is true, namely, that the teacher is as much responsible for listening as for telling. In this way, a two-way communication can be achieved and more rewarding interrelationship brought about.

The reference to instruction with and without learning is a direct way of mentioning the concept of impact and response that is characteristic of management and that depends on a forward thrust by one and a response by the other. Here again, two-way communication is essential. This is linked closely with the idea that participation of all parties involved is essential if coordination is to be achieved. A common target or purpose is an essential element of a successful interrelationship. This is true for instruction and learning and also for impact and response that constitutes the total picture of management and coordination in a group enterprise. Consideration of this type evolves clearly to a concern for the various aspects of appropriateness of the impact and response relationships. Appropriateness has eight sides that have been selected as important to the impact-response situation.

The first side of appropriateness is *purpose.* Purpose is one essential element of successful coordination, which is another way of referring to successful impact and response.

A second side of appropriateness is *content.* It is not enough just to have a target or a purpose. There must be substance to the procedures by which the impact and response come about in order that all involved can know when a purpose has been achieved.

The third side of appropriateness is *behavior.* It is not enough to say or provide for the right things because that in itself might not stimulate response. How communication takes place is almost as important as the purpose and content. The old song that went, "It isn't what you do, it's the way that you do it," still has much meaning for people considering any type of interaction that involves what must be considered coordination. Coordination is a successful impact-response situation.

The fourth side of appropriateness is *process.* Again it is not enough just to have purpose, content, and a pleasant behavior. There must be a system, which is process. Process is an organized way of using the best abilities and skills of all people involved so that they are related in a combined action that brings about successful coordination in the pursuit of a purpose.

The fifth side of appropriateness is *support.* People may know what is to be done, they may know why it is to be done, they may have a strong desire to do it pleasantly, and they may be well organized. But unless the space, time, and material are available as supports, the whole process of impact and response will not result in successful coordination in the pursuit of a common purpose.

A sixth side of appropriateness is *credit.* The whole process of management that involves the impact-response interrelationship calls on differing kinds of assignments as individual contributions to achieving purpose. It is important that, when there is differentiation in the assignments and in the accepted subresponsibilities, proper credit be given to those who have fulfilled the assignment successfully. Assignment here is not seen just as something imposed by someone else, because many assignments are self-designed and self-imposed. The person who does the work should be recognized as having done it.

The seventh side of appropriateness is that when credit has been recognized, there be *acknowledgement* of that credit. Acknowledgement is a form of commendation that is not a sign of weakness but rather a stimulant, as indicated in the previous chapter. Acknowledgement, then, is most appropriate for the successful impact-response stimulation and interaction.

The eighth side of appropriateness is *validation.* When people have entered into the efforts of achieving a common purpose, with each contributing something unique to that achievement, it is important that the true accomplishment of goal or purpose be verified by validation criteria. Validation leaves no doubt that it was a successful enterprise and was successfully carried out.

Certain priorities must be recognized at selected times in order to use the eight sides of appropriateness. One person does not say, "I will determine purpose and you will determine content." Everyone must be involved and with a set of priorities. Priorities should not be seen, however, as absolute. Blends must be recognized as appropriate at various times. At times, for example, the impact-response patterns may determine when priorities need to be combined, blended, or reversed.

Examples of Strategy

1. Ask a curriculum committee to analyze the eight sides of appropriateness in its responsibilities for determining the sequential attack of course updating. Share the results with other curriculum committees.

2. Select staff members to review your district's classroom supervision practices. Relate the practices to the eight sides of appropriateness of impact and response.
   a. Identify forms of desired commendation.
   b. Identify validation criteria that will improve the verification of goal accomplishment.

3. Attempt to define additional sides of appropriateness and place them in the proper scope and sequence of the original eight sides of appropriateness.

IDENTIFICATION OF LEARNERS

Considerable space has been given to discussing instruction without learning and with learning. This discussion leads to the concept of impact and response as it relates to management acceptance in achieving coordinated action towards commonly accepted purposes. Note that the plural has been emphasized throughout. No one will have the exclusive rights of imposing impacts and no one should be encouraged to provide only responses. It is interactive and must remain that way.

Schools long have been burdened with what might be called a "teach me" myth. This also is true in the management field. It is a myth to say "manage me." It is impossible not to recognize the plural nature of coordination in management as defined in terms of impact and response. Learning and managing in this sense can be termed *directionalism*. In other words, one person at one time may initiate an impact action and at another time be a person who receives impact and, therefore, becomes the one who is the responder. It is important to remember that goals change as conditions change; and since individuals apply unique abilities to actions toward a common goal, directionalism must be pliable. Stimulation of mutuality is emphasized in this concept of the management experience. People who want to be a part of the group action are likely to be substantial contributors. It takes courage to admit the need to learn just as it takes courage to admit the need for direction. Therefore, the response may be the result of an invited impact.

The idea that it takes courage to admit the need to ask for help may be related to the status concept of the individuals involved. Some people in power have to resist thinking that their contributions and abilities are superior to those of people with different status in the bureaucratic model. Individuals can and should overcome this feeling of superiority. People are named to management positions because some of their unique skills can provide proper management activities that result in impact-response interrelationships, which lead to productive coordination.

If the bureaucratic model is overemphasized by any of the people involved, people who need direction may not want to ask for it. In this case, the impact-response relationship breaks down because of some individuals' concepts about the importance of people in different positions and assignments. All people involved in an organizational action should be acknowledged learners. Just as there must be two-way communication if instruction or influence is to take place, so people in any particular assignment in the educational organization must be willing to be learners. In this way, the interrelationships become more productive and the impact-response description of management appropriateness is well placed.

Examples of Strategy

1. *In a conference of administrative staff members, ask each person to identify areas of knowledge that need expanding in order to perform administrative tasks more effectively.*

2. *Reveal weaknesses as well as strengths in two previous managerial decisions that you have made. This openness may encourage similar behaviors and the seeking of assistance by others on the management team.*

3. *Identify examples of isolated decision making in which it might be productive to involve others on the line-staff chart in order to strengthen or improve the quality of the decisions and to give greater assurance that the group will pursue the requirements in fulfilling the decision.*

AREA OF PURPOSE

Each of the eight sides of appropriateness constitutes an area involving impact and response. Some consideration will be given briefly to each area as impact-response concepts evolve.

The area of *purpose* presumes that there are goals and purposes. This differentiates the general and the specific. The goals are the broad targets chosen for institutional or group action, and the purposes become specific guidelines to behaviors and relationships that make the people involved in the group enterprise move toward the commonly accepted goals.

The purposes chosen as guidelines to action affect the organizational or structural pattern of management. A purpose indicating that the pupils are viewed as individuals will incline the instructional program toward uniquely individualized purposes. This program would require a certain type of specialized help that would be available at all times. The relationship between the specialized assistance of help offered by people in the organization constitutes a structure of relationships. Organizational structure is a pattern of relationships between people that is determined, in this case, primarily by the purpose that the total group intends to achieve.

Purposes also affect the operational pattern of management. Individualized purposes are chosen so that each one can contribute to the total action. The arrangements made for time, material, and people relationships constitute the operational pattern and are largely determined by purpose; if they were not, the individuals in the organization as well as the organizational pattern itself would seem to drift to no organization at all.

The area of purpose must recognize the need to protect individuals. Many people may select goals for the institution. The purposes that constitute the guidelines within which each individual makes a unique contribution to the accepted goal must be considered as essential protection for the individual.

The purposes in a school organization must be anchored to the learner. It is often now heard that some purposes within the school organization must take priority over the welfare of the learner. The learner (the student in this case) must be a central figure in the choice of purposes for individual as well as for group action. This means that the system of relationships that evolves in the schools must be based on purpose. The system of grouping students, assigning teachers, scheduling time, and making space and material available must all be related to the purposes that have been selected.

A purpose-based system provides a definition for competence expectations. Too often, expectations show up at the end-of-line evaluation. Competence must be defined at the outset, scrutinized during the process, and evaluated at the end of the effort. Defining competence expectations becomes a definitive way of interpreting the specific purposes that guide the efforts toward goal achievement. Defining competence expectation leads to accountability.

The important thing in accountability is that the criteria to be used with the data that would be acceptable in the procedure by which the data would be collected must be known when goals and purposes are determined. The accountability system that is designed when competency expectations are declared and are purpose-based constitutes the screen for priority determinations of things that will be done day by day. This makes a compact area in which so much depends, from the standpoint of program design, on the proof of accountability in achieving competence expectations.

Examples of Strategy

1. Ask teachers to identify the purposes that they infer from a recent central office bulletin.

2. Create a matrix with identified purposes of a recent action on the horizontal or vertical axis. List the goal or goals on the other axis and distribute for staff reaction. Seek suggestions for altering the list. Distribute to teachers with the option of signing or submitting anonymously. Use the results to improve on the past action and look for indicators that could improve future decision making.

3. List a district goal that might have been discussed or agreed on recently by the school board. Then ask some employee volunteers to determine a set of acceptable purposes that would identify group action to fulfill the goal.

4. Assess the goals and purposes of a school and develop an organizational and staffing pattern in order to accomplish these goals and purposes.

AREA OF CONTENT

The side of appropriateness labeled *content* is a transition from purpose to substance. Purpose may give direction to people's actions, but purpose is anchored to the competence expectations that eventually will be achieved in the objects of the institution itself, namely, the students. When considering the area of content, sources and resources should be identified.

The purposes should lead to a wise selection of the kinds of substance that will be offered in the instructional program. Organizing for instruction becomes a selecting of what will be taught and what will be needed to support the teaching. Thus, the identification of sources and resources can be determined as the area of purpose is studied, particularly as the effort to define competency expectation proceeds. Content decisions must be made almost continuously. The priorities referred to earlier become not the priorities of how to perform the actions that lead to good learning but rather the priorities that constitute the decisions on what will be taught and to what extent and purpose it will be taught. The popular notion that content predicts outcomes is not very sound. Content should predict the outcome only if it is anchored to the purposes for which all efforts have been designed.

Many militant special interest groups exist both in the school and the school's environment. To the extent that a militant special interest group can impose a content on people who have not participated in a selection, a conflict may develop that will work against the best system-wide type of planning that would get the best purposes and substance to achieve those purposes.

Militance in special interest groups affects priorities that may have been established earlier. It becomes necessary to be prepared at all times to negotiate emphases in terms of the decision of substance that will be involved in the instructional program. Emphasis also can be related to the time allocations that are devoted to any substance as directed to a given purpose. The decisions about substance thus are under continuous challenge, which may be a good thing. The requirement of not freezing into a particular position will keep the options open for the review of priorities in purpose and in substance. As the decisions about substance are made and the emphases determined, a sequencing of activities becomes a part of the responsibility of the strategies for instructional management in the area of content.

Sequencing needs a value determination as to how much emphasis each element will receive. There must be a criterion that helps determine what to keep and what not to keep in the instructional program. This is a part of the instructional management responsibility, and the impacts and responses in the content area must work according to an acceptable plan if these choices are made about sequencing and also about what to keep, discard, and substitute.

The management related to content has tremendous influence on instruction. How management is designed and carried out can make instruction a very important area of appropriateness in the study of instructional management. The evaluation responsibility now is in the area of content as it is in the areas of purpose, organizational design, and operational pattern. Evaluation responsibility must be met when content decisions are being made, not at the end of content presentations. In this way, evaluation and accountability programs can be relevant to the intent of the total institution.

Examples of Strategy

1. *Review several years of school board actions and ask the administrative and teaching staffs to describe the impact on the instructional program.*

2. *Ask teachers to identify within their department the effect of recent policy decisions that are strengthening or weakening the emphasis given to the subjects they teach.*

3. *Review the priorities of purpose to determine necessary adjustments required in order to include a recently identified piece of content to be added to the curriculum. Identify background requirements needed by the student that must precede the new content being added to the curriculum.*

4. *Review past evaluation procedures and determine if they were designed before or after content decisions were made. Develop a policy relating to evaluation procedures.*

5. *Specify strategies used by a militant special interest group to impose content in an area of your curriculum. Develop guidelines for analyzing pressure tactics.*

AREA OF PROCESS

Instructional management obviously requires the interaction of many people. The in-school population is composed of administrators, supervisors, teachers, students, specialists, and service personnel; in addition, the out-school interest includes community leaders, parents, and other citizens. The instructional management task involves the impact and response of many and varied combinations of people. The concern for the *processes* by which the instructional management will occur is important.

Process indicates action. There are literally hundreds of starting gates for any type of activity or enterprise that might be instituted. The relationships within the school among the administrative and teaching staffs assure that any one in either group may be an initiator of some action. The pattern of relationships becomes important and is a process by which the instructional management can succeed. When one starting point has been selected, the direction toward the selected goal must be maintained. It is not a good concept of process when a change in the process, approach, or even the goal occurs after a start in one direction and before that direction has been completed. This does not mean inflexibility to the extent that once the process is started it cannot be modified.

Flexibility is needed in process just as in any type of activity. Flexibility in the relationships among people in the instructional field supports the desired interaction that brings about an impact-response result that can achieve goals of instructional programs. When expansion is in order, the starting place and direction can be determined through the relevance of the expansion of the current program to the purposes and goals of the school.

Expansion is not just an "adding on"; rather, it is an adaptation that brings about the extended or included areas of concern and responsibility that may not have been envisioned at the outset. People should watch for the special pleaders and special interest people and also for those who speak as oracles. This might facetiously be called "medicine man" assistance. Close scrutiny should be given to the people who know all the answers for every activity that have a ready made remedy for any difficulty that comes along. Such people do not contribute to the expansion of a program through relevance to purpose and unique capacities of the people involved.

The people who are involved in process must have some choice of the type of tools or specific activities that are chosen to accomplish the goals selected and are within the accepted process of interaction. The availability of the support facilities becomes a part of the process arrangement that is designed primarily to support the people involved in the action. Management extension should come, primarily, not from the desire to control more people and activities, but from an increased choice and availability of the tools required by those on the "firing line." Management extension is not the concept of control and direction nearly so much as the concept of support. If management is well organized, and if the structures are satisfactory to all participants, the benefits will accrue from the designed system.

Smooth working relationships become an important part, perhaps the main supports, of the process and system of continuity. As has been indicated, the relationships of these various areas are of concern. In this instance, the process must be related to the content, the content having originated from the purposes. Thus a continuity is achieved in the various areas of impact-response relationships.

Examples of Strategy

1. *Ask staff members to keep a log for one week in which they record the operational experiences that supported or thwarted their assigned responsibilities.*

2. *Seek staff assistance in identifying content areas that are deemed valuable and necessary, but where there are no special interest or support influence groups. Upon identification, decide whether professionals in the district are willing to continue support of such content and at what cost.*

3. *In small group discussions, list several methods that can be used to allow process procedures to remain flexible. Compile results and distribute copies to staff and board.*

4. *Review the strategies of "medicine men" in your district and list alternatives to their actions that would better meet the goals of the district.*

AREA OF BEHAVIOR

The discussion of process in the previous section defined the kinds of interrelationships that would be most productive in the instructional management concern. It is also important to consider that an individual has a *behavioral pattern* that becomes important in the development of the coordination necessary for carrying forward an instructional program.

A modern and popular declaration states that each person should just be himself or herself. This approach may deny an opportunity to achieve the interaction necessary for a group enterprise. Freedom is not necessarily lost when individuals find it necessary to change their own behavior in order not to interfere with the behavior of an entire group that accomplishes the institutional purpose. So the behavior of management, as well as the behavior of teachers and students, becomes a concern relevant to the achievement of instructional purposes.

Program declarations that give organization and defined purpose to the various elements of the instructional program become important in determining the kinds of behaviors on the part of all involved. Selecting those declarations that bring about the best total approach to the instructional program is a proper effort. A specific illustration is that of coordinating the office directives. Many administrators need to communicate with all personnel in a school building or a school system but feel too outnumbered to communicate through one-to-one relationships. Often, the office bulletin is used as a quick and ready means of communicating various aspects of the operation that need to be shared with all members of the staff. The real problem comes when, for instance, a central office sends out directives that relate to the curriculum, to the school schedule, or to the control of support supplies. At the same time, a principal may issue directives to teachers in the same way. A teacher may not have time to read all the directives, or may find the directives in conflict. The various offices in a central office setup, for instance, pupil director, personnel director, and curriculum director, may be sending directives that are not consistently uniform to represent the central office or the individual school office. Many times, the expectations declared in directives, such as the institution of new programs, the evaluation of other programs, and various types of things envisioned by the central office, become a real time burden for the individual classroom teachers. There is a feudal temptation on the part of administrators who tend to issue the directive and then mentally envision every reader of the directive conforming to it. Such conformation probably does not happen and, even if it did, it is a weak assumption for any administrator to make.

Recently, some emphasis on management by objectives (MBO) has developed to challenge administrative personnel. Administrators and supervisors often overlook MBO overtones, but the teachers are the ones who have to produce so that a principal or supervisor can achieve the MBO negotiated with the central office. This results in pressure from the principals, supervisors, and other administrators in in-service types of activities. Many of the in-service procedures develop into a sort of pressure chamber, forcing the teachers to conform to a central plan. Perhaps the time limitation was determined with teacher participation, but timing and expectations often constitute a severe burden for the teacher who is committed to the productive instruction of students. School systems must institute teacher time-action analyses. Perhaps, then, the directives and expectations emanating from the school offices would be coordinated and sequenced to keep undue pressure off the teachers who should be devoting more of their time to pupil instruction. This can be best defined as *expectations sanity.* Expectations can be declared by an administrator or supervisor in thirty seconds. But the teacher's accomplishment of that expectation might take many weeks. If a number of administrators and supervisors declare expectations, the teacher has to wonder what kind of sanity permits such unreasonable expectations to emanate from the administrative offices.

Examples of Strategy

1. *Ask a committee representing all major position categories to make a quantitative analysis of distributed bulletins and directives with estimates of time required for response or compliance.*

2. *Review the most recent half dozen memos written to determine whether the information could have been transmitted more clearly in personal discussion.*

3. *Analyze a recent written directive to see if individualizing the directive through discussion would generate the information or cause the action. Were you "pulling it out" or "pouring it on" in the directive?*

4. *Review teacher directives given to students enrolled in a specific discipline to determine any conflict of direction. Discuss the reasons for any conflicts of direction with persons involved.*

AREA OF SUPPORT

The previous section discussed some of the behavior characteristics that cause destruction or encouragement of rewarding interactions among the various position holders in the total organization. Here, emphasis is on those behaviors that may result in *support,* primarily for the teacher. The teacher is the central figure in directing the instruction of students, a focal point for much of the concern as well as for the dependence to get the right things done. If the question is raised of support for whom and of what, the quick and direct answer is support for the teacher. Support is essential if the teacher is to use unique abilities to direct instruction and bring about pupil learning.

Strong reference was made previously that action analyses would be appropriate. The purpose of such analyses is time protection, primarily because the sequencing of instruction activities in the classroom must be based on the time available to or required by the teacher and pupil to accomplish the purpose of the classroom. Time protection and interruption control have been illustrated many times by questioning how any teacher can teach with the disruptions of a two-way public address system in the school building. Whenever someone in the school office hits the chime for a particular classroom and says, "May I interrupt please," interruption has already occurred. More consideration must be given to time protection and to the kind of time made available to the teachers and pupils in the classroom.

Many distractions cause interruptions in the classroom. Noise in the halls, the inaccessibility of projectors, or the delivery of materials during the teaching and learning periods are some. Many of these distractions could be handled before or after school sessions. The real concern for time protection and interruption control, and protection against distraction for teachers and pupils, is that teachers and pupils be free to use initiative that would provide the most direct support to the learning goals. Instructional management is responsible for providing just this type of support service. The tools and materials referred to need to be appropriate, of sufficient quantity, and available. This direct support by the management positions frees the teacher to direct instruction to the best results in the classroom.

Another type of support occurs when teachers become somewhat frustrated and want someone to hear about their problems. Perhaps management's ears do not hear the real things that teachers want to declare with respect to classroom and instructional support. This results in complaints to other teachers or to people outside the school. Here again is the necessity for two-way communication at all times and not just one-way communication limited to directives.

The mutual concern of the management contingent and the teachers for the problems that occur in the development of successful instructional programs might be one of the best avenues to the needed support. Acknowledging strength has been emphasized as a way of stimulating teachers. Perhaps if the teachers acknowledge management strengths, improvements in the instructional management of a particular school or school system will occur.

Examples of Strategy

1. Ask all teachers to record, for one week, the time, nature, source, and result of interruptions during teaching-learning sessions in the classroom.

2. Prepare an in-service opportunity to review the time allotments made in the existing schedule for each subject offering. Ask teachers, by department or subject area, to determine and substantiate the optimum time needed to fulfill the assigned instructional mission. Compare the differences in current time alloted with time preferred or needed.

3. Seek employee suggestions for alternative ways of accomplishing day-to-day housekeeping responsibilities without interrupting classroom instruction. Query support staff as well as professional staff for suggestions to reduce classroom interruption.

4. Describe various methods administrators can use to support teachers that do not contain monetary involvement.

AREA OF CREDIT

The discussion of support focused on the teachers' needs in order to achieve the kinds of learning hoped for in the classroom. Goals are established as common targets for all people involved in an activity. Purposes are defined to give direction to action in the pursuit of goals. When goals are achieved, credit should be given to those responsible. It seems simplistic to suggest it, but considerable evidence exists that goals are declared and left to stand without anyone giving them further attention.

Goals are usually general and there may be many facets to goal achievement. Achievement may involve many people. Instructional management is responsible for bringing about the proper relationship of people that gives the greatest probability of goal achievement. When many people are involved in goal achievement, there must be a differentiation of assignments in order to maintain control of the many facets involved in the activities of these people. Differentiating assignments means that, even though people know their own assignments, they need to know the assigned responsibilities of others involved in the total operation. Nonetheless, it is easy to get lost in the crowd as an individual pursuing the unique assignments that may be different from those of colleagues in the organization.

It is important that some sort of recognition become part of the behavior system of all people involved in the operation. Most individuals have a personal desire to be recognized for the contributions that they make. Nonrecognition is destructive of the individual's enthusiasm, hope, and sometimes even of aggressive efforts. There can be a great waste of talent if teachers feel that they are not being recognized as providing an absolutely essential part of the instructional program. Recognition by others, whether it be a superior officer, a peer, or a layman in the community, does constitute a type of therapy. Recognition of worth stimulates people. Recognition of worth builds self-respect. Recognition of worth is justice.

The need for recognition must be kept in mind as the instructional management design is established and carried out. It is a part of the behavior pattern of all involved, and giving credit where credit is due must be a part of the maintenance of organizational purpose and effort.

Examples of Strategy

1. As a school administrator, keep a record for one week of the conversations you have with others. Who were they, what was the occasion, and what were the reactions?

2. Create a good news file recording achievements of staff for possible use in periodic conversational or written feedback.

3. Create an in-service experience for supervisors to promote sensitivity to signs of successful achievement of unique teacher assignments.

4. Encourage, through example, informal gatherings where students display their work in areas of participation as a method of supporting the product of teaching efforts.

5. List as many methods as possible to give credit to various categories of positions within a district. Discuss the worth of this credit with representatives of the various categories.

AREA OF ACKNOWLEDGEMENT

The previous section dealing with credit presented a way of giving effective support to the teaching-learning situation. *Acknowledgement* becomes an implementation of the worth of credit. If recognition is not given, an overt acknowledgement is made impossible and all the benefits of recognition acknowledgement are lost. Reciprocity as a characteristic of interaction within the group organization becomes essential. Chapter 4, "Reciprocities as Building Blocks," really originates in this activity of acknowledgement. Without acknowledgement on the part of those involved in an interaction, reciprocity becomes impossible.

Reciprocity is one means of developing an "otherness" on the part of all the people involved in organizational activities. Otherness means the removal of selfishness so that peers are able to reinforce not only their own activities but those of their associates. This gives the solid foundation for a mutual awareness of group effectiveness. It is likely, that, when effectiveness is designed and each contribution to it is recognized and acknowledged, mutuality will be retained. There is no room for jealousy within the organizational activity.

Jealousy destroys mutuality and otherness, and the strength of support that comes from the acknowledgement of work well done is lost. Power is gained from the acknowledgement of one's own as well as others' effectiveness. Power comes to the receiver of acknowledgement as well as to the giver of that acknowledgement. Acknowledgement is a foundation for recovery from failure, as well as a stimulation to creative action. It is the type of behavior that can continue to reinforce all who contribute to the instructional program. Acknowledgement is one commodity that increases in amount and potency as it is used. The increase comes in terms of satisfaction with the task to be performed and insurance that the task has been performed well, as well as the security of knowing that one is a member of a team in the institutional organization.

Examples of Strategy

1. Ask teachers to observe the effect of their success acknowledgement on the behavior of students.
2. Write a letter to parents of outstanding teachers identifying the personal and professional qualities that have been revealed and the district's appreciation for their outstanding work.
3. Write a letter to the spouses of teachers who give an inordinate amount of time and energy to their work to cement relationships and understanding between the teacher's home and the school district.
4. Encourage student groups to recognize the good work of their teachers.
5. List specific examples when credit has been acknowledged or not. Analyze the different behavioral outcomes in each situation.

AREA OF VALIDATION

Validation is the eighth side of appropriateness in determining and judging instructional impact-response characteristics. This is a determination of whether instructional management has used the organizational structure and operational procedures that bring about the maximum contribution of each individual to the effective end of achieving the selected purposes and goals.

All agree that learning is the right thing to accomplish, that seeing is a good thing to achieve, and that judging is a proper thing to do. An important concern is whether learning, seeing, and judging are controlled by an acceptable purpose and thus can be validated properly for the instructional management responsibilities.

The criteria for determining validation in the total instructional impact-response area should be mutually selected. The mutuality extends to those who are involved in the organization as well as to those who are present for the purpose of personal gains, such as learning. It extends to members of the community who should have some opportunity for criteria selection to make certain that schools are accomplishing those things for which they are created. Open covenants, discussed and openly arrived at, are the preferred approach. Criteria can and must be mutually selected by all people involved in the total instructional program.

Validation is related to evaluation. The criteria selected for validating the various aspects of the instructional management program can aid in determining proper criteria for evaluating the outcomes of the instructional program.

Examples of Strategy

1. *Select a committee of laymen who will address themselves to the task of enumerating and evaluating what laymen say they expect from the schools.*

2. *Design and implement a plan for periodic review of (a) the goals of the district, (b) course goals in the curriculum, and (c) community expectations to determine the degree of accomplishment.*

3. *Develop a needs assessment program that involves students, professional staff, other employees, and citizens to insure that agreed on purposes and goals are achieved.*

A reunion of goals and processes will be discussed in greater extent in chapter 8. The eight sides of appropriateness are concluded at this point of exploration as a means of judging the kinds of materials, relationships, activities, and outcomes that are appropriate instructional improvements.

This chapter has stressed the necessity for people in a group activity, such as school, to seek a commonality of goals. Such commonality gives strength and purpose to the impact-response phenomena. It is a short step from the impact-response logic to the melding of purpose and effort. Chapter 3, "Synthesis of Purpose and Effort," explores the nature of such a synthesis.

MORE READING IMPACT

Bolden, John H. *Developing a Competency-Based Instructional Supervisory System.* Hicksville, New York: Exposition Press, 1974.

Bureau of Business Practice, Inc. *The Magic Meeting-Minimizer.* Waterford, Connecticut: Croft-NEI Publications, 1975.

Milstein, Mike M. *Impact and Response.* New York: Teachers College Press, 1976.

Stradley, William E. *Administrator's Guide to an Individualized Performance Results Curriculum.* New York: The Center For Applied Research in Education, Inc., 1973.

Synthesis of
Purpose and Effort

Management acceptability, discussed in chapter 1, disclosed the authors' belief that individual attitudes of all participants are fundamentally important in the organizational mode. People's feelings are as important as their actions. How they think is as important as what they think. These things affect the impact-response phenomena (chapter 2). The eight sides (areas) of appropriateness constitute the anatomy of the impact-response phenomena. These phenomena are conditioned by and are conditioners of the *relationships of purpose and effort*.

The wants of people originate in what they perceive as being advantageous to them in the way of emotional satisfaction, professional intent, or physical needs. The varying perceptions of people result in different origins of wants. Many of those wants combine in complex ways. The experiencing of want, however, constitutes an origin of purpose for each individual; the purpose selected promises to satisfy the want.

A particular set of wants is developed by the individual and, consequently, the subsequent purposes may or may not be related to the wants and purposes of other people. The individuals in a school organization, each having individualized wants and purposes, must operate within a group of professionals. A group may develop group wants and purposes, but individuals must reach some relating agreement so that individual wants do not conflict with the common purposes of individuals who constitute the group.

The purposes that grow out of the commonly accepted wants of individuals in a group provide one of the best origins of effort. Effort is related to the strength of the purpose and the urgency of its achievement and satisfaction. The individual behaves in this manner both as an individual and as a group member. Effort for the individual is related to wants and purposes. The efforts of individuals acting in a group situation are related to and have their origins in wants and purposes. The effort expressed by individuals or by groups must have some direction or that effort may not achieve the purpose. Purpose determines the nature and amount of direction needed for the proper use of individual and group effort.

Specific skills are needed if the purposes and efforts of individuals and groups are to be synthesized into a relationship that can satisfy a purpose. Synthesis is a unification of elements, in this case purpose and effort. Synthesizing purposes and efforts of individuals within a group having common purposes constitutes a basis for coordinating the efforts of group members. Coordination affords individuals in groups a personal satisfaction through a sense of group contribution. Strategies are needed to continue synthesizing so that efforts can be sustained. These strategies are implicit in (1) defining teaming requisites, (2) setting up the diversification of tasks, (3) common purposing, (4) nurturing expertise, (5) developing understanding of the tasks in delegation, (6) seeing therapy in analysis and appraisal, (7) promoting the ways of unity, and (8) using a strategy model for a referent point.

TEAMING REQUISITES

The coordination of individuals in a group effort assumes a working relationship between the positions of group members and the purposes chosen by that group. This leads to a concern for the requisites that bring about coordination or teaming. People who bring their unique abilities to a group action usually have an identifiable position in that group. These position expectations must be related to the purposes of the group as well as to the purposes of the individual. Much depends on the sequencing arrangements of the efforts of individuals if they are to be brought into coordinated group relationships. Individuals cannot proceed independently without endangering the success of group action. Sequencing with the efforts of others is essential to the coordination characteristic of team operation. (Sequencing, in this context, implies a logical timing applied to the delivery of services to a common or related action target.)

Those members who would help sustain the sequencing of efforts in the group organization must provide frequent mission reports for the entire group. The mission report should include a review of the purposes that directed the choice of processes designed to achieve the purposes, and the status of progress toward acceptable outcomes. A generous amount of reciprocity is required in a group. Sequencing assumes that each person may approach a task at a different time but according to a recognized plan. The reciprocity of standing aside to let another proceed is a support to the sequencing requisite of the achievement of group purpose. Each person, regardless of the stage in the sequence of effort contributing to the group purpose, needs to feel recognized by others who have responsibilities in the organization. This is membership recognition. If a person is to behave as a creative group member, membership recognition must be felt and acknowledged. The significance of reciprocity is the topic of chapter 4.

Sequencing in the effort to satisfy a purpose might have a series of checkpoints. The checkpoint identifies a time and situation that permit all members in the group to stop for a review of each individual's contribution to the organized effort. At the checkpoint, determine if the sequencing was well-planned and if the effort was well-directed to the selected purpose. At this point, for individuals to maintain a reciprocity of support, each one must develop some objectivity in criticism and sincerity in commendation. Criticism, presented in a proper manner, is an observation of the contribution of the individual's efforts to the group enterprise. Criticism is primarily an objective review of the planned sequence, as it relates to the effort and the individuals who must exert that effort to achieve the purpose. When the sequencing of effort has not been appropriate, corrective measures can be taken. When the effort has been achieved, words of commendation can induce added effort and more careful practice of the skills of sequencing an individual's unique efforts.

Examples of Strategy

1. *Make an inventory of the teaming efforts observable in your school system. Select a successful effort and an unsuccessful effort. Analyze the sequencing steps. Are these related to the success or failure of the effort?*

2. *Hold in-service meeting(s) with committee chairpersons to develop concepts of the significance, use, and abuse of preplanning and sequencing.*

3. *Develop operational policies and procedures for committee activities that reflect the synthesis as discussed in this chapter.*

DIVERSIFICATION OF TASKS

The efforts in a sequence of activities leading to a selected purpose represent a series of tasks to be performed. Each task must be related to the purpose or the individual and group enterprise cannot achieve satisfaction. Just as the positions in an organization must be related to the purpose and sequencing of efforts, so the task must be consistent with the identity and the purpose of the positions created within an organization.

Individuals must be placed properly in the organizational pattern. In order for each member to make the best use of unique talent, the task must be appropriate to the individual as well as to the nature of the selected purpose. Just as effort cannot be applied without a sequencing plan, the tasks in an organizational enterprise must have a high degree of interrelatedness. Many tasks can be isolated in the total organizational effort and still have a support function. But even when the task has a support function, it would not be so identified unless its performance contributed to the performance of other tasks.

The interrelatedness of tasks, which grows out of a purposeful sequencing of effort, brings about a type of reciprocity between individuals in the organization that might be called *purposeful independence.* This means that an individual probably could not achieve a group purpose single-handed. Few group organizations can be simplified to that stage. The individuals in the group enterprise must be interdependent. Full dependence is not required, but isolated independence cannot be assured to selected individuals. The degree of independence and dependence must be determined by the purpose to be achieved and the array of tasks essential to that achievement.

People may think that the degree of autonomy experienced in any group enterprise or individually selected effort is the base for creative action. Autonomy is seen by some as not only a God-given right but a constitutional one. It is dangerous to harbor the idea that an individual can be wholly autonomous, either as an individual or as a member of an operational group. There are strengths and weaknesses in autonomy. Sufficient autonomy should be given to allow for creativity in tasks that lead to an appropriate individual or group purpose. Autonomy is weak when it is seen as a measure of freedom, freedom being interpreted as an absence of restraints imposed by self or others. Such an attitude toward autonomy weakens group effort that depends on coordination. Chapter 4 contains a more extended discussion of autonomy as it affects the interrelatedness of individuals in group activity.

A work ethic must be observed by the individuals performing tasks in a group enterprise. This work ethic must be based on a recognition of an appropriate contribution of individual effort to the group goals or purposes. This work ethic must also include an imposition on the individual, self-directed or alter-directed. It must allow each individual to be supportive of others in the total sequencing of efforts. This work ethic leads to a high degree of coordination of tasks. Coordination is achieved through an appropriate selection of tasks that keeps overlap and interference at a minimum. It also keeps the interrelatedness of those tasks directed toward group purpose. If the tasks can remain coordinated, if the individuals can find freedom and satisfaction in participating in group efforts, and if the individuals can merge or synthesize their purposes with group purposes, the outcomes are related through the synthesis of purpose and effort.

Examples of Strategy

1. Select a group activity that you felt was extremely successful. Have the group members analyze it from the points listed above. Develop a set of criteria to be used as guidelines for setting up other group activities.

2. Tabulate the present number and type of tasks for each staff member. Analyze the overload, underload, overlap, and balance.

3. Develop an on-going wall chart containing the tasks for each project to be undertaken. Color code different types of tasks. As delegations are made to staff members, consider appropriateness, interrelatedness, degree of autonomy, coordination, and balance.

COMMON PURPOSE BUT UNIQUE EFFORT

The emphasis on the agreement of individuals on a satisfactory group purpose does not mean the loss of the uniqueness of individuals. The very process of selecting a group purpose can be a challenge to individual inventiveness and vision. Recognize that groups, in order to achieve the sequencing of effort with purposeful tasks involved, must have some sort of organization. In group organization, people should agree not only on common purposes but also on a diversification of tasks making it possible for the organization to proceed toward its selected goals. These agreements reduce duplication of effort and increase complementary, diverse individualized performance.

The purpose of the organization influences the status of individuals in various organizational positions. A sense of contribution depends on explicit recognition of some authority. It also depends on submission to group constraints or directives as essential to the coordination of group effort.

An organization is made up of individuals merged into a total group, but also into many subgroups. A subgroup usually is constructed through the recognition of a related series of tasks. The relatedness can be achieved and maintained by the agreements of individuals and subgroups on certain prerogatives. Accepted prerogatives promote a central identity of a subgroup's contribution to the total enterprise. Individuals must feel that unique effort has been required and contributed in the sequenced activities.

The inclination of individuals and subgroups to revert to a desire for independence may lead to a separativeness of small groups within a total organization. There is a tendency to believe that a subgroup is a world with its own unique purposes, even though these purposes originated in the determination of total group purposes. Rational thought must be given to the limits of separativeness that can be permitted to evolve from human inclination. Necessary constraints, however, do not have to be applied by those who are not part of the organization. It does mean that organizations function best when the individuals of a subgroup are willing to recognize the lines of autonomy, separativeness, and individual action as they relate to the total group enterprise.

An orchestration of responsibilities is necessary in the operation of a successful group. A symphony orchestra is not started by a director and then left to produce music according to individual rhythms, keys, and interpretations. Orchestration is achieved when an individual, subgroup, or the entire organization accepts direction. But even when the entire organization has a sense of responsibility to operate together, there still needs to be direction if proper sequencing and interrelatedness of performance are to be achieved.

The orchestration of efforts in a group may raise the question that membership in a group offers limited opportunity for appeals and arbitrations. Such procedures should be built into the organizations at the time that purposes are defined so that the individual's freedom of creativity is protected and supported as an integral part of the group procedure. Perspectives of contributing individuals require an open forum that fosters ease of review, re-evaluation, and redesign. This also provides for an appeal to reason and encourages the art of compromise. Appeals and arbitrations thus become a part of the group process, not dependent on outside power as a source of justice. The discussion of coordination will be continued in more detail in chapter 10.

Examples of Strategy

1. Select one unique effort of an individual staff member that has been very successful. Analyze the success considering (a) the purpose of the effort, (b) the amount of time involved, (c) the cost, (d) the response of persons involved, (e) the response of persons not

involved, (f) the relation to group purposes and goals, and (g) the relation to the other tasks in the position description for this individual. Is
there a balance? Develop guidelines for future efforts.

2. Select one unique effort of an individual staff member that has been
   successful. Analyze according to points listed above.

3. Select one unique group effort that has been successful/unsuccessful.
   Analyze according to the points listed above. In addition, analyze the
   satisfactions of each individual member.

NURTURE AND CARE OF EXPERTISE

Earlier, this chapter discussed the individual efforts needed to carry
out the tasks required to achieve group purpose. Individuals, when
selected for a position in the organization, must accept tasks assigned
to that position. The assignment and the *acceptance* is related to
unique ability or skill called expertise. Individual expertise needs to be
identified so that the assignment fosters a maximum contribution to
group purpose. Expertise, once identified, must be committed to
appropriate tasks. Misassigned people will never achieve the purposes
of the positions for which they were selected. Persons who are misassigned are almost certain to lose their expertise, for lack of application or lack of spirit to continue to exercise it. One way to develop and
maintain expertise is to make the proper assignment and give recognition for contributions related to the output of the expertise.

Supporting conditions such as recognition of other people, time
allocation, space and material, and an array of other elements, make
effort more productive. A worker with expertise will not exercise those
skills if, at the same time, a feeling is harbored that no one recognizes
or appreciates the contribution to the group effort. Expertise cannot
stand still. It does not exist in a particular form and amount forever.
Expertise must have the opportunity of extension through application
to new and challenging tasks within the organizational effort. Opportunities to experiment with the application of expertise and with new
challenges to different purposes that evolve, are stimulants. They nurture expertise and make the best use of it.

Protective policies may cause the individual with expertise to
explore developmental activities. Anyone who applies expertise to the
extension and application of a purpose, apart from its origin, must
have the opportunity to experience failure as well as success. Protection to the group and to the people being served by the group is
assured, providing success and failure are defined. A decision must be
made on how long uncertainty of outcome can be permitted in the
group organization so that the individual with expertise has ample

ópportunity to extend and apply that expertise. One group protection is a periodic summary of the unique contributions of each individual. This provides an opportunity to determine whether creativity has led to a more productive outcome. If it has not been productive, the summary makes it possible to select revisions in the application of expertise.

The summary of contributions made by individuals, subgroups, and the total group must have some measure of reward attached to it. Rewards often have been limited to monetary advantages. Perhaps this will work for many in a crass material community and age, but only to a limited extent. The rewards of recognition and commendation are equally important in maintaining the expertise of individuals and relating them properly to the activities of a group seeking to achieve its purpose. Using, not abusing talent is the subject matter of chapters 6 and 7.

Examples of Strategy

1. *Make an inventory of the areas of certifiable expertise of each staff member. To what extent is your school district utilizing these talents?*

2. *Make an inventory of other areas of expertise and talents of each staff member. Include hobbies and areas of major interest. To what extent is your school district utilizing these talents?*

3. *Make an inventory of the areas of expertise and special talents of non-staff members in your school community. To what extent is your school district utilizing these talents?*

ASSIGNED VERSUS USURPED DELEGATION

The use of expertise of individuals assumes that expertise has been recognized as a contribution to the purposes of the group. The assignment of expertise to a specific task can be called *delegation*. The process of delegation has its own peculiar nature. Someone must make a proper assignment of expertise to a specific position and task in the organization. This means that the delegation is orchestrated by someone recognized for expertise in delegation, but this is not enough. Individuals must accept the delegations or the invitations to apply their expertise to the tasks of organization. Delegation as a management skill will be discussed in detail in chapter 9.

A relationship of the acceptance of delegation to what might be called *self-assignment* is needed. When a delegation is made it is not necessary to assume that the individual assigned, even though it is a recognition of expertise, has been put into constraints. Rather, the assignment and acceptance should be regarded as self-assignment.

The synthesis of both elements in the process of delegation brings about the best performance of the individual as well as the best contribution to the group purpose.

The orchestration referred to above states that there must be management skill applied to task distributions and delegations. Assignment takes planning and orchestration requires insight into the interrelationships of the contributions of individuals and subgroups in the total operation. Management skill must include the authority to relate delegations to organizational purposes. Authority can originate in those who will be subjected to it in the process of coordination. If the members of a group accept the authority of an individual to distribute tasks, that authority no longer connotes control and penalty. Nonetheless, acceptance of authority often erodes with the time extension of the assignment. Some people feel that, if their expertise is making a particular contribution to group effort, they may be doing the work of someone else. This type of mental aberration needs to be cured with a fresh reintroduction to the purposing of individuals in a group enterprise.

Coordination happens not only as a result of well-planned sequencing of purpose and effort, but also because the individuals contributing to the total enterprise accept the relationships in a wholesome spirit. This is the spirit of coordination and it is essential to a good working relationship between people. Again, the opportunity for periodic review should be guaranteed to every individual. The periodic review, in this case, would review the delegation that had been assigned or usurped. It is possible to be an empire builder and to keep adding specific tasks to one's own array of responsibilities, sometimes to the exclusion of other productive contributors. Once the periodic review has been conducted with respect to delegation, there is a base for making a "tactful redistribution of assignments and delegations." *Tactful* because the people involved recognize that the group purpose determines the criterion as to whether delegations were properly made, properly accepted, and properly executed. This is a synthesizing of individual and group purposes, achieved through the process of delegations assigned, usurped, and/or accepted.

Examples of Strategy

1. *As each staff member's effort is evaluated, include questions that relate to task assignment in the criteria for assessment. Are the individuals carrying out assigned responsibilities? Are the individuals usurping responsibilities of others? Why?*

2. *Check your communication system. To what extent are you keeping staff members informed of their various assignments and those of others?*

3. *Delegate the task of coordinating assignments to one staff member. Include the responsibilities a system of communication, a system for feedback, and a system for ongoing appraisal.*

THERAPY IN ANALYSIS AND APPRAISAL

Participation in group activities can create situations in which individuals overexert or underexert themselves, and develop feelings of imposition by or antagonism toward their peers. Coordination does not prevent some individuals within the group from becoming dissatisfied, disenchanted, and otherwise a burden to the process of communication and action. Observations of the successes and failures of others may stimulate some individuals to seek jealous or comparative reprisals. These problems that individuals may develop as members of a group can be termed, in some ways, a pathological state. Sometimes these states are temporary, but at other times they tend to rechannel the efforts of the individuals who succumb to them.

The potentials for the development of these pathological states may reside in the group patterns of operation. Thought must be given to the kind of therapy that might reduce the complexities and levels of anxiety or other pathologic states that might develop. Very often, the individual is unaware of the motivation that seems to encourage the pathologic state. This motivation becomes a problem for those trying to apply some appropriate therapy. A revision of procedures might help individuals disillusioned with their roles in the group action.

Great power exists in the definition of feelings, problems, and issues. The process of defining what has gone wrong and what the current state is may be one of the primary ways of correcting it and of preventing recurrences. The power of definition becomes the base for respected evidence that can be gathered to assist in the resolution of any difficulties. A lack of respect for evidence reduces the inclination to collect information for its potential assistance in resolving issues and problems. Such lack of respect for analyses may incline the decision process toward conclusions based on inadequate evidence and toward action by expediency.

Evidence can be secured only through an analysis of the variables present in individual and group action. There is a tendency for groups to establish norms without adequate evidence. There is nothing wrong with establishing norms as the basis for judging the behavior of individual and group activity. Those norms, however, must constitute acceptable criteria for judging the evidence of achievement that leads to a common purpose. Norms often can be evaluated in terms of ideals held by the individuals in a group. Psychopathic states may occur because the norms and ideals have become too widely separated. When this is true, tension develops, the norms are no longer satisfactory, and the ideals may be unattainable. It is important that each group contain many who can qualify themselves as judges of evidence collected in relation to any issue or problem of individuals and groups. The qualifications to judge are based primarily on respect for analysis and appraisal of all relevant evidence. (Auditing as continuous evaluation will be explored intensively in chapter 12.) Occasionally, individuals should review their own qualifications to make judgments. The main therapy perhaps can be summed up as the conscious effort to move sequentially from definition to evidence to decision to action. This therapy is only a part of wise individual contributions to the group enterprise. Directed self-management is discussed in chapter 15 and extends the concept of therapy consistency in self-direction.

Examples of Strategy

1. *In staff development meetings, work on the concept that analyzing and appraising the positive as well as the negative aspects are essential in the process of evaluation.*

2. *Develop a set of criteria for assessment at the outset of each activity. When the appraisals are made, never use a negative result for reprisals, in order to maintain a positive outlook on the part of the staff towards evaluation.*

3. *Make a special effort to see that the evaluation techniques for each project are carefully defined at the outset of each activity, not at the end.*

THE WAYS TO UNITY (OPTIMUM SYNTHESIS)

The preceding sections suggest the development of ways in which unity of action and coordination of purpose and efforts can be achieved. These might be viewed in terms of a series of wants. These wants are (not priority ordered):

1. Purposing
2. Cooperating
3. Coordinating
4. Supporting
5. Helping
6. Relieving
7. Commending
8. Suggesting
9. Planning
10. Evaluating
11. Rejoicing

These wants may serve as a roadmap for individual and group actions that can lead to a synthesis of purpose and effort, not only for the individual but for the individual in the group. In this way, a high level of coordination can be achieved and there can be an optimal synthesis of purpose and effort of the group members.

The action indicated in the words above is dependent on the stimulation and guidance of one or more members of the group involved in an organizational activity. This presentation is primarily concerned with the group activity that is focused on the instructional program. There must be some products of leadership that bring about the desired kinds of effort leading to a realization of the accepted group purposes. The products of leadership can be visible. That person who helps others to achieve a coordinated action leading to a common purpose can be acknowledged as creating the conditions under which such coordination occurs. It means that a leader is an influencer of people, a person who can stimulate people to action, and a person who can evaluate the products of individual and group action as they relate to the purpose accepted by the group.

A leader can bring about stability in action to produce coordinated activity and purposeful achievements. Stability is not a matter of establishing one way of relating. Rather, it is a process that makes the best use of individual expertise for the needs of any particular time. However, it must keep everyone interested in achieving the common purpose. A program of action is the product of this kind of leadership. Leadership that brings about this coordination can be identified also as a synthesizer of people and purpose, of purpose and effort, and of effort and product. This type of program of action will be explored in greater detail in chapter 14, "Direction through Indirection."

Examples of Strategy

1. *Pursue the meaning of the terms listed in order to show how these leadership characteristics can bring about unity. Include use, misuse, and abuse, in discussing balance.*

2. *Characteristics of leadership are often misunderstood. Use in-service meetings to define or redefine leadership and its many ramifications.*

3. *Be aware of the leadership roles assumed by many of your staff members. Make a special effort to commend those who use the leadership role in a positive manner to promote the purposes and efforts of your system.*

A STRATEGY MODEL

The Purpose-Effort Strategy Model presented in Figure 1 was developed to summarize the point of view expressed in this chapter. It focuses on the strategies of instructional management with a major concern for the humanistic approach. Humanizing, in the context of the model, is defined as:

> Humanizing in education administration relates to the elevation of human dignity. Identifying, cultivating, and developing personal qualities that result in a feeling of self-worth are basic to growth and perpetuation of the administrative effort and the good health of the educational system. School system cohesiveness of effort toward goal or mission achievement is dependent on the interpersonal esteem and respect that is shared by the individual members. Personal respect and esteem are basic to group respect and mission cohesiveness. Humanistic approaches instill feelings of self-worth through the harmonizing of individual needs, interests, and aspirations with those of the system.

The strategies of instructional management focus on the school's instructional program, with full realization that many personalities must be involved in the total enterprise. There are instructional impacts that must be accounted for if management is to be achieved. These antecedents to action are discussed extensively in chapter 11.

The arc providing a cover for the central part of the Model is identified as Instructional Impact Sources. All of the sources obviously cannot be identified in any one model or even at any one time. Three major sources of impact are identified in circles 1, 2, and 3. Circle 1 constitutes the purposes generated by the people in the environment of the school. Since they have personalized purposes for education, and since they have not entered into conscious coordination of their purposes, they can be seen from the school's point of view as Multiple Competitors. Individuals seek to put their personal imprints on the school's program, based primarily on the kinds of purposes generated in the individual's mind.

The Normative Prescribers indicated in circle 2, Institutional Purposes, provide an impact source that may be a coordinated or consolidated expression of the Environmental Purposes indicated in circle 1. It is obvious that an institutional purpose cannot be a complete amalgamation of all of the purposes from the community sources that are competing for impact on instruction. Normative prescribers include the legislative branches of government, the local municipality boards and council, and the school administrative boards. Each of these are aided by their respective executive officers. There may be, as shown by the double arrow between circles 1 and 2, an exchange between the environment and the institution. This denotes a facility for compromise so that the local board of education in particular might be an appropriate interpreter of the interests of the environment for the schools. The Multiple Competitors of the Environmental Purposes may have a direct impact on those individuals who must carry the decision forward to Management Strategies. As indicated above, these

Figure 1.   *The Purpose-Effort Strategy Model.*

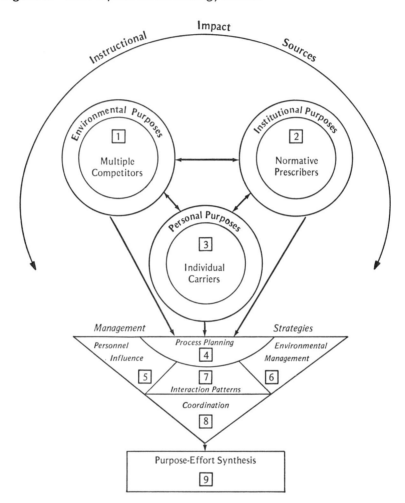

Adapted from Fig. 7 (p. 143) in EDUCATION, ADMINISTRATION, AND CHANGE: The Redeployment of Resources by Lanore A. Netzer et al. Copyright © 1970 by Harper & Row, Publishers, Inc. Courtesy of the publisher.

often have been channeled through the institutional purpose development whereby the many prescriber demands are formulated into policy. Eventually these purposes and policies come to professional people, who also have personal purposes. These professionals are called the Individual Carriers of the purpose to effort and action.

Professional personnel normally would be the ones represented by circle 3. The impact then must go through the process of planning. In this instance, the planning is for a process that carries forward the purposes generated, and possibly coordinated and consolidated, by the purposes emanating from circles 1, 2, and 3.

Process Planning, number 4, becomes one of the major efforts of consolidating, in a realistic way, the wishes of those who have the sources of impact on instruction, and developing those wishes into an implementable program. Process Planning must include Personnel Influences, Environmental Management, and Interaction Patterns. Personnel Influence comes primarily from those professional workers who have unique ways of seeing the purposes of education. But they also have a responsibility, as indicated in number 6 of the Model, to bring about some realistic management of the environmental impacts. If Personnel Influence and Environmental Management can operate successfully, then an Interaction Pattern, number 7, is shown as a means of harnessing the various sources of purpose.

The purposes and the processes provide the power for Interaction Patterns to lead to Coordination, number 8. When coordination has been achieved, there is direct entry to the effort to achieve the purposes that were generated, accepted, and implemented. This is called the Purpose-Efforts Synthesis, number 9, which is the purpose of the descriptive model shown here and which provides the focus for this book as it seeks to develop the strategies of instructional management through a major emphasis on the humanistic approach.

Humanism is seen in this presentation as being something far more desirable and effective than the earlier model called the Line-Staff Model. The Line-Staff Model was based primarily on authority, control, constraints, and rigidity. It was believed that this kind of management was the only way to achieve institutional purposes. It has been discovered over the years, through experience and research, that this kind of control of intelligent human beings in a free society does not work. Creativity that is possessed by school personnel is lost as is the stimulation that can be generated by pursuit of individual purposes, as opposed to the purposes imposed by a rigid organization.

The power sought in this publication is that power generated by stimulating and directing the purposes of individuals, working in a group or institutional arrangement, to gain major effort as a result of their own purposing. Stimulation and direction achieve effectiveness through planned action or strategies. All chapters include "Examples of Strategy" to relate the discussion more closely to the instructional management responsibilities of all school personnel. The next chapter presents analyses interrelating examples of strategies that encourage development of the skills of reciprocity.

STIMULATION IN MORE READING

American Association of School Administrators Yearbook. *Profiles of the Administrative Team*. Washington, D.C., 1971.

English, Fenwick W. *School Organization and Management*. Worthington, Ohio: Charles A. Jones Publishing Company, 1975.

Kirschenbaum, Howard, and Sidney B. Simon (eds.). *Readings in Values Clarification*. Minneapolis: Winston Press, 1973.

Mitchell, Vance F., Richard T. Barth, and Frances H. Mitchell (eds.). *Proceedings of the 32nd Annual Meeting of The Academy of Management*. Minneapolis, 1972.

Netzer, Lanore A., Glen G. Eye, Marshall E. Dimock, Matthew P. Dumont, Lloyd Homme, Fremont E. Kast, and Stephen J. Knezevich. *Education, Administration, and Change,* New York: Harper and Row, Publishers, 1970.

Reciprocities
as Building Blocks

Chapter 3 dealt with the synthesis of purpose and effort. This synthesis can be achieved only when people constitute the media through which the two work in close coordination or are synthesized in action. Purpose and effort can only combine through involved people to be a force in any organizational activity. *Reciprocity* between people is one way that purpose and effort become synthesized in action. People determine the content of reciprocity as well as the procedures that nurture and maintain it. The content of purpose and effort, as well as reciprocity, in this book is focused on the instructional program sponsored by schools.

The fact that an organization called *the school* requires many different kinds of tasks to be performed and services to be rendered does not remove the necessity for all people in the organization to work toward a common purpose and in a reinforcing manner. Task differentiation is essential to the successful activities of an organization. Task differentiation, however, permits individuals working in the organization to deliver their own unique contributions to the common purpose, namely, the development of young people, the pupils or students. Task differentiation is a way of organizing; it does not infer that, once a task has been isolated and a person(s) assigned to it, that person must work unrelated to others in the organization. Differentiation need not lead to the isolation of individuals or groups of individuals as they go about their specific assignments within the total organizational effort.

Teaching and learning are very complex tasks. There is no set of skills or procedures that all teachers, supervisors, and administrators use to contribute to the teaching and learning enterprise. Complexity demands different kinds of abilities from the personnel employed by the school. In this way, complexities can be mastered and effectiveness can result. Understanding and direct support among the personnel carrying on the activities of teaching and learning are important aspects of reciprocity. Understanding is essential so that persons can relate their own assigned unique tasks to those assigned to others. Direct support is essential; the total enterprise cannot succeed if individuals or groups work against each other's particular assignment. In this sense, reciprocity is both a process and a product: it describes a way that people can understand and support each other in the total enterprise; and it is an achievement of the conscious efforts of people to understand each other and to render assistance.

MEANING OF TERMS

Two key terms are used in this chapter, *reciprocity* and *building blocks*. Reciprocity is a mutual exchange among people involving many different kinds of activities essential to the accomplishment of the complex tasks of teaching and learning. A principal provides instructional materials to the teachers and the teachers, in turn, exercise some conservation in the use of these materials. Thus, reciprocity in support has been gained; the principal performs an administrative function of materials supply and the teachers respond by putting those materials to good use.

A teacher is thwarted by a disruptive pupil and another teacher or administrator suggests the legal alternatives for the resolution of the problem. Thus, one teacher is confronted with a problem and receives reciprocally an assist from those whose unique contributions are the knowledge of and communication about the legal alternatives.

A teacher has the privilege of selecting instructional goals and another teacher provides information on related goals in the learning sequence, namely year-to-year, grade-to-grade, or course-to-course. Thus, two teachers have reciprocated to provide a better base for achieving continuity in learning. A superintendent releases the results of system-wide testing and the principal prepares teachers and community for a proper interpretation of those test results. The superintendent is not acting alone and neither is the principal. Rather, they complement each other's efforts to bring about maximum advantage from the information released.

A principal supervises the transfer of pupils from one school to another and, in the process, supplies information pertinent to the teaching and learning continuity. Reciprocity is achieved via the actions of the transferring administrator and the receiving administrator, and the learning situation is supported by these actions.

The second term, building blocks, represents the elements essential to coordination and purposeful action. Building blocks can be identified by words such as: *respect, confidence, clarity of expectations, autonomy, compromise, analysis*, and *ethics*. These terms or building blocks will be used to structure the presentation of the rest of this chapter. Reciprocity will provide support as the building blocks to better teaching and learning situations are explored and applied.

CONSISTENCY GENERATES RESPECT

Lack of respect is not a beneficial state between two or more persons committed to fulfilling parts of the responsibility for a common goal. Uncertainty about what those goals are and how to achieve them can deter the contribution each individual makes to the organizational enterprise. Uncertainty about what the purposes or goals are, as well as uncertainty with respect to personal contributions to those purposes, breeds fear in the individual. Fear prevents people from achieving their maximum potential, and leads the individual to make decisions and choose behaviors on the basis of expediency.

Expediency means that the individual, rather than performing on the basis of predetermined and self-selected behaviors, yields to the real or imagined expectations of others. Expediency tends to exalt the wishes and behaviors of others. Those who choose behaviors on the basis of expediency will find those behaviors inconsistent simply because the people in the environment have different purposes and ways of acting. Individuals, rather than acting on the basis of self-chosen behaviors, try to guess what the other person would like them to do. In any organizational endeavor, there are many other persons. Each individual receives a multiplicity of impacts from many other people and acting on the basis of expediency results in highly variable ways of acting. The dependence on outguessing others for the sake of expediency destroys the individual's consistency. The variability generated by trying to behave as other people would have you behave destroys the stability in individual patterns of action.

Stability is the base of consistency, and consistency is the only way that people eventually can understand a pattern of performance generated or chosen by an individual. Consistency cannot be achieved on the basis of expediency. Consistency can be achieved only if the individual has a referent set of values on all occasions when alternative behaviors are possible and when individual choice of behavior becomes necessary. A particular behavior choice must always have an answer as to why. That why is better answered in terms of a value system. The person who can act with consistency and who knows why the acts were chosen communicates to others by the action itself. Behaviors communicate as well as words. Other people will have a basis for extending respect if a consistent pattern of behavior is established based on good reasons. The respect of others is the greatest support to self-respect, and self-respect leads one to consistent patterns of behaviors based on acceptable values.

Examples of Strategy

1. *A periodic diary might be kept to record the outstanding actions of a particular day with some speculations as to why the particular actions were chosen as performed.*

2. *Make queries about the uncertainties that exist among your colleagues on a staff. What are the things that cause people to wonder about their own roles in the action to which all are committed, and how much of the time are people performing without being fairly certain as to the nature of the outcomes that might be anticipated? Anyone can set about raising these questions and thereby cause an analysis of the kinds of uncertainties that exist.*

3. *List some of the volitions and compulsions as various members of the staff perceive them. A comparison of volitions and compulsions might bring insights into the extent to which a consistency of relationships exists and thereby provide a support for mutuality of respect.*

4. *Conversations, formal and informal, about the value patterns held by various members of the organization give rise to analysis that could help meet the requirements of consistency of action. Such conversations could hasten the achievement of self-respect and respect for others as a supportive state among all people in the educational enterprise.*

OPENNESS STIMULATES CONFIDENCE

Consistency in action, as indicated in the previous section, can lead to *confidence*, in oneself and in others engaged in a common task. The basis of confidence could be full information about the purposes and procedures of others. Secrecy about one's purpose or procedures can easily produce suspicion. What people do not know can easily be supplanted by what they can imagine. Imaginings can be incorrect, providing a weak basis for proceeding with the task at hand.

Suspicion traffics in assumptions. If people have to imagine what others are purposing and doing, the imagination creates assumptions. When people make assumptions about their own work or the work of their associates, these assumptions can be as satisfying as facts. Assumptions, however, often fail careful scrutiny. Assumptions can be discarded, of course, but they also can be the basis for choosing action before they are discarded. On the other hand, scrutiny can reinforce facts. If facts can not withstand scrutiny, they can be discarded just as assumptions can. But assumptions are much more volatile than facts. Scrutiny, then, is one way of determining whether people are operating on the basis of assumptions or facts.

The refinement of assumptions and facts can occur through review and report. It is highly advisable for people to review their assumptions and facts periodically and to report them to someone else. Refinements achieved through reviewing and reporting can constitute a pattern of openness occasioning confidence in oneself and in others, as well as in the purpose of the total organization. Openness, however, must be recognized as multidirectional. It cannot be characteristic of only administrators, supervisors, or teachers. It must be experienced throughout the activities of the enterprise. Since openness is multidirectional, it must be a characteristic of all people who have a responsibility in the activity.

Examples of Strategy

1. *A monthly review of the why of behaviors of all participants in one satisfactory incident can establish a pattern of thinking causing attention to be focused and refocused on the whys of what is being done. The habit of questioning of why a thing is being done in a particular way can bring about a basis for confidence in the purpose of the enterprise, as well as among those who are participants.*

2. *Develop a form for gathering information on the reasons appearing vital in any decision event. This could be a very simple memo or data-gathering instrument that would make it easy for all persons involved in a decision activity to register the reasons that seemed most important when they took a position on the issue. It is not necessary that these forms be signed; the reasons are more important than who held those reasons.*

3. *Use all media to invite declarations of "What I would like to know." This has a tendency to focus attention on the kinds of information that people want. Teachers might want to know why a particular decision was made in a board of education meeting. They are entitled to know not only the decision that was made but the reasons for that decision. This would constitute an openness that would eliminate the feeling that secrecy was the mode of operation, and would stimulate confidence in the fact that decisions were being made wisely.*

4. There might be substantial gains in group discussions on "What I like most about a listener." This would direct some thought to the fact that it is just as important to be a listener as it is to have an opportunity to speak. If people are happy having their statements challenged, it is important to know this about their particular way of entering into group action. It might provide an opportunity for all people to become more sensitive to the things a listener can do to bring out the best suggestions from those voicing their beliefs and opinions.

PERFORMANCE AND EXPECTATIONS

Expectations placed on persons tend to condition not only the things they do but the quality of the performance exhibited. There are many sources of expectations and all of these condition performance.

Some expectations are established in the employment contract. The directives provided at group meetings and the individual contact with colleagues and peers, who indicate the kinds of things they wish other people would do, constitute expectations. These are expectations that come from people involved in the employment process as well as from colleagues who share some of the differentiated tasks required in the conduct of the school educational program.

Expectations originate in other people as well as in the targeted individual. People develop ideas of what they would like to do and what they would like to become. Self-imposed expectations are conditioners of performance as much as those imposed by others. The many sources of expectations may induce individual variability in their acceptance and recognition, thereby resulting in variability of performance. There is nothing wrong in variability of performance but it may lead to complications in checking the quality of performance. Variability may be controlled by maintaining a close relationship to the purpose at which the performance is aimed. There needs to be conscious effort to bring about harmony between expectations and performance.

Wisdom is not found in the acceptance or imposition of expectations without some evidence that the expectations can be or have been fulfilled. This is the essence of evaluation. Too often, job descriptions for school positions may indicate the expectations of the formal management of the organization. At the same time, it is necessary to determine what kinds of performance constitute evidence that the expectations have been fulfilled. Without these performance anticipations or behavioral outcomes, the process of evaluation may become unfair and misleading. Confidence can be established through a full review of all expectations and the kind of performance relevant to those expectations. Evaluation, in this sense, is not as objectionable as it often is when performance is judged unrelated to the expectations that should have been stated at the beginning of the employment activity.

Expectations also can be effective instruments for planning. If expectations are assessed in terms of relevant performance evidence, they may lead to a decision to maintain the performance as observed. On the other hand they can lead to a design for new and better ways of accomplishing the goals of the organization and the expectations placed on each individual.

Examples of Strategy

1. The analysis of job descriptions in terms of expected performance might be an activity that could be entered into by administrators, supervisors, and teachers with great benefit to all. In this sense it would bring about a revelation of hidden expectations that may have existed at the time of employment or that might have been self-chosen by the employees.

2. Have position incumbents revise their own job descriptions in terms of the kinds of things that they see themselves doing in order to accommodate the original description as prescribed in the employment process.

3. Institute an open search for hidden expectations. This does not mean that people harboring hidden expectations are necessarily seeking to harm someone else. It simply means that they, perhaps, have not had an occasion to review them.

4. Ask teachers to draft model job descriptions for all administrative and supervisory positions. This would provide the teachers a vehicle for expressing what support they would like to have from the administrative and supervisory staff.

LIMITS OF AUTONOMY

Much emphasis has been placed on the individualization of teaching and learning. There is no doubt that individualization is necessary, but there must be an orderly way of achieving the goals established by an organization.

Autonomy basically is self-determination. It is assumed, however, that a person who achieves some autonomy or self-determination in school tasks possesses goals that are in harmony with the school goals. It does not mean that accepting the purposes and procedures of another person necessarily destroys autonomy. Patterning after other people might be a self-determined way of acting. It is still autonomy, even though there is a commonality of pattern.

Autonomy, in itself, should not be a goal of an individual's activity. In this case, it could not be realized until the individual was free of all expectations and patterns established by others. This age of negotiation and bargaining has established a concept of autonomy that grows out of adversarity. Leaders on each side of the table seem to abandon the spirit of reciprocity and seek instead to substitute group guarantees of autonomy. (It is hoped that the negotiation process will mature into a less guerilla like relationship.) The inclination to feel that a person is wrong just because others are behaving in the same way is not a satisfactory way to judge the level of autonomy that is experienced.

Some people may speculate that there is only one way of achieving complete autonomy; that is to be in an environment devoid of people. This is hard to accomplish and highly undesirable in a modern world. But even if the individual were free of expectations and constraints imposed by other people in the environment, there still would be conditions imposed by nature. Realistically, a person who chooses education chooses an activity that involves other people. A proper view of the relationship between the individual's purposes and the organization's goals is needed. These cannot be too disparate or the purposes and goals of education would not be realized. Entering into an employment contract assumes that the individual examined the conditions under which the employment takes place and accepted them. The acceptance is autonomous for that individual. But the employment contract itself becomes an instrument for determining priorities between individual purposes and organizational goals. There are personal as well as interpersonal aspects to purposing. Certainly, individuals who find satisfaction in seeing the personnel in an organization accomplish the goals of that organization have achieved a perspective on personal and organizational priorities that could be rewarding.

Autonomy cannot be achieved by invading the rights of others. It is intolerable for one person to achieve autonomy if associates in the activity or organization lose it. These rights have been defined in codes of ethics, the regulations of the school district, the laws of the state, and the decisions of the courts. Their priorities are well established and the individual is free to accept or reject them by accepting or rejecting the contract for employment.

Autonomy is both a process and a product. It is a process in the sense it provides an opportunity for the individual to assess personal priorities as they relate to the organizational priorities. It is a product in the sense that with a balance of priorities between the self and the organization, it provides the sense of being a self-determining individual; thus, autonomy becomes a product.

Can a person without autonomy still be creative? Perhaps the creative person is under more constraints than the noncreative person, particularly since creativity often requires a great deal of self-discipline. Creativity is not something that occurs as if by magic. It occurs because an individual, possessing certain unique capacities and abilities, is able to apply those to a task at hand and to come up with unique outcomes. It is impossible for an organization to require creativity of an individual. The individual is the medium through which creativity takes place. The limits of autonomy are to be found in disciplined self-determination rather than haphazard or careless self-determination. Autonomy is determined by the limits of the purpose that one accepts and strives for in an organizational enterprise. Other aspects of autonomy were explored in chapter 3.

Examples of Strategy

1. Invite the staff to list the things that "cramp their style." In this way one can assess those elements in the organization that seem to be frustrating. Those individuals who believe they could be doing something better if they could apply more of their own self-determined ways of going about the task need a way and an opportunity to make their feelings known.

2. Stimulate buzz sessions on "What I would like to do if I could." Any one person in the organization, particularly at the administrative or supervisory level, may not be able to assess the kinds of things that people would like to be doing if they had the time to do them, if they had the permission or support to do them, and if they had the material required for what they want to do.

3. Distribute do-and-don't interpretations of the employment contract. Often there may be a hidden feeling that the employment contract is something to try to evade or contradict. This need not be so, but often there is little effort to interpret the kinds of intent that a board of education has in the provisions of the contract. In the present day of negotiations, there are many opportunities to bring about more discussion and common interpretation of the employment contract.

4. Ask for cooperative effort in defining autonomy levels. This means that there are some areas in which perhaps no autonomy should be granted. For instance, in the case of health and safety there must be some commonality and constraints so that all people in the organization can work safely. There are other levels, such as the selection of the learning experiences to accomplish an agreed on goal, in which the individual teacher has a great deal of autonomy in selecting and pursuing the teaching procedure.

RECIPROCITIES IN COMPROMISE

The word *compromise* has come into disrepute primarily because it suggests a vacillation between choices of goals or behaviors. It is unfortunate because compromise is a phenomenon that can occur on an interpersonal basis and can achieve agreements possibly better than the self-selected purposes and activities of individuals.

Persuaders are found in all environments. Persuaders want to communicate a point of view that might influence the performance of others. Many people are persuaded and adapt their own behaviors according to the suggestions of others. Persuaders may find occasions when they communicate their points of view and desires to others who are unpersuaded. And so we have a pattern in group activity where a person(s) seeks to influence the actions of others who accept or reject the influence.

Instances in which the persuaders and the unpersuaded continue in the same activity leave little doubt that "something has to give." If the two points of view are so antagonistic in nature as to handicap the accomplishment of the organizational goals, something has to be done about it. Perhaps increased opportunities for interaction between the persuaders and the unpersuaded might bring about alternate decisions acceptable to both.

Unfortunately, many persuaders want to continue persuading without being persuaded by others. This leads to the problem of *one-wayism*. There are alternatives to one-wayism, but usually they have to develop as a result of an agreement between the conflicting points of view (conflicting thoughts). When the alternatives to one-wayism are explored, compromise is one way to break through the roadblocks that exist. Compromise means that one or both parties to the exchange has won and/or lost. When one yields to a persuader, there should be a gracious retraction rather than a vindictive acceptance. At the same time, the persuader, or that person who has influenced the new or alternate decision, should have the capacity for humble accession. There is no time for the person who wins the point to reflect on power over someone else as a source of satisfaction. It is more important to consider the original point of difference rather than the personal gains achieved by imposing a point of view on another.

Progress is achieved through the interaction of people—the vehicle for this interaction is compromise. Compromise is the intelligent way of resolving conflicting points of view or decisions in a way that all parties can gain as well as yielding particular points.

A suggested sequence in the reciprocity of compromise is compromise—time lapse—review. Whenever one person yields a point of view to the discussions of an interaction, there should be some agreement as to the time lapse that would be acceptable before a review is instituted of the new decision, so that once again a new compromise might be achieved. The equity of this type of interaction through compromise can prove satisfactory to all individuals in an organizational setting. Additional discussion of the meaning of compromise can be found in chapter 1.

Examples of Strategy

1. *Develop an alphabetized list of "points at issue" for periodical review. This would provide an opportunity to see if certain types of subject matter come into issue between individuals or groups more than others. At the same time, it would be possible to review what kind of compromise seemed to bring the most positive results to the interacting parties. This might chart a new way of resolving the differences between people or between groups. The important thing is not who wins or loses the point but what resolution to the issue is achieved.*

2. *Maintain a personnel frequency table of recognized concessions to points of view and decision issues. It is quite possible that this would expose to observance those who want to dominate in all decisions. It might, at the same time, provide a basis for discovering who is unable to make compromises or never has an individualistic point of view. Use this as a basis for encouraging a sense of security in confronting issues at hand and in seeking compromises that can satisfy the greatest number of people and at the same time accomplish a proper goal.*

3. *Establish a calendar of issue reviews. The time lapse to review becomes an important concession to those who engage in the act of compromise. Justice demands provision of an opportunity for the decision to be scrutinized to see if further improvements can be developed.*

ANALYTIC BASES FOR MUTUALITY

Reciprocity is the mutuality that can be achieved between interacting persons and groups. It was indicated earlier that the lack of openness often causes people to operate on the basis of imagination and to depend on assumptions rather than facts. *Analysis* is the best cure for the ills that might be engendered by a lack of communication or the secretive bases of operation. There is great power in definition. Whenever an issue is identified, and prior to initiating some efforts at resolution, people should make sure that they have the same understanding of the stated issue. Too often, a commonality of information is assumed that does not exist. Just because people work together in the educational enterprise, they do not necessarily have common perceptions of the things that should be done and the ways to do them. To cure this lack of commonality of information, define and search for relevant facts.

Issues should not be resolved, decisions should not be made, and goals should not be selected on the basis of expediency or notions of the moment. A search for facts is needed and these facts should be arrayed in a manner that induces comparative interpretations. A fact might mean one thing to one person and another thing to another person, but the differences in interpretation do not change the fact itself. The opportunity for the exchange of information involved in a comparison might be the best way to sort out the relevancy of facts and to establish the priority of those that might influence the decisions of individuals and groups.

The setting of priorities for facts relevant to any particular issue means that a weighting is given to those facts that ought to influence most decisions. In the end, there are bound to be some lingering differences. These can be more agreeable if they are arrived at following a careful definition of terms and issues, a search for relevant facts, and a compromise of the interpretation of these facts. This means that there would be a continuing process of mutuality based in the analytic procedures.

Examples of Strategy

1. *Formulate several analytic procedures to allow for flexibility as different kinds of issues and problems are confronted. This would give all persons involved in the discussion the feeling that a one-wayism had not been instituted by someone in the process of analyzing issues and problems.*

2. *Institute open group discussions with attention to the definition of key terms in the agenda items. This need not take more than a few minutes at the beginning of any group discussion, but it might tend to keep that discussion in focus and increase the exchange of information.*

3. *Discuss ways of "living with differences" when no issue is under consideration. Too often the inclination is to try to work out a stressful situation in the heat of argument. It would be better to open discussion on ways of working together in the face of differences in points of view when there is no specific difference at issue.*

ETHICS OF AGREEMENT
AND DISAGREEMENT

Ethics implies an acceptance of certain standards to judge behavior. In any group activity, there are many points of agreement as well as points of disagreement. It is important that these be faced in an ethical way; certain standards of behavior must be accepted by all parties in the group and seen as a facilitator of the interaction leading to group accomplishments.

One type of ethic that should be considered is that agreement does not constitute the basis for developing a power group. It is too easy for people who have achieved agreement to feel that they have a proprietary grasp on whatever that decision may affect. A power group may evolve that tends to impose that point of view on others who disagree. Agreement ought to be recognized for what it is and not as a basis for a power grab.

Recognition should be given to individuals and groups inclined to move from disagreement to isolation. Too often, the individual who was outvoted, lost an argument, or failed to achieve a particular point of view tends to withdraw from the group and its activities. This isolation and disagreement tend to preserve the point of disagreement and make future compromise less likely.

Recognition also must be given to those who have achieved agreement and assured that such agreement was based on fact and quality. It is just as possible to reach an agreement on a falsity as it is on a fact. These things need to be assessed from time to time so that no illusions develop with respect to the outcomes of group thinking.

Again, it must be recognized that disagreement, while leading to isolation—either self-imposed or alter-imposed—does not constitute an identity of danger. A person who disagrees is not one who should be targeted for destruction. Rather, the respect that constitutes mutuality among differing people can be the basis for achieving the best possible compromise. The respect that comes out of the ability to live with agreement and disagreement really becomes an extension of oneself. The kind of thinking one does about his or her own agreements and disagreements may be the thing that increases the communication between that person and others in the organizational setting. When respect is accomplished through an extension of self, there is almost certainly a purpose-supported understanding. In other words, the whys of points of view become the bases that reflect the kinds of purposes accepted by the individual or by the group. This supports the mutuality of understanding that can make a group enterprise thrive.

Examples of Strategy

1. *Develop a code that can produce an interaction among people who find themselves in agreement and disagreement. The code can be very simple. It can indicate that one person must not dominate the discussion time but rather should alternate between discussing and listening. Respect is gained as the orderliness of the interaction can be insured to all involved.*

2. *Maintain a record of agreements and disagreements. This provides the assurance that at some future time the agreements can be assessed and consolidated, maintained and strengthened. Or it can mean that, from the record of disagreements, reassessments can take place. Without the record, and with people operating entirely from a memory of agreements and disagreements, there may be many intervening distortions that increase the probability that constraints and conflict will develop rather than issues resolved.*

3. *Encourage all personnel to report promising procedures for reaching agreements. This will indicate a positive way of looking at the process of interacting. All personnel have found unique ways of achieving agreements with others. The procedures might be shared with all others and constitute a source for those who believe that reciprocity and mutuality is a strengthening factor for individuals in a group situation.*

BUILDING DIRECTION

Building blocks are for building toward a purpose. The purpose here is the development and maintenance of a good educational program. The thesis is held that all professional participants in the school have unique contributions to make to goals. These contributions cannot be accomplished without reference to the others in the school environment. This implied coordination requires conscious effort by all personnel. Reciprocity as a process of mutual supportiveness is offered as facilitator. The building blocks having the best promise of coordination are: respect, confidence, clarity of expectations, autonomy, compromise, analysis, and ethics. The reciprocity motive and these building blocks lead us directly to the substance of chapter 5, "Loyalties and Influences."

SOME SUGGESTED READINGS

Bennis, Warren G., Kenneth D. Benne, Robert Chin, and Kenneth D. Corey. *The Planning of Change.* 3rd ed. New York: Holt, Rinehart and Winston, 1976.

DeCecco, John P., and Arlene K. Richards. *Growing Pains: Uses of School Conflict.* New York: Aberdeen Press, 1974.

Loyalties and Influences

The reciprocities discussed in chapter 4 were viewed as building blocks to group achievement. The emphasis was on the interactions among people, reciprocal reactions and interactions that strengthened the processes people use to achieve their common or individual purposes. The motivations that stimulated reciprocity were not discussed but considerable attention was given to the ways that interactions were conditioned by organizational structures and operational patterns. That chapter defined reciprocity as a pattern of interactions among people, developed and maintained through the structures of organization and operation.

This chapter emphasizes the individual as a person operating within a group of persons. Loyalties and influences will be analyzed in terms of the reactions of persons to persons. This chapter complements the preceding chapter in that organizational structures and operational patterns cannot exist without the people who occupy the various structural posts and implement the operational pattern. How people influence people as persons, rather than as occupants of hierarchical statuses, in an ongoing effort to achieve the goals of the institution will be discussed. The focus is on people reacting to and interacting with people.

NATURE OF LOYALTY

Loyalty in its simplest and most direct form can be called *adherence*, adherence to a purpose, a person, a pattern, and/or a promise. The most frequent occurrence of adherence is to persons. Persons may have diverse or common purposes and may pursue diverse or comparable patterns of action. The person varies in adherence to a promise according to the origin of the promise or to other reasons that may govern the degree of adherence.

The primary concern is with the loyalty that occurs between persons. The person may be a peer, a subordinate, a superordinate, or even a stranger, as well as those mythical people identified as a movement. At any rate, the nature of loyalty is highly personalized.

Loyalty to persons can be aggressive or passive. In the case of aggressive loyalty, patterns of action may be characterized by high levels of vigor and possibly of dominance. Submission, on the other hand, is a passive type of loyalty, although it may be seen as a condition that can be identified with either aggressive or passive types of loyalty. Normally, the passive type of loyalty is expressed by those who exhibit no strong feelings of adherence and yet do adhere. The individual expresses no reasons for loyalty or lack of loyalty. The individual who is not particularly active may still be loyal even though it is less obvious than in the more aggressive type.

Loyalty can be said to be stronger than love or hatred. There are those who feel an emotional love, a common love for a cause, or a common commitment to a goal, yet, the love of these things may not be a true measure of loyalty. Loyalty seems to override aggressive or passive types of love. As for hatred, there are individuals who hate other individuals yet, for reasons of their own, remain loyal to that hated person. Hatred is not a good basis for loyalty, nor is it developmental in the sense that loyalty based on love can be. Loyalty to those who are hated may have a personal motive, such as, some anticipated benefit. Nonetheless, the joy of loyalty will not be as great when expressed to the hated as to the loved.

Some myths about the nature of loyalty seem to persist. One of these myths is attached to *hierarchical status.* There is a culture base built into the minds and sensitivities of many people that loyalty is due a person who holds a higher status in the hierarchical structure. Hopefully, those in the high hierarchical status also are loyal to those who hold lower posts. But the myth seems to be that loyalty is less obligatory for those in the higher status than it is for those in the lower status. In recent years, there have been some solid efforts to move beyond this concept of hierarchical status as it relates to loyalty. At the present time, there are indications that, while the culture still imposes loyalty in the hierarchy, performance has been able to displace much of this older concept. Because of this, there is more participatory action and recognition of individual contributions to an enterprise. These contributions have become the bases for loyalty rather than hierarchical status.

Another myth is that loyalty is generated by the promise of *monetary rewards*. It is assumed that those in a higher status, who have been rewarded more generously for contribution to a cause, would be more loyal than those who receive lower levels of rewards for service. A related myth holds that loyalty is generated through *status rewards*. Those in the upper hierarchical status positions can give some recognition to those in lower level positions, thus stimulating the flow of loyalty from lower positions to higher positions. This is not the case presently, except as a residue of cultural inheritance.

Some people support another myth that loyalty occurs because of *fear* generated in the individual who is expressing loyalty. The fear may be for the security of the future, the penalty of the present, the loss of status and money rewards, or the separation from group activity, in this case, the school as director of educational programs. Many movements in the past few decades, primarily through the process of negotiation, have removed much of this fear and, thus, loyalty has to be generated by different means.

Still another myth about loyalty holds that, if the working conditions are sufficiently favorable, the individuals in the organization will be loyal to peers, subordinates, and superordinates simply because of the *pleasures of working*. These conditions probably do not generate that much loyalty and there are other much stronger bases.

Regardless of all the myths involved in the nature of loyalty, and all the other things that may describe it or bring it about, a mutuality in loyalty will bring about greater satisfaction and greater continuity. Mutuality of loyalty becomes one of the most important characteristics to develop and preserve in a relationship that involves loyalty. Mutuality and continuity can be gained much more readily if loyalty is based on rational thinking and conclusions. Blind loyalty is a way of identifying many of the characteristics of loyalty, but these are related primarily to the myths described above. Rational behavior has no counterpart in blindness, particularly when loyalty between people is the concern.

Examples of Strategy

1. *Invite all staff members to describe a few specific instances in which they were aware of a growing sense of loyalty to a purpose, a person, or an action pattern because of the manner of interaction.*

2. *List first principles that you would uphold during the course of collective bargaining that might promote loyalty with employees while representing the goals of the employer (school board). Invite teachers to react to the list.*

3. *In small group discussions, list specific examples of loyalty based on love of a person or hatred of a person. Attempt to define the reasons for each situation.*

NATURE OF INFLUENCE

Influence primarily is an other-person response. A reason for loyalty to another person constitutes a source of influence. On the other hand, the first person may simply react to the second person without any real interaction. The generation of influence, however, is one type of reaction and, therefore, could be termed an interaction.

Influence can be induced. It can be induced by some of the means cited in the previous section on the nature of loyalty. Perhaps the oldest concept is that of training people from childhood to adhere to a certain pattern of behavior and belief, a concept presumed to be followed in countries highly dictatorial in nature. But influence occurs almost continuously. Even though the individual has been indoctrinated almost from birth, there is a continuous bombardment from a multitude of influential sources. There are as many different ways of inducing influence as there are people to be influenced. This can be multiplied by the many variations in individual personalities that provide an endless array of reasons for accepting influence or being influenced.

Many influences are self-chosen. People are subjected to many impacts that sometimes result in rational choices of the nature and target of influence sources. The self-chosen influence may be the best descriptor of freedom. On the other hand, a self-chosen influence could be destructive to the individual, as well as to the organization and environment in which that individual exists. If possible, it would be best if some influences were induced and others self-chosen, or each influence might be both induced and self-chosen.

The question of what is influenced is closely related to the substance of the influence. For example, influence might be focused on the association with a person or persons. The person might be influenced with respect to goals and purposes, with respect to beliefs, or with respect to ways of doing. These are examples of what is influenced. It is not enough to say that an individual has been influenced by another individual; one must describe the nature of the influence and the subject matter or content of the influence. This makes a great difference in the matter of loyalty and influence in the instructional organizational setting.

Caution must be exercised against the assumption that conformity is perfect influence. People may submit to a particular association because there are no other people available. A person may conform to the goals and purposes that beliefs and even ways of doing are means of maintaining employment and livelihood, or even a personally desired status. Influence is greater than conformity and perhaps that is the way it should remain.

One of the greatest influences is found in the *role of appreciation.* One individual may appreciate another not necessarily for having served that individual, but rather for what the other individual was doing or intended to do. This role of appreciation is one of the best descriptors of the finest type of influence. Appreciation can override the myths of hierarchical status and fear, and other kinds of things that describe loyalty that results in influence.

Closely related to appreciation is *acceptance and rejection.* Acceptance is positive, rejection is negative. In all probability, acceptance perpetuates a particular influence on the individual whereas rejection of the person, the goal, the beliefs, or the ways of doing tends to erode any influence that might occur.

A person can put together the ideas of appreciation and acceptance, reject the role of dominance, and move to what is called the *rule of indirection.* One of our great writers told the story in one sentence. "Teach people as though you taught them not, and treat things unknown as though forgot." Thus, the more positive aspects of influence are described as an indirect type of relationship between people. This makes it unnecessary to choose a myth to demand loyalty and exert influence. It becomes a positive type of interrelationship, not one of dominance or impact.

Examples of Strategy

1. Stimulate small group discussions on the topic, "What or who influenced me most in choosing education as a profession?"

2. Identify areas of recent professional success achieved by associates and extend appreciation.

3. Encourage teacher discussion identifying influences causing students to make unusually great effort in positive behavior in their classroom.

4. Identify about one percent of the student population that might be considered "troubled youngsters." Have small groups of teachers identify the influences that might be negative and thwart student success. Use this experience as a forerunner to a one-to-one voluntary teacher-student relationship to reveal caring and concern as an initiated plan of positive influences.

5. List specific examples of indirect methods of positive influence between teacher and student and administrator and teacher. Share such a list with the persons involved in the incidents.

REINFORCING-THWARTING INTERACTIONS

The loyalties and influences that characterize the interactions among individuals usually do not follow a common pattern. Individuals have preferences and this is proper. Individuals are at their best when they have their own pattern of preferences, whether it is association of people, the subject matter of the task assigned, or working conditions, along with the many other things for which people express preferences.

Preference becomes important as a promoter or inhibitor of the action and contributions of people. Some preferences may bring about a receptivity to reinforcement by interaction with other persons. Some preferences, however, may result in a thwarting of personal activity because of the nature of the interaction with others. Reinforcing and thwarting, are terms that describe the results of loyalties and influences that may occur among people.

Loyalties and influences may bring about changes in the individual with respect to people, assignment, subject content, or ways of doing. It must be recognized, however, that a preferred change is not necessarily traumatic. Sometimes the preferred change is a result of observation or suggestion. The preferred change may be neither reinforcing nor thwarting to the activities of an individual. The speed of the preferred change, and the cause of such change, may be either reinforcing or thwarting. It may be traumatic if persons have to change while feeling thwarted in not being able to do things they would like to do. The manner in which the loyalties occur, and the influences that result, can be reinforcing or thwarting to the individual responding to an influence. Persuasion as a change agent can be reinforcing or thwarting. Certain types of rewards, particularly the personalized kind such as recognition, accommodation, and acceptance, are likely to be reinforcing to the individual who has experienced a preferred change. Persuasion can result from threats that generate fear or from withholding recognition, acceptance, and support. Either the reinforcing or the thwarting pattern of persuasion will bring about change. The important thing to recognize is that, when change occurs, it remains a positive force for the individual. A negative force destroys much of the unique contribution that an individual might make to the educational enterprise.

Many believe that loyalties and influences can be subjected to manipulation. Most manipulation is offensive to the individual subjected to it. Yet there are those who believe that the political strategy that is appropriate for any kind of group activity is an acceptable way of influencing other persons. Manipulation, which is most likely to be offensive, probably will never be reinforcing and most likely will be thwarting to the individual, with respect to the employment expectations in the educational enterprise.

Interactions have content and process. This was inferred in many of the previous statements, as well as in some of the previous chapters. The content of interaction often deals with the selection of purposes and goals, the exposition of beliefs and preferences, the selection of the content for instruction, and the determination of the criteria by which evaluation can take place. The process of interaction is described in terms of the kinds of interactions that occur among people, particularly in a group enterprise such as the instructional program of a school. Process will be given more attention in other chapters of this book since both process and content are important in maintaining the reinforcing concept of stimulating individuals to make their best unique contributions to the education program.

Explicit and implicit influence patterns exist. The explicit patterns are perhaps the most reinforcing. There are those kinds that can be characterized by an openness of the consideration of policy and operational regulations. They are explicit when the opportunity is provided for any person to discuss, question, or approve some previously adopted practice. The implicit influence occurs because an individual gains some insights that had not been gained earlier. The new insights may bring about a change of preference in the selection of purpose and process. The most undesirable type of implicit influence comes from another person in the form of withheld information, implied threats, or communication by facial expression rather than by words. Whatever the pattern, it is well to analyze it frequently to determine whether it has a reinforcing or a thwarting effect on the interactions of the people in the organization.

One thing in the school's instructional program that must be considered is the disposition of needs of the individual and the situational demands of the organization. An illustration of this concern is a teacher who prefers to work without frequent interruptions. Some teachers may wish to work on a rather loose schedule rather than a highly structured one. There are times when the school situation demands rigid regulations with respect to time, distribution of materials, evaluative procedures in the classroom, and changes in programs that are pressured by a central office or organizations within an environment. There is perhaps no way to indicate a procedure to bring dispositional needs and situational demands together. The disposition of individuals and the demands of the situation, however, may be brought closer together through a concern for those interactions that are reinforcing, as opposed to those which are thwarting.

The role of rational motivation is based on the procedures by which influences can be the result of mutual interactions, mutual desires, and cooperative efforts. Thus, the probability of individuals arriving at self-chosen rational motivations will be increased, proving more reinforcing to the individual as a member of the group.

The merits of acceptance and approval need not be repeated here other than to indicate that acceptance and approval are practically always reinforcing and almost never thwarting in the interactions among people in an organization. The central focus of efforts to analyze interactions should be to determine whether they reinforce or thwart the individuals who are involved.

Examples of Strategy

1. *Open the discussion of a change need in the instructional program by listing procedure preferences of each participant.*

2. *In small group discussions of teachers and administrators, state examples of how the negotiated agreement reinforces and thwarts individual preferences.*

3. *Seek reactions from teachers on a one-to-one basis as to the type of classroom visitations that might reinforce the teacher's work.*

4. *Arrange for a team-teaching experience where an administrator or supervisor teaches with the regular teacher in a nonmonopolizing, nonthreatening supportive manner. This could take place on a given day or series of days, i.e., a unit relating to economics or taxation might be ideal for the participation of the district business manager or superintendent, in cooperation with the regular classroom teacher.*

ASSUMPTION-BURDENED PEERS

Many descriptions of peer relationships have appeared. A few are analyses that indicate the kinds of things that peers do to each other, and some are simply discussions of the place of peers in group activity. It is well to recognize at the outset that there are many types of peers. There are peers with respect to position status, to general and unique ability, to purpose, and to the ways in which people go about achieving their educational commitments. Regardless of the type of peer that may be identified, there are some conditions that apply to all types.

The one condition of major concern in this section is that assumptions seem to burden one's perception of and reaction to peers. Knowledge can be a director of behavior. Knowledge about peers can be the basis for determining behaviors toward those peers. The behavior need not be reinforcing or thwarting, but knowledge of another person does affect the way one relates to that person. Just as knowledge is a determiner or director of behavior, so are assumptions.

Whether there is knowledge or assumptions about peers, attention should be given to whether the knowledge is accurate and whether the assumption is destructive, both of the character of behavior as well as the influence of behaviors on peers. Assumptions are more hazardous than knowledge. Knowledge can be dealt with objectively; assumptions originate in the subjective and usually are treated subjectively. Many people deal with their own assumptions as though they were basic fact and knowledge. This is most unfortunate because of the influence assumptions have on those behaviors that accomplish a group determined and sponsored enterprise.

Assumptions about others often determine who will exercise influence and who will be influenced. To reiterate, some kinds of treatment among peers are reinforcing and some are thwarting to the major contributions that an individual makes to the instructional enterprise. Also recognize the fact that all people may have assumptions about others. When individuals try to evaluate and determine why other people behave towards them as they do, recognize that those other people's assumptions are the main determiners of that behavior. Here again, the best antidote for an assumption is an evaluation of it in terms of whether it is a fact and should be retained as knowledge.

The assumptions held about others, and the perceptions of the assumptions that others hold, may make a difference in the assumptions one has about oneself. Whether or not individuals see themselves as persons who must submit to the wills of others, without being able to participate in major group decisions, is important. The assumption might be that individuals see themselves as worthy contributors to the instructional enterprise and, therefore, gain a reinforcing sensation. Recognize that assumptions about self need to be analyzed just as vigorously, if not more so, than the assumptions held of others. Assumptions can be eliminated, revised, or substituted by the substantial type of knowledge.

Some favorite assumptions that have been extant over the years about the relationship of peers and the instructional programs can be indicated here. Individuals may have heard that, if a person feels particularly successful, this feeling should not be communicated to others. The purpose of keeping it in confidence is that, if the individual lets others see or be informed of things that have been done particularly well, it will be classified as boasting, thereby destroying status. Another assumption is that all people are basically selfish. Perhaps this reflects the fact that selfish people ascribe this assumption to other people. On the other hand, individuals have grown up in a society in which survival is based on the practice of selfishness; selfishness may be so ingrained that it is seen as a noble trait. The authors of this book are unable to accept that perception.

Another favorite assumption is that frequent association with a particular person or persons develops disrespect. Trying to remain somewhat aloof from the closer associations that might become a social pleasure illustrates this. On the other hand, if a few people tend to increase the frequency of their association, excluding others from that association, it is charged that a clique has been formed that is unhealthy in a group enterprise. Assumption patterns lead to that type of labelling.

Another favorite assumption is that if an individual asks for help it indicates an inadequacy. The fact that individuals recognize the possibility of gaining help from someone, makes it doubly unfortunate if they are deprived because of this assumption. The other side of this assumption is that an offer of help is condescending to the person receiving the offer. This is another assumption that deters progressive and rewarding interaction among people.

The last illustration of favorite assumptions presumes that all people can be typed. There has been much talk in recent years about stereotyping with respect to sex, color, and other characteristics. The assumption has held for a long time that people can be typed as generous, selfish, or as having a closed or open mind. A whole array of characteristics can be assigned to each type. This is done without analysis of whether other persons possess such characteristics.

Some type of assumption therapy needs to be developed. The authors prefer team activity—well directed, well purposed, and well processed. This is a pattern of interaction that has a purpose. It usually involves peers in a common enterprise. Here again, the careful procedures, which will be discussed later at several points, are worth reviewing in order to make a team activity a truly reinforcing experience for all involved.

Examples of Strategy

1. *Suggest that all administrative and supervisory staff members develop a list of assumptions about the quality of the instructional program as gleaned from contacts with school patrons.*

2. *Have each teacher complete an anonymous paragraph regarding how well the basic subjects are being taught in your school. Select such subjects as science, mathematics, social studies, and language arts where student assessment results are available. Compare, in the presence of the respondents, the test results with teacher assumptions about the condition of education in these chosen areas.*

3. *Check your needs assessment results and take an item of indicated concern such as discipline. Identify internal employee and student attitudes about the current conditions and compare with external community attitudes. Once the comparison of data is made, identify the differences in feeling as compared with fact. Then identify steps that might be taken to improve conditions and communication regarding resolution, both within the schools and within the community.*

4. *List several characteristics about yourself and present them to your peers to determine if they are assumptions or knowledge as perceived by you.*

PEER INFLUENCES

The preceding section dealt with assumption-burdened peers. A concern was whether characteristics of peer relationships could be influenced by knowledge or assumption. In approaching the discussion of peer influences another assumption can be made, namely, that one's peers are assumption free. This often is not true but it does give a positive note to a discussion of the types of influences that may be characteristic of peers.

A number of sources seem to be important in peer influence. Sources tend to be reinforcing points-of-view that lead to a reinforcing type of interaction. This certainly is desirable and this section is concerned with those positive sources that provide reinforcing peer influences.

The first source of peer influence is *acceptance*. A sense of belonging is important to almost everyone. A few people may indicate that they would like to be left alone, or that they prefer isolation, but it is a rare individual that really means it. Acceptance by persons in an organization is supportive of a satisfactory ego status.

Another source of influence from peers is *affirmation*. The fact that actions, beliefs, and goals, as well as products, are affirmed by peers constitutes an influence on the individual receiving the affirmation. Affirmation tends to be an evaluation that is reinforcing to the individual. Affirmation does not mean that the individual can ignore the necessities for change; rather, at any moment in time, an action seems to be acceptable and the subject of recognition and applause.

Another source of peer influence is that of being available for *assistance*. Few people can get through hours and days of work without welcoming some help from another. Peers who are willing to assume that peers are coworkers can find a mutual reward in assisting one another.

Another source identified with peer influence is *security*. The feeling may exist that acceptance, affirmation, and assistance are continuing. There is a sense of security in that there is no need to be apprehensive about termination, either of support or of opportunity to work.

Another influence from peers provides a source of *association*. Again, it is the modes of acceptance and affirmation that stimulate the opportunity for continuous interaction. The association with peers becomes a source that can influence the individual. The influence is that of determining, if possible, the pattern of behaviors that will provide continuity to the association. In this sense, individuals feel compelled to discover what makes their presence acceptable and desirable so that association will continue.

Stimulation is another source of peer influence. Certainly acceptance, affirmation, assistance, security, and association are reinforcing. But the reinforcement constitutes a stimulant to the individual who is the recipient. The source of stimulation is not just one person's stimulation; others may find mutuality in stimulation to be a source of influence.

Peer influence also may result through *increased knowledge*. Everyone cannot survive on the quantity and quality of knowledge possessed at any one time. The world moves on, the classroom moves on, and individuals are confronted continually with the necessity to adapt classroom instruction to changes in the environment. Increased knowledge can come faster and more accurately through peer influences.

A final example of peer influence is that of *problem solution.* In a group action, many problems occur just as they do in individual action. It is important to emphasize the opportunity to define the problem, to assess the unique contributions that individuals can make to the solution of the problem, and to maintain the association during the problem solution activities. Peer influence can be a tremendous source in the solution of problems.

Examples of Strategy

1. *When an instructional policy committee or team completes a careful definition of a task, ask each member to identify other staff members who might bring unique contributions to the policy consideration.*

2. *In a self-evaluation session, rank in order the peer sources of influence and then compare the rank order with those developed by administrators.*

3. *Create faculty show-and-tell opportunities that relate to areas of student activity, i.e., encourage staff to display their artistic accomplishments during a student art show. Invite faculty who play musical instruments to sit in with the students during a band or ensemble public performance.*

4. *Schedule a time during an in-service session for staff to bring an item or object that represents a favorite recreation or pasttime and create small revolving discussion groups to discuss and share their interests.*

HIERARCHICAL NUANCES

The various sections of this chapter are arranged in alternating fashion between the reinforcing types of influence and the thwarting types. The purpose is to make sure that the various aspects of loyalty and influence are observed.

An inclination to develop title worshippers is found in any organizational type of activity, both by actual observation and by cultural accumulation. Many people may say that they have freed themselves of this inclination. Freedom from title worshipping is not achieved simply by transferring the worship from a position in the hierarchical structure to someone within the peer group. It is important to see hierarchy as it is, whether it exists at an all-district level or at a professional organization or union level. In all probability there are hierarchical tie-ups in all parts of an organizational activity.

Title worshipping stimulates speculation that history discriminates between what might be identified as sun and shadow. If the individual worshipper becomes sufficiently appreciated and needed by a hierarchical status leader, that individual is going to be in the sunshine. The assumption is that certain benefits flow from this state, either in working conditions, recognitions, or rewards. On the other hand, it is assumed, rightly or wrongly, that if individuals are not in good graces with a hierarchical leader, they are relegated to the shadows. In this case, the individual might as well walk insignificantly through the professional life or go elsewhere. Thus, there is an inclination to look at hierarchical beneficence as either sun or shadow, with no twilight or dawn.

The idea of being in the sun or shadow raises the question of whether any person is "in" or "out." This means that if you are in, you have the benefits of the organization and its power. If you are out, you are on your own and little or no help will be forthcoming from the organizational hierarchy. There is a power also in the alphabet and age. Many people assume certain prerogatives because the initial of their last name is in the first part of the alphabet. A lifetime can be built on "firstness" preferences based on the alphabet. Eventually it can constitute an elitist self-image. Some persons assume that being a little older than others constitutes a hierarchical status, and that age represents a seniority of more experience and better knowledge. This viewpoint is often challenged by younger members of an organization who may think that anyone who has been in the profession ten years already has one foot in the grave. Alphabet and age hangups are hierarchical in nature.

An idea seems to persist that whatever individuals hate, will not be hated once it becomes possessed. If there is a certain type of restriction on an individual's activity within the organization, hate may be generated toward it. On the other hand, if the same person can make a restriction, it will not be hated but will be possessed. Therefore, somebody else will hate it.

Reference was made above to title worshippers who find themselves in one type of hierarchical organization or another. The within-peer group structures often provide just as rigorous a hierarchy, with many and varied status postures, as does the general organization of the school system. The head of a teacher committee or union can have as rigorous a hierarchical grip on the individuals within the organization as superintendents, principals, and supervisors do in the school organization. To treat within-peer group hierarchies, apply the same type of analyses and concerns as those applied to the organizational structures for administrative management. The attitude has been that as long as the peer group imposes the structure, it is much more palatable. This is not necessarily true, viewing some of the more informal and formal aspects of within-peer group structures.

Many decades ago, the organization of the school system in this country was described as an educational ladder. It began with kindergarten or first grade, went up to high school, and on through college. The highest rung on the ladder was graduate school. Unfortunately, this concept of the educational ladder was applied to the degree of recognition and unique contribution of those who worked at the various steps of the ladder. It took a long time to get a salary schedule that treated first-grade teachers equally with senior high school teachers. It was not only the grade level, but the subject matter taught that set this hierarchical construct. This is particularly true in the high school where some material is considered a solid subject and other material (e.g., vocational material) is considered a support subject. Often an elitism is attached to such concepts. This type of hierarchy is just as unreasonable and influential as that of the administrative organization of the school system. Academic elitism is a type of hierarchy that has to be dealt with and must be described in the same kind of problem terms that hold for the administrative organization.

Recent decades have revealed a sort of superstructure of developing equalitarianism. The superstructure refers to those who hold positions traditionally assumed to yield only power, but now assumed to provide leadership in supplying working conditions and other services that are beneficial to the teaching act. Equalitarianism occurs because there is a growing recognition that the skills required of kindergarten teachers are as great, if not greater, than those teaching skills required of a professor in graduate school.

The point of this section on hierarchical influences is to analyze some of the hangups that people seem to develop as the result of what always has been called hierarchy. People should stop abusing themselves with respect to the horrible things that appear in others. Perhaps putting a stop to this self-abuse can help people to recognize, as indicated in the previous section, that peer influences provide sources for many things that are needed.

Examples of Strategy

1. *Analyze a sample of a year long accumulation of board minutes, administrative bulletins, and teacher union minutes to see if there are real differences in hierarchical inferences by the categories of management.*

2. *In a group setting, discuss the following question, "Can a person alternate between the sun and shadow status with the same person, or is it either one or the other?"*

3. *Select an educational goal to be achieved at all grade levels, kindergarten through grade twelve, and develop a public information article or series of articles revealing the coordinated responsibilities at each grade level. Use this vehicle to let the public know that substantial teacher expertise is demanded at each grade level.*

> 4. Set up a "forward with the basics" parent openhouse. Reveal the fine arts and practical arts, along with other curricular fields, as basic to the instructional program and the mission of teaching young people how to live as well as how to make a living.

THERAPY OF INTERACTION

Some preceding sections emphasized the thwarting type of influence that may occur at the hands of peers, as well as others in the hierarchical structure. Interaction can be therapy for those who seem to have developed the sense of being thwarted by some of the undesirable types of influence. Some, on the other hand, find action and interaction with peers and hierarchical status leaders reinforcing. The therapy of interaction, however, is more than simply reinforcing or thwarting.

Therapy is achieved because interaction involves an interrelationship among people. It provides everyone an opportunity to feel part of the action involved in the management of the instructional program. Being a part of the action is the sense of participation that provides many people with a sense of freedom by virtue of the fact that they have an opportunity to share in the selection of goals, processes, and evaluative strategies.

A person who feels a part of the action finds therapy in helping others and receiving help. This alternating experience tends to keep the individual from the complete internalization that often antagonizes the other people in the action. Alternating the using and contributing of help develops a sense of individual and group strength. Interaction provides the individual an opportunity to make, as well as to receive, contributions. The individual and the group are strengthened as the result of this sense of close relationships.

One of the best elements of the therapy of interaction is that it leaves little time for brooding. Brooding requires a certain degree of isolation to let people feed on their own miseries. But becoming a part of the group action, and being both a user and a contributor of assistance, yields a different outlook on one's place in the group. The tendency to withdraw from others and from the purposes and activities involved in an instructional program is deterred. To the extent that interaction reduces this withdrawal tendency, it has served as therapy for those who have found working with others a thwarting rather than a reinforcing experience.

One of the best parts of experiencing group action is that joint action seems to be habit forming. People who have good experiences as members of a group, and who have sensed a certain success because they joined together in action, are much more likely to seek the joint-action pattern when new problems arise. In this sense, therapy has been achieved through the interaction of the members of the group. When people achieve a certain type of "we-thinking" in group successes, probably more and greater opportunities to participate in the group will open up. Such participation provides a sense of individual contribution to the purposes of group activity.

Examples of Strategy

1. Stimulate small group discussion and speculation on the kinds of tasks that require group action and those that can be done better by individuals.

2. Ask for the identification of prevailing obstacles to teaching and learning, within each teacher's work station, that might better be resolved through group action.

3. Assemble employees who share facilities to discuss better ways of cooperating to serve the different needs and interests of students. Discuss the advantages of group action over individual courses of action.

4. Discuss the relationship between the concepts of therapy of interaction and the concepts of management team. Determine where they are compatible and where they are incompatible.

ANTIDOTES FOR INTERNALIZATION

Previous sections referred to the inclinations of people to withdraw from group action, due to a sense of being thwarted by the dominance of others, and to internalize the difficulty. Internalizing means that one sets up patterns that bottle feelings inside and does not reveal them to others for interaction that might provide needed therapy.

The question might be asked, however, why not internalize? Some might argue that internalization can build inner strength. They also consider that it is a build-up of things that are self-selected. On the other hand, internalization may represent resentment, both to what someone else is doing or to what oneself is doing. The chances are for the reinforcement of added resentment that will not stimulate the pursuit of the major purposes for which one joins the staff of an instructional program. Those who internalize tend to deprive themselves of the benefits of peer influences and group action experiences. As previously stated, there is therapy in the interaction among people. This section discusses some of the other antidotes for internalizing that can be used with ease and effectiveness if there is willingness to do so.

One antidote for internalizing is to test for objectivity. The point is not to test just the objectivity of the others in the group, but of oneself. It is wise, on occasion, to test the objectivity of group decisions, group actions, and group products. Objectivity means directly and simply that whatever is considered a need, whatever is done, and whatever ways of doing are used must be subjected to analyses that compare the action to known criteria. Testing for objectivity determines the extent to which the action has been freed from emotional control and is based on identifiable facts and organized knowledge.

Another antidote for internalizing is to develop the habit of searching for alternatives in the quest for right. It is easy to say that I want to do something differently in order to make it right and this is the way it will be done. If this way was not chosen from a group of alternatives, there is the possibility that objectivity has been lost and that better ways of doing may have been overlooked by the immediate choice. One must recognize that when alternatives become the pattern of the quest for right, or just the quest for the problem solution, there will be differing points of view. Objectivity helps to prevent differing points of view from becoming the cause of internal strife.

The development of the art of compromise becomes a very important aspect of interrelationships. The art of compromise was discussed in an earlier chapter and reference is made here simply to indicate once again that the search for antidotes for internalizing, as well as for other types of organizational activities and compromise, may become necessary. One outcome of the use of alternatives in the quest for right and the development of compromise is that of selecting the goal of knowledge acquisition. If this is a goal, people can improve their own intellectual stature as well as the pattern by which problems will be solved and operational strategies designed within the group action. The goal of knowledge acquisition can be a real support to the identification of alternatives, as well as to the choice of the best alternative.

Development of the art of compromise is based on the recognition that the acquisition of knowledge is a continuing goal for all. If the goal of knowledge acquisition is precise, it is an easy step from that goal to the use of the research approach to decisions. What is required is objectivity in the identification and choice of alternatives, knowledge acquisition as a means of approaching the most difficult or simplest decisions, and decisions based not on emotional or internalized approaches but on factual information tested by the research approach. From time to time, take this research-approach decision and turn it on one's own actions. We have to analyze the cause and effect of our own actions. It would be goal-revealing if we paused at the end of a day occasionally and said "What did I cause somebody to do today and what was the effect of that action on me?" Perhaps we are saying again that we should take the research approach to decisions, this time decisions with respect to personal behaviors.

Some of these ways of using the antidotes for internalizing can be achieved by turning to the much more productive job of trying to balance personal responsibilities of self and others. This helps in keeping a proper perspective on our contributions as peers and also supports positive factors in the management of the instructional program.

Examples of Strategy

1. *Provide an opportunity for teachers to have individual conferences with principals and supervisors. Use the conferences to discuss the teacher's goals and explore the kinds of help that principals and supervisors might provide in the achievement of goals.*

2. *Arrange for a meeting of teachers who teach the same subject to students at the same grade level to review grading procedures, criteria used, and longitudinal records of grading practices over the past one or two grading periods. Identify through discussion and compromise the practices that will serve logically and fairly the best interests of all students taking the same course offering as to:*
   a. *The affect of individual actions on the group.*
   b. *The affect of group action on the individual.*
   c. *The place of compromise in this area.*

3. *Ask the social studies teachers if they could lead discussions with other faculty members regarding due process as it relates to student and faculty rights. Related state and federal legislation could provide useful direction, as well as a review of case law, to recommend district policy.*

4. *Schedule an opportunity for staff to reveal the advantages and disadvantages of required subjects at grade twelve. Prepare a list for each and circulate to the group for further discussion at a later date in an attempt to encourage evidence-based decision making.*

SKILLS OF OPENNESS

This chapter began with reference to the previous chapter on reciprocities as building blocks for group achievement. This chapter does not dwell on the reciprocity that could be generated through organizational structure and operational patterns. Emphasis here is placed on the individual as a person operating in a group of persons. Concerns are with the loyalties that have developed and the impacts of those loyalties as influences on individuals within the group.

Patterns of loyalty and influence exist. These might lead to a desire for developing the skills of openness in an individual operation as well as in group activities. Observation of the patterns of loyalty and influence is one of the skills of openness that is worth pursuing. Develop the skill of analyzing personal emotional tendencies that characterize individuals and that are observable among individuals and in the work group.

The developing of analysis skills can be shared with other members of the group and can help to maintain a positive goal in the determination of loyalties and influences among peers, as well as others in the school environment. The analysis of personal emotional tendencies might lead to a definition of the perceptions of issues. If people can identify an issue, and declare their perceptions of and their various involvements with that issue, they are on the way to maintaining the openness of interaction. This is a skill worth developing.

A part of the skills of openness encourages the reports of actions and beliefs. It is not enough to limit reports to the things that are declared as group goals and to report only on those group activities and outcomes. It is important that individuals feel free to report feelings, beliefs, or problems to anyone of their choice or to an entire group.

Another skill of openness is to develop a system of reports on individualized assignments and responsibilities. People often drift away when they do not have an occasional reminder of the original intent of the position activities and services envisioned when the position was accepted. Individual assignments and responsibilities need to be reviewed openly from time to time. If there are differences of opinion, it is possible to use the skills of problem identification and of perception of issues, as well as some of the other skills referred to previously. Another skill of openness that can move group action along tremendously is that of setting ground rules for the decision process itself. This provides full information at all times and the sense of membership that comes from knowing.

Another and final example of the skills of openness is the development of instruments or data-gathering devices for evaluation of interaction behaviors. These should not be imposed from the outside, but developed within the group itself. In this way, it is possible to move from the study of organizational and operational patterns to the real study of the interactions among individuals. Moreover, individuals can make a valid assessment of the loyalties that exist and their impacts and influences on the individuals within the group.

Individuals differ in the time and manner in which they achieve a functioning status in a group. This chapter has explored some of the characteristics that account for this differentiation. Decisions are essential to group functioning and individuals must develop the skills of decision making. Chapter 6 will present some thoughts about the relationships of talents to decisions.

INFLUENCE READING

DeBruyn, Robert L. *Causing Others to Want Your Leadership.* Manhattan, Kansas: R. L. DeBruyn and Associates, 1976.

Goens, George A. "A Study of the Interactions Between the Individual and the Formal and Informal Organizations." Unpublished doctoral dissertation, University of Wisconsin-Madison, 1973.

Heck, Shirley F. "Teacher-Peer Interactions." Unpublished doctoral dissertation, University of Wisconsin-Madison, 1972.

Jensen, Gale E. *Problems and Principles of Human Organization in Educational Systems.* Ann Arbor: Ann Arbor Publishers, 1969.

Koehn, John J. "A Study of the Interaction Patterns of the Formal and Informal School Organizations." Unpublished doctoral dissertation, University of Wisconsin-Madison, 1972.

Owen, Robert G. *Organizational Behavior in Schools.* Englewood Cliffs: Prentice-Hall, Inc., 1970.

Talent and Decisions

The active life is characterized by a continuous array of decisions. In the passive life, persons may choose to live out a lifetime on the basis of only one or a few decisions. It is impractical to assume that passivity can help one to achieve personal or professional satisfaction in an environment that is active and changing continuously. The active life characterizes most people in any sort of responsible position or with responsibilities apart from a position. The challenge of new and persisting demands or decisions occurs day by day, if not moment by moment.

Many types of decisions can be identified in this decision continuum. There are "off-the-cuff" decisions, some of which may be sound and some facetious. The designation "off-the-cuff" or "off-the-top-of-the-head" suggests that little thought and, therefore, little mustering of knowledge goes into the choice of decision. Some decisions might be termed *appropriated*. A person, rather than take the initiative and responsibility for making an independent personal decision, chooses to appropriate a decision already identified and accepted by others. There are *tentative* decisions when people wish to keep the options open because they do not have adequate information and an adequate ordering of information to make a careful and more permanent decision. There are *deliberative* decisions that approach the type that calls on the individual's talents and basic knowledge, as well as the strategies of ordering knowledge, to reach rational decisions. Deliberative decisions are the most desirable type, particularly in dealing with the major activities of life and of a profession.

The benchmarks of quality decisions are related closely to the types identified above. Quality in a decision, however, might be found in any type, regardless of the classification terminology used. At the very least, quality is going to be related to *relevance*, that is, relevance of the decision to the problem identity. Relevance of the basic information or knowledge used to make the decision includes the focus on the application of that decision. Another benchmark of quality in decision is *stability*. The decision must anticipate a number of current as well as evolving facets in the environment in order to endure. Another mark of quality can be referred to as *endurance*. An enduring decision is able to withstand the erosions of evaluation, application, and explorations for alternative decisions. Still another benchmark of quality is *acceptance* by others. The others in this case constitute a jury that evaluates the quality of the decision in order to determine whether they will accept it as their own. Thus, quality is related to relevance, stability, endurance, and acceptance. Other benchmarks can be identified, and individuals should feel privileged and obliged to select their own benchmarks for judging quality.

The role of individual talent is one of the most potent elements in good decision making and good decisions. Talent is ability that is many-faceted. Talent is more than a particular narrow line of thinking and of acting. Talent is a personal attribute that helps an individual to envision other elements in the environment and to bring that expertise to the choice of decision. The benefits of high intelligence must be seen as the essence of ability and, therefore, of talent. The person of high intelligence possesses more and better knowledge, and better strategies of relating knowledge to the demands of a personal life or a profession, than those of low intelligence.

Intelligence and knowledge selection is most important in assuring that decisions will be of high quality. Intelligence and knowledge can be as useful for people with evil purposes as for those with noble purposes. Safety can be guaranteed only through a value-based choice of purpose that gives direction to the application of the decision process. If the decisions are based on the kind of characteristics identified in talent, and given proper purpose through value-based information, the decisions can be applied to the demands of the action foreseen as a part of individual responsibility.

The intention is not to indicate that decision is an end in itself. Decision is a stage in the process in which the talent of people can be applied to the kinds of purposes and processes that seem best characterized by achievement. In the following sections of this chapter, there is a continuing analysis of the relationships of talent and decisions.

PURPOSE ORIENTATION

The talent's capacity must be focused on challenging tasks and stability must be supported through value-based purposes. Talent, as discussed here, has the capacity to deliver action toward good purposes and goals. People are stimulated to apply their talent to making good decisions through self-motivation, the motivation of others, and the motivation gained by membership in an organization.

Organizations can be said to have altars of power. These altars of power often are found in some of the bureaucratic modes that exist. They also may be found in the desires and behaviors of individuals who are active in various responsibilities within the organizational structure. References to bureaucratic modes almost invariably bring to mind the fixed arrangement of responsibilities that have hierarchical relationships. This means that some of the elements observed as the orientation of purposes are analyzed as imposed or chosen purposes; imposed in the sense that an organizational structure and design may have built-in purposes for those who carry various responsibilities within the organizational structure. There are many opportunities, nonetheless, for individuals to choose purposes that, if arranged in proper relationships to the institutional or organizational purposes, can accommodate highly individualistic characteristics.

The primary concerns of this book are the professional responsibilities of teaching and the professional outcomes of learning. Administrators and supervisors have teaching responsibilities just like teachers. The idealized purpose of the school as an organizational structure, bureaucratic or not, is teaching and learning. Within this central purpose, there can be negotiated weightings of individualized purposes. Negotiation, in this sense, means primarily an exchange of thoughts, information, and desired decisions with respect to purpose among individuals who do not abandon their institutional responsibility. Professionalism can be identified by the weighted purposes that characterize the individual within the group enterprise more than by any isolated pattern of characteristics used to describe an individual member. Individuals have much latitude in determining the weighting of various purposes attendant to the achievement of the major purposes of the school. The important point is that the school is an institution with a built-in general goal or purpose. The legitimized survival of the institution must be achieved through the talent and talent-based decisions of those who staff the superstructure of the organization, as well as the highly specific responsibilities that are essential if the major purposes are to be realized. What are some of the benchmarks of talent?

TALENT IS IMAGINATION

Many people see nothing except what has substance and structure and is within the range of the eye. Seeing things in the mind that are not seen by the eye is a simplified definition of *imagination*. Imagination can range only within the confines of the intellect or talent possessed by the individual. The broader the array of things that can be brought into mind's view, the greater the substance of an imagination that can structure the relatedness of things in a total area of responsibility or operation. This same imagination may find in the structuring of relatedness some gaps where nothing appears as a contributing factor. At this point, imagination leads to the creation of the new.

Creation of the new needs to appear in the total structuring of relatedness of all elements of the total operation, thus, providing a better total than the original. Imagination working in this manner can be considered a sharpening of the accuracy of anticipation. If the mind can see beyond present reality, there is a possibility of identifying not only the gaps and the operating supports that exist but also anticipating other elements that may occur and the possible conflicts among them. Talent, which is imagination, can see some of the consequences beyond the horizons of the present operation. This is something much simpler than the kinds of futurism that have been envisioned in recent years. This is an operational type of concern that sees consequences that may exist in the operational supports and strategies.

Imagination provides the opportunity to identify alternatives, not only of decisions but also of operations. Talent is facilitated by the imagination that provides opportunity for greater choices from alternatives, and these choices should lead to a better selection of purposes and processes. When imagination operates within the total talent repertoire of an individual or of a group, an improved quality of decisions is certain to result. Talent, supported by imagination, should provide the opportunity for individuals to serve more effectively within their own assignments and as their assignments relate to those of others.

Examples of Strategy

1. Initiate an informal speculation on the "way out" things that might happen in education. These informal speculations are more than a way of passing time. They constitute an opportunity to speculate on some of the things that may show up in the future that seem very improbable at the present. Having them in mind may help to identify those or similar ones that eventually may be there and make an impact on the educational structure.

2. Share the decision process by communicating problems or issues with two or three alternative decisions. It might be helpful to call a formal meeting in which an agenda is stated, each item in the agenda having two or three speculative alternatives of decision. This might open the way for all members of the group engaging in the decision or analysis process to feel that there is no one way being imposed and that the imagination each one possesses may be rewarding as a talent that can support the best conclusions and decisions in face of the stated issue.

> 3. Ask members who participate in the decision action to speculate on how a number of other specific people might react to the decision. This means that you are seeking to structure an opportunity for all people involved to exercise their imagination as a means of releasing their talent to contribute to the total enterprise.

TALENT IS STIMULATION

Most people can recall encounters with ideas that have impressed them greatly or "left them cold." This state of coldness may result from envisioned responsibility that accompanies the idea or from the envisioned obstruction that may come with the idea. At any rate, whatever the idea is and does, it does not stimulate the individual or the group to active pursuit of goals and purposes.

Dependence on the evaluations of ideas that occur in the observation of other persons comes easily. There is great power in *emulation*. This power of emulating, however, might become either active or inactive. Most people recognize a part of their own behavior as a response to others who constitute a stimulation for the individual. In an organizational enterprise like a school, the talent of *stimulation* must be recognized for the power that it possesses. It is essential that the power of emulation, or stimulation of other people, be directed in a coordinative manner toward the organization purposes.

Challenges to action and to inaction exist as indicated above. Stimulation is not a description of inaction, it is a characteristic of action. Stimulation can provide the desire to achieve an interpretation of the significance of each person involved and the informational items that can be used to accomplish the purposes espoused. This does not mean that stimulation envisioned here is limited to a type of control over another person. It is just as important for stimulation to result from differences of opinion as from acceptances of opinion. Some security is generated in the process of differing within a group. This does not make differing a goal of the organization nor a purpose for the individuals in it. It is an open relationship within the group that makes possible an exchange of ideas that constitutes stimulation to the participants.

The dramatic character of a purpose of an organization or of individuals becomes a stimulating agent of organizational activity. The interrelationship of people should be emphasized in a group enterprise, not the fixed relationships that might be encountered in the bureaucratic mode. The character of purpose is dramatic because of its capacity to stimulate. Purposes that are inviting and challenging can result in dramatic stimulation.

Reference has been made several times to the interrelationship of people and their ideas. It is important that a mode of operation within the group responsible for the school activities develop the capacity to recognize the "assist" that comes from others. This talent is stimulation to both the individual and the group enterprise.

Examples of Strategy

1. Ask the staff to list some characteristics of people who stimulate them to action. This would provide an opportunity to assess the power of the interrelationships of people as a means of stimulating greater action in the pursuit of purposes.

2. Pause occasionally during group discussions and ask each member to indicate at that point the greatest concern that each has in the issue at hand. This must be done in a manner that does not invite the use of this information for any type of reprisal or disciplinary action. Rather it is a vehicle for each member to offer a thought that might constitute an additional alternative to view as the group tends toward the process of decision.

3. Secure anonymous indications of persons who offer much help to others. This would provide an opportunity to identify the power of the talent on the staff that provides stimulation to many individuals and certainly to the group enterprise. The anonymous indication is wise since it would reduce the suspicion of some that it was a "back-scratching" process from the beginning. The intent here is to provide some way for people to identify those who stimulate them most. There also is the opportunity to observe the talent possessed by these people so identified.

TALENT IS DIRECTION

A firm relationship must be established between purpose and the *direction* that a group moves within the school organization. Talent in selecting those purposes that invite direction constitutes a contribution worth nurturing. Whenever there is a recognition of relationship between purpose and the direction of movement, there are certain requirements of implementation that must be recognized. If purpose is to give direction, it requires talent to see the possibility of implementing appropriately selected action.

Support needs to be provided by facilitating the various elements of the implementation process. The choice of support action is a form of direction, not a control over direction. The productive type of support recognizes the difference between purposeful direction and creativity-destroying control.

Talent is direction and direction assumes a process of movement or implementation. There must be certain determiners of progress toward the achievement of the direction pursued. This progress is seen best in the degree of coordination that exists in the process of implementing those actions leading to the selected purpose or goal. Coordination is multifaceted; there are many persons involved and many inputs from the school environment. It takes much skill and talent to pursue directions coordinating the efforts of those who are participating properly.

One of the concerns that needs to be registered at this point is that talent in direction must include the ability to know when the purpose has been achieved. The emphasis is on the processes of facilitation. Too often, the process characterized as coordination of people and facilities seems to constitute people satisfactions rather than an assessment of whether the purpose has been achieved. Whether or not the purpose has been achieved, a great deal of agility is required to modify the directions to be pursued. Talent is direction, and this talent must be combined with the ability to modify not only the process but the purpose.

Examples of Strategy

1. Ask participants in an innovative effort to evaluate the implementation plan. This would provide an opportunity for the individuals to become aware of the direction being pursued and the extent to which the coordination of action has been mastered. It would be necessary in this case to separate the consideration of purpose and direction from the specific actions that constitute the implementation plan.

2. Develop job specifications for each person involved in an implementation effort that are specific to that particular project. This would permit each person to become better aware of the ways in which the members of group action supplement, complement, or support each other's unique responsibilities.

3. Distribute a description of things that might be observed when a specific purpose has been achieved. Here is a case in which direction is analyzed at the outset so that the achievement of purpose will be recognized. It also would provide a beginning to the process of evaluation, not only of the implementation procedures but also of the evaluation of the purpose achieved.

SKILL IS TALENT-BASED

Reference was made in the two preceding sections to the concept of talent as imagination, stimulation, and direction. Effective practice demands the achievement of all three. *Skill* is related to those individual talents that result in progress toward the chosen purposes. Skill is the expert way of applying those specific and unique things individuals contribute because of their talents and assignments. Skill is extremely specific with relation to each person's contribution to the total coordinative action.

Skill is possessed by individual participants in the group, rather than by a group. Keep in mind that the group, while powerful as a group, is nothing without the contributions of the individuals that compose it. Skill, however, is possessed for a purpose, and that purpose can be a group possession. In the instance of a school, skills are applied to those things necessary to make teaching effective in terms of the product, namely, learning. Application of skills requires talent. A mechanized routine, even though highly skilled in process, is not sufficient unless directed to the purposes accepted by the organizational group. This application requires talent that can be translated into skills of coordination.

Coordination is not imposed from above or from peers. It describes the way that people relate as they apply their unique skills and talents to the tasks at hand. An illustration of the variety of skills required for one task can be found in the research done by McAllister.[1] She studied the transition of a library into an instructional materials center. Emphasis centered on the way principals, teachers, librarians, and audio-visual directors perceived their respective roles in the structural and operational patterns of the school as the transition evolved. Audio-visual specialists and librarians saw the task as much more difficult than did teachers and principals. Principals saw a centralized system as more manageable than did those in other positions. Teachers saw the whole process as easily managed, except for their own adjustment to the new concept of media service. It was found that individual role concern was related closely to the probabilities of a potential weakening of previous specialties.

McAllister's research findings dramatize the problems of coordination among several skilled groups when a proposed change requires modifications of previous expertise. Specific efforts are required of all participants to accomplish coordination during and after a transition is experienced. Talent and skill are strong, needed elements in the school operation, but coordination can be fragile unless specifically treated by the talent-based skill of personnel management.

Examples of Strategy

1. *Make an inventory of staff uniqueness in expertise by various areas of responsibility in the school. Here is an opportunity to show that the unique skills possessed by each person can be orchestrated into a well-coordinated effort that leads to the achievement of a purpose or purposes espoused by the school as an organization.*

2. *Initiate a staff analysis of the skill requirements for an impending task. Here is a suggestion that good strategy might lead one to anticipate the requirements needed rather than to analyze them after they occurred. It would help to plan the implementation program with built-in coordination rather than to control it step-by-step and item-by-item.*

---

1. Jeanne Ployhart McAllister, "The Transition of a Library into an Instructional Media Center," (unpublished doctoral dissertation, University of Wisconsin-Madison, 1974).

3. *Present to the staff your own list of skills required for coordinating the total reading program. Here is an opportunity to analyze each person's responsibility for contributing to something as specific as a total K-12 reading program. Zinski researched the role of the elementary school principal in the administration of a total reading program.[2] Zinski found that principals rely primarily on specialists for program impact and see their own roles as matters of teacher selection, budget, and organizational structure and operation. But, even in these responsibilities, the object of the coordinator is program improvement rather than development or maintenance. The school organization, nevertheless, affects program planning and evaluation. Expertise in communicating and coordinating skill requirements is a unique expertise of principals.*

DECISION IS THINKING SKILL

The emphasis throughout this chapter has been anchored to the idea that decisioning is a highly intellectualized activity. It is a *thinking skill*. The thinking can involve certain assumptions, the most important of which is rationality. The previous reference to value-based purposes and decisions is closely related to the concept of rationality. Decisions cannot be made unrelated to other aspects of a total program.

A wide range of vision is needed in the thinking process to keep all aspects in a rational relationship. This range of vision does not exist as a dormant skill but as an active process of relating one element to another within the decision process. The search for alternatives in decision making is a thinking skill. It provides various ways that thinking can proceed in the search for the wisest choice among alternatives. This is the decision. When a decision is made, it must be recognized that it likewise contains many decisions. There are many elements involved in the target of the decision action; each of these elements require some decision with respect to its inclusion, its relationship to others, and its general utility in the major decision that is of maximum importance.

The wide ranged vision indicated above means that part of the thinking skill is to anticipate the impacts and outcomes of any major decision or subdecision that is made. This view of the horizon makes it necessary to anticipate what one decision may stimulate in the way of decisions needed in other and related areas. This thinking process cannot be carried on without a good knowledge base. It is essential that persons involved in decisioning regard their thinking processes not as a manipulation of former knowledge but as a creation of new knowl-

---

2. Ralph J. Zinski, "The Elementary School Principal and the Administration of a Total Reading Program," (unpublished doctoral dissertation, University of Wisconsin-Madison, 1975).

edge. Along with the demand for thinking with both imagination and anticipation of impact and outcome, there must be a continuous search for the certainties of knowledge that can be used. This thinking skill might be viewed as a management of information. The information must be discovered and organized. Management applies it in a proper manner to the focus of the decision process.

Examples of Strategy

1. Develop a matrix pattern for identifying the pertinent elements in a decision area. Seek to identify in each row and column of the matrix sheet the things that seem the most important to have in proper relationship. This kind of two-way comparison makes it possible not only to identify the pertinent elements but to speculate on the various relationships that may have to be controlled if the decision is successful.

2. Schedule thinking time for those involved in the decision process. This means giving emphasis to the thinking skills that are a basic part of decisioning. So often, we want to do our thinking as an interactive process within a group. Emphasize occasionally that alternatives come from a thinking process more than from the exchange of ideas within a group. There is need for both, but thinking time needs to have more emphasis.

3. Call brain-storming sessions for cause and effect agenda. The purpose of this is to speculate on the alternate decisions that might be made in the particular area of concern. These speculations might bring out some of the qualities of the various alternatives, in terms of the speculation as to what effect they might have on something or someone else.

4. Circulate an open-ended list of "things that need to be known" before a decision is made. This would tend to bring the matrix pattern back into a very active process of analysis. It is easy to solve an academic problem while forgetting entirely the problems of space, budget, or financial support. The open-ended list might cause many to think of elements in a decision that would otherwise be left to the responsibilities of others and not to the decision itself. Such a list also would reveal the needed information to be acquired by members of the group before they participate in the final action of decision.

DECISION INTERRELATEDNESS

Mention has been made of the probability that decision making involves many persons, many aspects of support, and many possible outcomes. It is essential to relate all of these things at the time the decision process is instituted. The school operation is a multitude of tasks. It is improbable that any decision can be made, even in a highly specific area such as facilities planning, that would not impinge on other aspects of the school's operation. Certainly the teaching and learning process is affected by the pattern of available facilities wherein such tasks are implemented.

Recognize each task as related to a common purpose. It is too easy to assume that this common purpose automatically makes the tasks related whether or not there is constant effort to relate them. Be a little more realistic with respect to the relationship of tasks. Try to see that decisions within each of them and over each of them must be related through active attention, with the common purpose of the total organization in mind.

Different people have different tasks. This is an over-simplification of an obvious point. But it is not so simple when you realize that individuals approach their unique tasks with a human variability that may not be predictable. Human variability may bring about a great difference in the way one task influences another. In other words, human variability can cause a loss of *interrelatedness* of people as well as the things they are doing. When these things impinge on others and create a handicap, there is definitely a conflict potential within the organization. Entire treatises have been devoted to conflict management. Conflict will occur, but recognize that there may be some way to reduce conflict to a minimum by giving more attention to the decision process in the early stages of action.

A certain amount of managed reinforcement may be appropriate in accomplishing decision interrelatedness. Certainly, there can be policies broad enough in nature that give general direction to many of the specific individuals engaged in the unique tasks. This management reinforcement comes through the predetermination of orderly relationships, either of people or of tasks. Managed reinforcement does not call for power over others but for a central clearing agent that can keep the lines of communication open. With full knowledge of what others are doing, most people are inclined to try to carry out their own tasks in harmony with others. Our biggest problem in education, as well as in other organizations, has been the absence of an active, central clearing agency that can bring information to the appropriate people at appropriate times in order to increase the interrelatedness of the total activity.

Examples of Strategy

1. *Establish a sequence of dependencies or progressive prerequisites for a K–12 program in some chosen field. Try to anticipate the ways that one person would be dependent on another, that one purpose would be related to another, and that one task would be related to all others. This is the progressive prerequisite identification that might bring about greater relatedness, not only in decisions but in the implementation of decisions.*

2. *Post a diagram of joint, parallel, and intersecting responsibilities of five selected staff members. It depends on the occasion as to what the criteria should be for the selection of five or any other number of staff members for such an analysis. The important thing is to develop a procedure by which people could quickly gain an understanding of how each has unique tasks to perform and how they are or must be interrelated in order to achieve the reinforcement of accomplishing a common purpose or goal.*

3. *Institute a communication system to broadcast policy decisions. Too often, policies are made and only those who make them know that they have been established. A communication system is needed to carry quickly all information with respect to the major policy decisions throughout the total operation. Eventually, some of the more minute or specific policy determinations might be welcomed by all people in the organizational effort.*

DECISION COMPETENCE

The fact that a decision has been made is not evidence that it is a competent decision. *Competence* can be shored-up and perhaps even predicted by keeping in mind some of the elements of decisioning discussed earlier in this chapter. It might be well to view competence as being an action that moves from open information on a decision, to a periodic review of that decision, to a restructuring of the decision. Perhaps there is no other way to keep decisions updated as required by the purposes they are intended to achieve.

A decision is more volatile and easily reversed than is a principle. A decision is involved when a principle is determined, but a principle usually has more lasting power than operational decisions. A principle usually takes into account many anticipated environmental and conditional aspects that place it farther in the future than a decision with respect to any operational action. New insights and changing environments are good reasons for reviewing and restructuring decisions. This calls for alertness as to how the operation is going, as well as the invention of some facets of an activity that might make the old responsibility move toward the common purpose and specific objectives with greater certainty.

The need for open information, for evaluative reviews, and for redesigning calls for the perpetual pursuit of wisdom. The wisdom needed here is based on reliable information, controlled observation of the decision outcomes, and a continuous review with respect to the environment that the decisions are supposed to serve. As the decisions are restructured and become more relevant to the purpose for which they were made, the quality of the decision is improved.

Quality develops power. The power of a decision is something other than the power of the people who make the decisions. The quality of a decision engenders confidence in all of those affected by it.

Acceptance on the part of people is the inherent power and quality of a decision. People are the media by which decisions are brought about and implemented, but the power is not in the person nearly as much as in the quality of the decision. The nurturing of the decision process toward a state of competence is best evidenced when the decision can be terminated in an achievement that is related to the purposes for which it was made. Perhaps there is no other adequate determination of the competence of decision other than the achievement of the purposes for which it was designed.

Examples of Strategy

1. *Classify decisions by such types as major, minor, support, dependent, and so forth. The advantage in trying to type decisions is to support the desire to review and to restructure. The weighting of a decision as to its need for restructuring may vary with its type. Thus, typing can be one of the processes by which competence can be achieved in decisioning.*

2. *Establish policies on periodic review for each decision type. The major decision, perhaps, would take an entirely different kind of policy review than would the dependent or minor type. At any rate, it probably is not an advantage to give equal attention and weight for review to all types of decisions.*

3. *Assign decision review committees composed of nonparticipants in the action as an occasional evaluation of decision quality. The selection of nonparticipants for an occasional review would help in freeing the evaluation from the personalized concern to prove that good decisions had been made by the initiating group. It is good to get greater objectivity into the decision review and an occasional committee of nonparticipants can provide this.*

DECISIONS GO TO WORK

This entire chapter has been devoted to talent and decisions. Both terms have been defined and discussed. The purpose of relating talent to decisions is to get on with the work at hand, namely, education. Decisions must have a process of action. Determining that process of action involves subdecisions under the decision of concern. Decisions are not instituted in isolation; they are instituted for the purposes of giving direction to action and moving toward it. The process itself requires continuous decisioning, and the various aspects of this process will be discussed in chapter 7, "Categories of Work Process."

DECIDING TO READ MORE

Combs, Arthur W., Donald L. Avilla, and William W. Purkey. *Helping Relationships: Basic Concepts for the Helping Professions.* Boston: Allyn & Bacon, Inc., 1971.

Sergiovanni, Thomas J., and David L. Elliott. *Educational and Organizational Leadership in Elementary Schools*. Englewood Cliffs, New Jersey: Prentice-Hall, Inc., 1975.

Wilson, John A. *Banneker: A Case Study of Educational Change*. Homewood, Illinois: ETC Publications, 1973.

Categories of Work Process

Decisions of all magnitudes constitute a major demand on those who are responsible for professional work. There are decisions dealing with management, reinforcement, evaluation, and planning. Those engaged in programs of education must make decisions continuously as an integral part of the regular work process.

Decisions are the result of thinking. Decisions may be borrowed from others, but even the process of choosing a source is itself a decision. Thinking must be reinforced with solid information, viable ideas, and defensible purposes if the decisions are to support work obligations. In a practical sense, work is the implementation of decision. At the same time, there must be decisions about implementation. Thus, decision making underlies almost every act and state of those who work in the educational process.

Few would argue that decisions are made for their own sake. They exist for a purpose and to achieve that purpose some systematic way is required to proceed from the original idea (decision) to the conclusion the decision envisions. There must be a close relationship between decisions about *goals* and decisions about work *processes*. Work processes are determined primarily by the nature of the goal that is sought. Thus, two different types of decisions are involved in the implementation of a determination or decision—what goals are desirable and under what conditions they will be sought.

A sequence of decisions exists in work implementation. The first decision is related to a goal or an anticipated outcome. This leads to a series of decisions or choices among alternative designs in order to select the work process that will lead to the desired goal. The sequence of decisions can be most helpful when the person making the decision and directing or engaging in the work process is aware of the type of process involved. Categorization of the work processes helps keep the various alternative ways of proceeding in proper context and in proper relationship to each other. The categorization of processes supports the efficiency of action.

This chapter proceeds from the discussion of the nature of process to the specific categories of work process, the chief target of this presentation. The nature of process will be discussed in terms of *activation, origins, isolationism,* and the *melding of specializations.* These constitute a prelude to the specific discussion of the four categories of work process: (1) Managing, (2) Influencing, (3) Evaluating, and (4) Planning. Each of these categories of work process is related to the Model presented in chapter 3.

PROCESS IS ACTIVATION

The preceding section indicated that practically all operations start with some decisions of determination as to desired outcomes and some concern for the procedures used to pursue the outcomes. It is clear that ideas and decisions must be communicated. Communication is the work process by which responsible individuals carry the idea and decisions through the various media of interaction required in order to achieve a defined and declared outcome.

The communication of ideas must have a plan; ideas do not generate communication systems of their own. They might suggest possible alternatives from which the communicating process can be chosen, but some plan is essential or the decision will remain uselessly at its point of origin. The system inferred here might be called the institutionalization of group activity. This means that there must be some systematic behaviors designed and maintained if the ideas and decisions are to find proper fruition. The action inferred in the work plan and in the systematic behaviors constitutes the bridge between the plans and the products, sometimes referred to as ideas and outcomes. Regardless of the terminology used to identify the beginning and end of any proposed activity, it is necessary to bridge the gap with some sort of planned and organized action that involves people.

Ideas and decisions cannot be generated without people. People develop the communication system for ideas so that they bear fruit in terms of the anticipated outcome. People have a major role in work action. Roles must be related so that they are mutually supportive and based on a value system defensible to others in the environment who are less occupied in the action process. Ideas that have a strong value orientation affect the vigor people apply to their action role. Confidence is increased if the program to be pursued is desirable and defen-

sible, and individuals are stimulated to identify the unique contributions they can make to the group enterprise.

Just as the value orientation of ideas can stimulate vigor in
individuals, ethics can stabilize the direction people move in their
work effort. Ethics also are chosen by people and must be carried out
and observed by people. The outcomes of any declared enterprise
constitute the measure of the quality and effectiveness of the work
processes chosen and pursued in the activity. The people, the ideas,
the values, and the ethics suggest that all processes have some common sources. Some of these sources will be explored in the following
sections of this chapter.

ORIGINS OF PROCESS

The definition of terms and of goals constitutes one of the basic *origins* of work process. Definition is essential even if only one person is
involved, since that person must have a clear notion of what the task is
and what desirable end is foreseen for that task. It is even more
important to define terms and goals when several or many people are
involved. This becomes the base of development of an orderly communications system to expedite specific tasks necessary in a work
goal.

The definition of terms and goals leads immediately to another
kind of clarification, namely, *relevant information.* It is unwise to
choose a goal and the work processes of implementation without having at hand all of the information that might help in the choice of
alternatives and interim and sequential decisions required in any work
performance. Relevant information encourages the identification of
alternative choices of action. But relevant information certainly does
not fit a formula. Individual judgment is still needed whether to go this
way or that way, whether to involve this person or that person, and
whether one alternative is more promising of success than another.

Another origin of process is found in the *philosophy of action.* If
one person feels that the philosophy of action must be sought on an
individual basis, then, in all probability, it will be difficult to achieve
agreement on goals, term definitions, and alternatives that might be
the most profitable. Those persons who can find a sense of individual
contribution and satisfaction in the successful operation of a group
will be more helpful in choosing the alternatives of action and carrying them forward to implementation of the declared goal.

The philosophy of action possessed by individuals in the group
determines in a large way the kind of intragroup structure that will
exist. Structure, or the pattern of relationships between people and
tasks, constitutes an important origin of work process. The disposition
to be mutually supportive within the group guarantees more desirable

and expeditious results than are possible in groups that fail to achieve this mutuality. This intragroup structure will determine in important ways the individual interrelatedness that exists within the groups. Individual interrelatedness depends on the individual philosophy of action and the extent to which group members have been able to achieve a commonality of purpose and goal. Individuals who are supportive within the group can be more helpful in identifying the origins of work process in terms of projection capacity. This indicates that individuals can project the effect of their own behaviors on those of others, and more particularly on the organized effort to which the group is committed.

A consideration of the origins of work process makes it necessary to recognize that a high degree of objectivity can be a real source of work vigor. Objectivity reduces the personalizing of successes of differences observed in others. It also permits people to examine their own contribution to the group effort without emotionalizing any of the relationships or activities of others.

Another powerful origin of work process is found in the many *environmental impacts* focused on the school. There is little doubt that the desires of parents and organized groups within the community affect the kind of work design that is developed. But they also affect the vigor with which designs are pursued in the purposes of the organized effort—in this case the school program. Recognize that there are individual and group desires operating within the work force. These individuals and groups can be stimulated more effectively through recognition of some of the origins of process indicated above. There is no indication that the individual must be sacrificed to group purpose or effort. The opposite is true; members must feel that they thrive as individuals as well as members of the group.

PROCESS IS NONISOLATE

The work process evolved from the origins indicated in the previous section affects people who are involved in the total operation. It is *nonisolate*. There is little opportunity for isolationism to exist in an organizational or institutional enterprise. No one person can achieve all the tasks and expectations required to carry out the purposes of the organization. The work process or work organization has a profound effect on those involved in the operation.

The complexities of work relationships increase as the number of people involved in the total operation increases. Complexity demands a closer review of the kind of work process most appropriate for the goal enterprise. People must acknowledge some acceptance of work expectations or organization. There must always be both a subject and an object in any type of organized group effort. The subjects are those involved in the work process itself; the object is found in the objective of the organization. When, in the process of work, one person influences another, the subject-object relationship exists.

The sense of group membership becomes essential if the subject of each type of relationship is to be accepted. The influencer and the influenced are involved in the membership of the organization. They must have a feeling of closeness to that group or organization. Each individual must include in the overall role of membership that of acceptance as a member of the group. The acceptance must reach into the self-images that permit people to see themselves making a contribution to the group effort. This role can be supported by mutual respect. Those who experience jealousy seeing others accomplish their purposes well will fail to exhibit the kind of respect that will support the group enterprise.

All groups are composed of individuals and individuals react in many ways. The differences in individuals constitute a potential for plus and minus effects; plus in the sense that there will be many differentiated types of abilities and expertise available and minus when the differences are seen as threats.

MELDING SPECIALIZATIONS

The inferred generalization was indicated above that individuals make up groups and are inclined to be more individualistic than group-minded. This is not necessarily true but, in this age of adversarity, it seems to be the more observed manner. The organizational effort or the work processes themselves must bring people into a more rewarding relationship than that of adversarity.

The individuals in any group possess unique kinds of talents and skills. The resources of uniqueness are something to be exploited rather than stifled in the individual interactions within a group enterprise. Uniquenesses themselves are not much help unless they are identified and related to other uniquenesses in the work process chosen for the accomplishment of the goals. The uniqueness of an individual becomes a base for differentiated contributions to a common enterprise. Differentiation can be achieved by arbitrary assignment or delegation unrelated to known expertise, but it is much more rewarding if based on the unique abilities of each individual. These contributions, then, can be made with a greater sense of self-pride and with a greater guarantee of success for the group.

The first step in melding specializations must be the *establishment of common goals;* the second, the *work process determination.* These can be achieved in the face of individual uniquenesses, resulting in the kind of interaction among people that will achieve a common goal with an effective work process.

Some tests of the extent to which the melding of specializations can be observed are needed. These tests of supplementation are as follows: (1) individuals find that the group experiences possess a stimulating outlook; (2) the work relationship is such that there is an observed tension reduction both on the part of individuals and on the part of interacting individuals; (3) when mutual respect has been established in the work process, there is a reduction or elimination of the envy of one person for the achievements or status of another; (4) the mutual respect that is established among people becomes a measure of the success in the supplementation of one individual to another; (5) when supplementation has been successful, there is evidence of self-pride as well as group pride; and (6) the individual's sense of accomplishment, which can be realized in the accomplishment of a group task or enterprise, is the ultimate test of whether supplementations of individual uniqueness and effort have been achieved.

Apart from the tests of supplementation, there are tests of the work process itself, and they are found in the extent to which goal achievement is realized. Goal achievements are the outcomes and products of individual and group effort.

Turn now to a closer study of the categories of work process. Each one will be discussed in a separate section. In each of the sections, each process will be explained in terms of two components.[1] These are structured as follows:

Managing is a work process with the two components of *directing and controlling*.

Influencing is a work process with the two components of *stimulating and initiating*.

Evaluating is a work process with the two components of *analyzing and appraising*.

Planning is a work process with the two components of *designing and implementing*.

Each of these processes with components will be discussed in terms of the identity of terms, their relationship to the work achievement, and with the aid of matrices that will help to detail the interrelationships involved in these processes and their components.

WORK PROCESS: MANAGING

Emphasis was given in chapter 3 to the synthesis of purpose and effort. It was indicated that such a synthesis does not occur by magic; it takes

---

1. Glen G. Eye, Lanore A. Netzer, and Robert D. Krey. *Supervision of Instruction,* 2nd ed. (New York: Harper and Row Publishers, 1971) Part Four, pp. 291–295.

the conscious attention of people who have ways of working that direct efforts to the goals or purposes set. When a group of people are involved, common goals are not spontaneous. Individuals come to a group with a set of personal purposes or goals, and they seek to direct their efforts to those goals and purposes. The individuals constituting a group must be willing and able to exchange points of view in surveying each other's goals, and must arrive at some commonality of acceptance of the goals and purposes of the organization—in this case the school system.

A reference early in this chapter was made to the joint sequencing of decisions required to achieve a common purpose. The sequencing of decisions is the orderly way of deciding on the processes to achieve goals and purposes. The sequencing of decisions assumes that there is an orchestration of effort. Here again, such things do not happen spontaneously but as a result of the leadership and acceptance of a person or persons who can bring order to the sequencing process. Order, however, does not come about by magic any more than does the achievement of common goals or the orchestration through sequencing decisions. Orderliness is another word for management. It also might be considered the result of management. Here again, the conscious effort of a person or persons is the basic ingredient for the achievement of orderliness by means of management. People frequently rise up against the concept of management as though it were a deprivation of personal freedoms that must take precedence over organizational and institutional purpose. Such a concept involves the inconsistencies of the individual's supremacy over the requirements of an organization and the organization's right to function.

The positive aspect of management will be emphasized in this presentation. Management is the nurturing of successful action. This does not imply that people lose their freedom, but rather that they gain a sense of success in an organization free of obstructive people pulling in opposite directions. Management is positive in the sense that it has the purpose of accomplishment. Certainly, successful action and accomplishment are outcomes to be sought rather than avoided.

The terms *management* or *managing* have this positive connotation, and this process of work is discussed here in terms of two components, *Directing* and *Controlling*. Here again there are popularized reactions against controlling, particularly in the sense that individual freedoms are assumed lost. Directing, a word less threatening than controlling, means to point the way rather than to deprive other people of choosing the way they wish to go.

These thoughts are put together as a use of management in the operational activities of a school system and are presented in Matrix 1,

Matrix 1 *Activating through Managing (Directing and Controlling)*

Examples of Management Targets	Examples of Alternative Action and Response Patterns					
	.1 Acceptance	.2 Rejection	.3 Defiance	.4 Modification	.5 Replacement	.6 Other
1. Living with Legislated Budget Limits	1.1 Explain mandate and noncompliance penalty.	1.2 Announce limits with no information on source of decision.	1.3 A bulletin on item limits to be observed.	1.4 Invitation to participation in item adjustment within limits.	1.5 Seek legislative amendments to correct hardships.	1.6
2. Declining Enrollment Staff Reduction	2.1 Policy review prior to decision date.	2.2 Announce staff reduction with no reference to enrollment problem.	2.3 Invite selected staff members to volunteer resignation.	2.4 Ask representative committee to explore alternative solutions.	2.5 Develop plan to relate staff reduction to staff attrition rate.	2.6
3. Participating in State-wide Student Assessment Program.	3.1 Review legislative discussions to ascertain legislative intent.	3.2 Announce state mandate without reviewing purposes or uses of results.	3.3 Memorandum announcing dates, participants, district comparisons, & potential norms related to teacher performance & staff replacement.	3.4 Request staff participation in developing local strategies for implementing assessment program.	3.5 Seek legislative amendments to avoid district comparisons and to consider variables such as in & out mirgration.	3.6
4. Other	4.1	4.2	4.3	4.4	4.5	4.6

Activating Through Managing (Directing and Controlling). Study first the labels of each axis. The vertical axis of the matrix figure carries the title EXAMPLES OF MANAGEMENT TARGETS. Three targets are suggested: (1) Living with Legislated Budget Limits, (2) Declining Enrollment—Staff Reduction, and (3) Participating in Statewide Student Assessment Program. The horizontal axis carries the designation EXAMPLES OF ALTERNATIVE ACTION AND RESPONSE PATTERNS. The thought in this axis label is that every behavior on the part of the person engaged in management brings forth a response from those working in the organization and subjected to management. The response pattern may be quite different on different occasions and for different people. The illustrations or examples used here include five types of responses, namely, Acceptance, Rejection, Defiance, Modification, and Replacement. There are open columns and rows in the matrix allowing readers to make designations appropriate to their particular wishes.

The specific behaviors in each cell of the matrix are classified as to the probable response that might be stimulated. Note cell 1.1 that contains the specific management behavior of "Explain mandate and noncompliance penalty." This is classified as a behavior that would gain acceptance in the operational requirements of a legislated budget limit. Note in cell 1.2 that the management behavior is "Announce the limits with no information on source of decision." This is classified as a response of Rejection at having any part in recognizing the operation as proceeding under the legislated budget limits. The action in 1.2 leaves no opportunity for an exchange between the administrator and the staff. It is simply an announcement of something that is going to happen, with no reason and no explanation. Very often, regardless of the propriety of action, Rejection can be the response if there is no effort to treat the staff members as intelligent people worthy of knowing the "why" of the situation. The third column indicates an action of Defiance, and the specific management behavior is "A bulletin on item limits to be observed." This is a cold and impersonal way of telling people to "knuckle under." Most people do not like to knuckle under to arbitrary mandates and, consequently, will defy the edict with all power available. The fourth and fifth columns are actions of Modification and Replacement. In these instances, the specific management behavior is designed to increase the participation of everyone in the operation to arrive at possible changes that should be palatable to all involved.

The other two management target areas will not be discussed in detail, but it is suggested that the reader follow through the specific behaviors in each cell, with their attending column classification, to get a feeling for the fact that management does affect people and that people do respond in somewhat predictable ways to the management behavior used. Many management targets might have been used in the illustration and it should not be assumed that the three used here are the most important or the only ones that need this kind of analysis. It is hoped that most management target tasks can be approached with sensitivity on the part of the administrator to the kinds of administrative behaviors used, and with sensitivity to the anticipated responses and reactions of those who are committed to service in the organization.

Examples of Strategy

1. *Distribute a list of target management items and ask all staff members to order them for a priority of attack.*
2. *Hold forum discussions at noncrisis times on the positive and negative characteristics of directing and controlling.*
3. *Ask for staff recommendations for identifying student contingencies that could be considered in optimizing the assessment environment inducing students to do their best.*
4. *Identify types of administrative behavior that would promote positive and receptive responses toward assessment on the part of students.*

WORK PROCESS: INFLUENCING

The preceding section presented a discussion of Managing with the emphasis on the positive side of the actions related to the components of *Directing* and *Controlling*. This section, dealing with the process of *Influencing*, is closely related to the positive aspects of Managing. It might be said that Influencing constitutes the most potent element of Managing. It is much better to have people influenced willingly, voluntarily, and happily than to have them influenced through the processes of compulsion and compliance.

Influencing, as a process, is more effective than Managing through the authority of command. The essence of this approach is that Managing and Influencing are both grounded in respect for and confidence in the leaders of group action. The influence by leaders is not necessarily a superordinate concept, but rather one of persons who are accepted as the best qualified in the skills of Managing and Influencing. The components of the Influencing process are *Stimulating* and *Initiating*. It is recognized that willful action results from stimulation, either from self or from others. Stimulating, then, seems to lead to a specific pattern of action that brings about a realization of the purposes and goals of individuals and groups. Initiating is a natural result of Stimulating. Initiating means that action has started and is based on the strong desire to do those things that will achieve the objective.

Matrix 2, Activating Through Influencing, is a presentaton complementary to Matrix 1. The labels on each axis are similar to the previous figure. EXAMPLES OF MANAGEMENT TARGETS are represented by three types of action targets. These are: (1) Living with Legislated Budget Limits, (2) Declining Enrollment — Staff Reduction, and (3) Participating in Statewide Student Assessment Program. The horizontal axis, however, is different from that presented in Matrix 1. These are representations of ALTERNATE ACTIONS and RESPONSE PATTERNS. The alternate patterns are shown at the head of each column as follows: (1) Expedition, (2) Endorsement, (3) Uncertainty, (4) Compliance, and (5) Inaction. Again, it is emphasized that these are not the only ones or the best ones, but rather the ones chosen to present the examples for the process of Influencing.

The matrix can be read in the following manner: the example of management target is "Declining Enrollment — Staff Reduction." The specific influencing action as shown in cell 2.1 is "Propose introduction of neglected services as an offset to staff reduction." This is classified as Expedition since it is believed that most memebers of the staff would view this specific action as one to be accepted, supported, and carried out. Cell 2.2 shows a specific action of "Pledge assistance to relocate released staff members." Here again it is classified positively as Endorsement. It is believed that most staff members would react favorably to the positive side of school management being concerned with the welfare of the individuals and, consequently, would be inclined to endorse such a move. The possible involvement of the teachers' bargaining agent in designing policy recommendations for reassignment might make the action even more acceptable. Cell 2.3, however, indicates an action that might result in Uncertainty. The action here is to "Cite published speculations on effects of declining enrollments." The problem with this action is to determine whether the published speculations are based on fact or whether they are related to the local school system and community concerns. Cell 2.4 indicates "Appoint staff committee to study pupil-teacher ratio trends." It is certain that most staff members would be willing to comply with a request of this type. It does not indicate any definite action, but rather an effort to gather information that might lead to the kind of action that would be expedited as well as endorsed. Compliance, however, in this case is not with a result but with a process. Influence, nevertheless, is occurring. Cell 2.5 indicates "Compliment staff on poise in face of a growing problem." This, of course, is a nice action but does not lead to any specific solution for dealing with staff reduction due to declining enrollments. This action of influencing might soothe the personnel on the faculty but it would not lead to any specific action.

Matrix 2 Activating through Influencing (Stimulating and Initiating)

Examples of Management Targets	Examples of Alternative Action and Response Patterns					
	.1 Expedition	.2 Endorsement	.3 Uncertainty	.4 Compliance	.5 Inaction	.6 Other
1. Living with Legislated Budget Limits	1.1 Present program alternatives for shared decisions.	1.2 Announce program adjustment with supporting rationale.	1.3 Indicate expectation of probable crises at future time.	1.4 Issue bulletin on budget adjustments and related expectation of staff.	1.5 Declare blamability of legislative bodies.	1.6
2. Declining Enrollment Staff Reduction	2.1 Propose introduction of neglected services as an offset to staff reduction.	2.2 Pledge assistance to relocate released staff members.	2.3 Cite published speculations on effects of declining enrollments.	2.4 Appoint staff committee to study pupil-teacher ratio trends.	2.5 Compliment staff on poise in face of a growing problem.	2.6
3. Participating in State-wide Student Assessment Program.	3.1 Invite all staff members to suggest preferred procedures for major tasks of assessment.	3.2 Hold general meeting to elaborate advantages of assessment information.	3.3 Reveal possible uses other than student comparison.	3.4 Issue list of specific assignments to tasks.	3.5 Announce probable delay in target dates.	3.6
4. Other	4.1	4.2	4.3	4.4	4.5	4.6

Examples of Strategy

The following strategies might be used to bring about the most positive results from those actions designed to influence people:

1. *Distribute a list of known management targets to a sample of staff members and ask them to record their opinions about progress status.*

2. *Ask principals to study teacher responses to differing types of subjects and communication procedures initiated in the central office.*

3. *Develop a longitudinal log of evidence of influence positively exerted to bring about compliance. Review the list annually as a base for charting a course of influence for the future.*

WORK PROCESS: EVALUATING

The process of Evaluating carries a burden of tradition based on attitudes generated primarily as a result of using evaluation to determine the rewards and penalties directed to people. It is difficult for people to see evaluating primarily as the effort to gather information that can serve as a basis for a judgment.

Judgments based on evidence certainly have a better chance of being correct and helpful than judgments made off-the-cuff or in an expeditious manner. One of the problems that surfaces almost continuously is that evidence, even though properly gathered and valid in character, has interpretation problems. People can look at the same information and arrive at different judgments to determine future action or to determine relationships between people. Evidence, nonetheless, does encourage objectivity. Objectivity, in turn, causes the evaluation, or evidence produced through evaluation, to be used in a positive manner rather than in a vindictive way.

Evaluating is closely related to Managing and Influencing. Earlier remarks indicated that historic attitudes toward evaluation influence people in a negative way or cause them not to do the things that perhaps evaluation is designed to do. Managing should not depend on subjective judgment if objective evidence is available. Evaluating has the two components of *Analyzing* and *Appraising.* Analyzing is seen by many people to be as threatening as the judgments based on the results of analysis. This is unfortunate since activities directed toward personal and organizational goals are better if analysis and appraisal are the primary base for making decisions that influence action.

Matrix 3, *Activating Through Evaluating,* presents examples of specific activities that can come under the process category of Evaluating. Here again, the EXAMPLES OF MANAGEMENT TARGETS, as shown in the vertical axis, are the same as those used in Matrices 1

Matrix 3 *Activating through Evaluating (Analyzing and Appraising)*

Examples of Management Targets	Examples of Alternative Action and Response Patterns					
	.1 Application	.2 Extension	.3 Validation	.4 Rejection	.5 Defense	.6 Other
1. Living with Legislated Budget Limits	1.1 Seek staff assistance in developing comprehensive educational needs study.	1.2 Predict possible effect of budget limits on instructional supplies.	1.3 Distribute report of tax-payer's league on feasibility of budget limits.	1.4 Suggest a cross-the-board percent cut on budget items.	1.5 Initiate staff-load study to determine personnel needs.	1.6
2. Declining Enrollment Staff Reduction	2.1 Secure outside specialist to define population trends.	2.2 Distribute chamber of commerce estimates of residence construction.	2.3 Report 10-year enrollment predictions from other school systems.	2.4 Ask staff to research tolerance of community support of reduced pupil-teacher ratios.	2.5 Summarize possible limits on fringe benefits in order to retain staff.	2.6
3. Participation in Statewide Student Assessment Program.	3.1 Secure psychometric expert to interpret state program and its potential application to the local school district.	3.2 Review other local and state student performance efforts experienced in the past decade.	3.3 Release experiential information from other states employing state-wide assessment programs.	3.4 Suggest that staff contracts not be renewed where lowest student performance is experienced.	3.5 List material and supply reductions required to pay for assessment costs.	3.6
4. Other	4.1	4.2	4.3	4.4	4.5	4.6

and 2. The EXAMPLES OF ALTERNATIVE ACTION AND RESPONSE PATTERNS on the horizontal axis are different from those presented in the previous matrices. The examples of specific action are shown in the cells that are placed in columns to classify the type of response patterns that might be expected. The response patterns chosen for these examples are Application, Extension, Validation, Rejection, and Defense. Here again, the column labeled Other indicates that each reader should assume the prerogative of changing the response pattern labels, as well as the specific action, or replacing them with those more appropriate to local interest and concern.

The third row will be used for illustrative purposes in discussing the way to read this matrix. The third row deals with the management target of Participating in Statewide Student Assessment Program. Cell 3.1 indicates an action of "Secure psychometric expert to interpret state program and its potential application to the local school district." This is put in the response column labeled Application. It seems logical that expert interpretation would be essential to design the kinds of group activities and individual contributions that could best aid in achieving the management target. Cell 3.2 indicates an action of "Review other local and state student performance efforts experienced in the past decade." This is placed in the column labeled Extension. The reason for this classification of response is that a review of such efforts for ten years does not lead to definitive action to achieve the management target. It would be necessary not only to conduct the review but to determine what other kinds of information would be necessary in order to project the kinds of actions that lead to an assessment program.

Cell 3.3 indicates an action of "Release experiential information from other states employing state-wide assessment programs." This is classified as a Validation response. The problem here is whether such plans that would be required would be appropriate to the kind of expertise possessed by the staff as related to the kinds of expertise needed for a successful assessment program. The validation would need to be carried forward to determine the extent to which the expertise previously required and used would be appropriate to the new plan of action. Cell 3.4 indicates "Suggest that staff contracts not be renewed where lowest student performance is experienced." This is classified under the response pattern of Rejection. The respondents, namely the teachers, properly could reject this since it requires teachers to take full and exclusive responsibility for the level of student performance. This does not account for many other variables that would need to be controlled if student success were to be measured adequately. Such variables might be the appropriateness of space allocated to the instructional materials center and the budget support for the teaching materials. Many other variables might be con-

sidered, but these are enough to indicate that the teacher could properly reject this action as an inadequate evaluation because the kind of
data developed would not be sufficient for or appropriate to the kinds
of judgments to be made.

Cell 3.5 indicates "List material and supply reductions required
to pay for assessment costs." This is classified under the response
pattern of Defense. The teachers quite properly might feel that, if the
program were to require funds needed for the regular program of
teaching, the assessment program should be delayed.

These are examples of some of the alternate actions that might
be taken in the process of Evaluating, and some of the possible
response patterns that might be encountered on the part of staff
members. Evaluation of the delegation process in chapter 9 is a
specific application of this general discussion of evaluation as a category of work process.

Examples of Strategy

1. *Submit one quite complete report on data collected on one target and ask staff members to indicate the validation evidence that would satisfy personal acceptance.*

2. *Invite suggestions from all staff members on how to submit evidence of learning outcomes in a manner that would be fair to teachers.*

3. *Present alternate application potentials on one set of data and ask staff to evaluate and support personal priority preference.*

4. *Use a master matrix such as Matrix 3 and ask staff members to submit reactions anonymously to a number of data summaries before choosing an action plan.*

WORK PROCESS: PLANNING

New purposes, organizational structures, and procedures can be
secured in a number of ways. One way is to look over the countryside
and, after finding a desirable pattern, simply adopt it. In the cases
where adopting a plan that exists elsewhere might cause too much dis-
turbance, there can be modification to adapt it to local needs and purposes. The more creative way, however, is to bring about those
changes, developed at the local scene, on the basis of a study of
needs, resources, and purposes that have been generated at the local
level. Regardless of whether one adopts, adapts, or develops, there is
substantial virtue in using pilot runs to test whether the innovation can
be managed as envisioned and whether it will produce the results
desired.

Plans, regardless of their source, often "die on the vine." The
problem, in many cases, is that people seem to think that the job is

finished when the plan is drafted. Implementation is one of the most neglected of the organized efforts in the whole educational enterprise. Unless careful implementation plans are made, good plans as well as bad ones never get off the ground. The time spent in planning programs is a total loss of effort if no time is spent on designing an implementation attack. The process of Planning is an integral part of the processes of Managing, Influencing, and Evaluating. Look on the development of innovative plans as a crescendo in the four processes, with Planning being the ultimate vehicle of change in an organization.

The components of the process of Planning are *Designing* and *Implementing*. Planning is seen as a total process beginning with the definition of purpose, continuing through the drawing up of a careful design or structure that seems promising for achieving the purpose, and then being completed through the process of implementing. Implementation should have a built-in evaluative process so that Evaluating and Planning really always work together. Evaluating should point to the need for the designing of new or modified plans. Implementing, then, is always based on a solid source of information gained from the Evaluating process.

Matrix 4, Activating Through Planning, is similar in design to the three preceding matrices. The column on the left contains the same three EXAMPLES OF MANAGEMENT TARGETS. The horizontal rows constitute the EXAMPLES OF ALTERNATIVE ACTION AND RESPONSE PATTERNS. The specific descriptions of response patterns are different from those in the other three matrices. They are: (1) Meaningful Reception, (2) Personalized Role, (3) Priority Sequence, (4) Validity Suspicion, and (5) Outcome Projection. In order to help in the use of this figure, MANAGEMENT TARGET 2, Declining Enrollment — Staff Reduction, will be used.

Cell 2.1 contains the specific action, "Explore extension of school services to adults in the community." This is categorized as Meaningful Reception. It is believed that information leading to an extension of services could create a situation in which the need for staff remains constant even though pupil enrollment declines. Teaching, administrative, and supervisory personnel would respond meaningfully to this kind of purpose, namely, to protect the professional futures of those employed in the school district. Cell 2.2 has a specific action, "Develop plan for staff sabbatical leaves." This is categorized under the response pattern of Personalized Role. The probable response of teachers to this sort of proposed action would be to think immediately of the effect on themselves. If they were the ones put on sabbatical leave for a year, how would that time be used? Do the persons have need to return to school or to travel, in order to come back professionally stronger, or simply to be employed in some other type of work? People would be concerned with how they could work out their particular concerns and welfare.

Matrix 4 *Activating through Planning (Designing and Implementing)*

Examples of Management Targets	*Examples of Alternative Action and Response Patterns*					
	Meaningful .1 Reception	*Personalized .2 Role*	*Priority .3 Sequence*	*Validity .4 Suspicion*	*Outcome .5 Projection*	*.6 Other*
1. Living with Legislated Budget Limits	1.1 Propose three-year plan for adjusting staff services.	1.2 Announce program modifications without indications of staff obligations.	1.3 Release Board of Education budget allocations without reference to needs assessment data.	1.4 Announce dropping of yet-to-be named non-basic program elements.	1.5 Discontinue Research and Evaluation Division of central office.	1.6
2. Declining Enrollment Staff Reduction	2.1 Explore extension of school services to adults in community.	2.2 Develop plan for staff sabbatical leaves.	2.3 Abolish all specialists as means of retaining classroom teachers.	2.4 Use data of past two biennia to set staff needs for next biennium.	2.5 Summarize industrial development estimates of business community.	2.6
3. Participation in a Statewide Student Assessment Program	3.1 Reveal an orderly plan for instituting the program from a positive point of view.	3.2 Announce the provision of personal assistance to staff that would relate classroom instruction to what is being assessed.	3.3 Adjust counselor work schedule to substitute counselor assessment responsibility for individual student counseling time.	3.4 Announce that program trade-offs will be made after each assessment experience to strengthen the "basics."	3.5 Provide student and faculty recognition for recorded high assessment scores.	3.6
4. Other	4.1	4.2	4.3	4.4	4.5	4.6

Cell 2.3 has the specific action of "Abolish all specialists as a means of retaining classroom teachers." This is placed under the response pattern of Priority Sequence. Certainly the specialist would not support this particular ordering of priorities. Teachers, likewise, might be reluctant to accept because of the expert aid that would be lost from the specialist. Thus, the main concern would be the ordering of those things that are most important and least important in order to accommodate the staff reduction. Cell 2.4 has the specific action of "Use data of past two biennia to set staff needs for next biennium." This is categorized as a response pattern of Validity Suspicion. It probably would be categorized appropriately by practically all people who are or are not affected by the need to reduce staff. Certainly the data of the past two biennia are not as predictive as needed to determine the staff needs for the succeeding biennium. The conditions of the past could not possibly be the same, and therefore some modification or waiving of the data would be required in order to achieve a valid base for making the final decision. Cell 2.5 has the specific action of "Summarize industrial development estimates of business community." This is categorized under the response pattern of Outcome Projection. This would be an appropriate designation since it is assumed that the industrial development summaries would be used as a projection of population increase in the future. The projection needs to be tested for validity since the type of industrial development might or might not be related to the number of school-aged children entering the community with parents who have been attracted by the industrial employment potential.

Examples of Strategy

1. *Review the unexpected outcomes of several recent innovative efforts.*
2. *Submit a major plan to affected staff members and ask them to estimate the probable impact on their time involvements and other potential hang-ups in the implementation demands.*
3. *Develop a chart detailing the provision of support requirements to assure staff assistance in implementation efforts.*
4. *Establish a set of policies to guide the multiple involvements in all planning activities.*

ASSURANCES OF SUCCESS OR DISASTER

The presentation of the matrices involving the four categories of process sought to interrelate the four work processes by cross-referencing. It is an elemental fact that no one process can act in isolation. The categories enable the more probable intent of the action to be focused in such a way that commonality can result in the naming of a category. To make certain that the crossing or interrelatedness of the processes is clear, Matrix 5, Activating: Assurances of Success, was developed. The left column or vertical axis contains the same MANAGEMENT TARGETS that characterized the matrices presenting the separate processes. The horizontal axis labeled EXAMPLES OF WISE CHOICE OF ACTION WITHIN PROCESSES and has the four major processes as column headings, under which the specific actions in the cells are classified. The four processes are (1) Managing, (2) Influencing, (3) Evaluating, and (4) Planning. The actions in each of the cells come from the matrix presenting the separate processes and, in this case, were selected as having the best promise for producing desirable responses. In this way, one can examine all of the actions, with respect to the best choices, and determine that the persons responsible for directing the activities, as well as those participating in the activity, have the most consistent plan for success. A practical thought on this matter is that, as the percentage of choices in the total operation of achieving targets is increased, so is the percentage of chances for success. Ideally, if every cell possesses the most favorable action, the most successful results will ensue.

The opposite of having the wisest choice of activities in each cell is having the worst possible choice in each cell. One might say that no one could be wrong one hundred percent of the time, and yet, in reviewing the activities of group enterprise, one recognizes that some people are exceptionally skilled in choosing the wrong way to do things. Because of this possibility, Matrix 6, Activating: Assurances of Disaster, was developed. Here again, the EXAMPLES OF MANAGEMENT TARGETS remains the same as in the previous five matrices. The EXAMPLES OF UNWISE CHOICE OF ACTION WITHIN PROCESSES is shown on the horizontal axis, and the same four categories of process are listed in the columns. This time, the most inept ways of doing things were taken from the four matrices on processes, and they provide combinations of the wrong ways to do almost everything. Since all four processes are highly dependent on each other, and highly interrelated in working toward selected targets, then, as the actions in each of the different categories tend to increase in similarity and in wrongness, perhaps disaster is the only predictable outcome. Emphasis on the wrong ways of doing things was included simply to alert those who tend to get careless in choosing from the alternate actions available in the direction of a group enterprise.

RELATIONS TO THE MODEL

The Model presented in chapter 3 started with instructional impact sources and proceeded through various purposes to the management

Matrix 5   Activating: Assurances of Success

Examples of Management Targets	Examples of Wise Choice of Action within Processes					
	.1 Managing	.2 Influencing	.3 Evaluating	.4 Planning	.5	.6
1. Living with Legislated Budget Limits	1.1 Explain mandate and non-compliance penalty.	1.2 Present program alternatives for shared decisions.	1.3 Seek staff assistance in developing comprehensive educational needs study.	1.4 Propose three-year plan for adjusting staff services.	1.5	1.6
2. Declining Enrollment Staff Reduction	2.1 Policy review prior to decision date.	2.2 Propose introduction of neglected services as an offset to staff reduction.	2.3 Secure outside specialist to define population trends.	2.4 Explore extension of school services to adults in community.	2.5	2.6
3. Participation in Statewide Assessment Program	3.1 Review legislative discussions to ascertain legislative intent.	3.2 Invite all staff members to suggest preferred procedures for major tasks of assessment.	3.3 Secure psychometric expert to interpret state program and its potential application to the local school district.	3.4 Reveal an orderly plan for instituting the program from a positive point of view.	3.5	3.6
4. Other	4.1	4.2	4.3	4.4	4.5	4.6

Matrix 6   Activating: Assurances of Disaster

Examples of Management Targets	Examples of Unwise Choice of Action within Processes					
	.1 Managing	.2 Influencing	.3 Evaluating	.4 Planning	.5	.6
1. Living with Legislated Budget Limits	1.1 Announce limits with no information on source of decision.	1.2 Indicate expectations of probable crises at future time.	1.3 Distribute report of Taxpayer's League on feasibility of budget limits.	1.4 Announce dropping of yet-to-be-named non-basic program elements.	1.5	1.6
2. Declining Enrollment Staff Reduction	2.1 Invite selected staff members to volunteer resignation.	2.2 Cite published speculations on effects of declining enrollments.	2.3 Ask staff to research tolerance of community support of reduced pupil-teacher ratios.	2.4 Abolish all specialists as means of retaining classroom teachers.	2.5	2.6
3. Participation in Statewide Student Assessment Program	3.1 Memorandum announcing dates, participants, district comparisons, & potential norms related to teacher performance & staff replacement.	3.2 Announce probable delay in target dates.	3.3 Suggest that staff contracts not be renewed where lowest student performance is experienced.	3.4 Announce that program trade-offs will be made after each assessment experienced to strengthen the "basics."	3.5	3.6
4. Other	4.1	4.2	4.3	4.4	4.5	4.6

strategy area. The processes presented in this chapter can be located initially in the Model in area 4, titled Process Planning. The movement from that point is to Personnel Influences, Environmental Management, Interaction Patterns, and Coordination. This chapter deals with the specifics of that first step of relating influences and purposes in such a way that the ultimate outcome is the synchronization or synthesis of purpose and effort as depicted in area 9 of the Model. Additional references in relation to the Model will be made at appropriate points in future chapters.

The four categories of work process presented in this chapter will be reintroduced from time to time as refinements are presented that lead more directly to the specific responsibilities of designing strategies for instructional improvement. The categories of process will also be helpful in the latter chapters that focus on auditing, evaluation, and self-management.

This chapter opened with a focus of attention on the decision process characterized by *thinking*. Thinking and decisions were related to the ways of attacking chosen tasks. The processes can be applied to indiscriminate tasks. The concern, however, is with the chosen processes and tasks determined by the goals of the instructional programs. Chapter 8 will explore the relationships of goals and processes.

RECOMMENDED BEST READING
(YOUR OWN MATRIX ANALYSIS)

Bureau of Business Practice, Inc. *The Magic Meeting-Minimizer*, Waterford, Connecticut: Croft-NEI Pub., 1975.

House, Ernest R. (ed.). *School Evaluation: The Politics and Process*. Berkeley, California: McCutchan Pub. Corp., 1973.

Sergiovanni, Thomas J. (ed.). *Professional Supervision for Professional Teachers*, Washington, D.C.: Association for Supervision and Curriculum Development, 1975.

Relationships of
Goals and Processes

The preceding chapter dealt with the categories of work process—
Managing, Influencing, Evaluating, and Planning. The actions that
constitute the processes can be categorized according to many different kinds of responses. Process in chapter 7 was defined as *ways of*
behaving. It was emphasized that the ways of behaving should be
selected so that they would lead to a goal, in this case, the selected
outcomes anticipated as a result of action.

Categorizing the processes provided a framework for examining
specific actions and their relationships to the kinds of responses elicited from those people involved in the operational program. The
responses that might be elicited from participants were shown in
Matrices 5 and 6 in Chapter 7. The matrices indicated common purposes of achievement and specific actions that might lead to the
accomplishment of selected outcomes. The specific actions then were
categorized or classified in terms descriptive of ways that people
respond. Matrices 5 and 6 are referred to now as starting points in discussing the relation of processes to goals. Matrix 5 indicated the
optimum selection of specific actions with respect to the responses
characterizing the participants. It was indicated that, when processes
are well related to the purposes or goals of the organization, there is
substantial assurance of success in the program. On the other hand,
Matrix 6 indicated what can happen when all of the processes are
poorly selected and unrelated to the goals or anticipated outcomes.

This chapter deals more specifically with the relationships between goals and processes, and includes suggestions for developing and maintaining the relationships between goals and processes. In the discussion, great care is taken to keep the goals and processes separated with regard to their identity, but related with respect to the operational pattern of the organization.

SOME ASSUMED CONFLICTS

The idea long has been held that the ideal and the real are separate entities, if not entities in conflict. The conflict becomes obvious when the ideal connotes desirability and the real means practicality, and results in a loss of guidelines for moving from what is to what might be better. A similar assumed conflict between theory and practice shows up repeatedly in the relationships between the university campus and the field schools. Unfortunately, it is assumed that anyone who teaches on the university campus is basically theoretical and that this position is antagonistic to practical things. The converse of this assumption is that the practical person has no time for theory. Again, it is unfortunate that the reinforcements to theory from practice, and vice versa, are lost to those who should seek better ways of pursuing their selected goals.

A similar unfortunate conflict has been assumed between goals and processes, and this conflict is the point of discussion in this section. It is unfortunate because goals can be the major guidelines to the selection of those immediate purposes, and related processes or actions, by which goals can be achieved. This discussion will try to separate the identity of goals and processes and yet establish a relationship that can guide more productive types of activity.

Goal achievement can be evaluated. The evaluation can be accomplished, however, only if the goals are well defined and the evaluative approach uses those criteria that best describe the accomplishment of the goal. Processes, on the other hand only can be monitored. Any evaluation of process must be in terms of the progress being made toward goal achievement. Process can be viewed as a contributor to progress toward a goal. Poor goals and good processes can operate at the same time. It is unfortunate when the selected action permits people to move progressively from one status to another and still find no improvement over what is being accomplished presently.

Goals must stand before us as targets of the selected processes. Perhaps, more commonly, good goals are selected and poor processes are used in the pursuit of those goals. The reason for this inconsistency is that proper attention was given to goal selection and they tended to remain fixed. On the other hand, a process may have been an off-the-cuff action assumed to be good primarily because it pursued a good goal. Processes, however, require just as careful planning and definition as do goals. If this is done, there is a good chance that proper goals and proper processes can be established concurrently.

The indication above that more careful thought is given to goals than to processes reveals the different attitudes people hold toward a target or goal and the action or processes of goal realization. Action is more easily personalized. Thus, processes seem much more real and intriguing to the participants in an organizational effort. Too many people think that the target is established by someone else and that they simply have to act as they see fit to achieve the goal. This attitude deprives the individual, who selects and implements processes, of the benefits of directionalism that come from the study of goals.

Many people think the goal sits there but action gets there. This attitude must be changed if a good relationship between goal and process is to be established. Nonparticipants in an organizational activity are more inclined to see the *what* of the operation than the *why*. The what is the process; the why is the goal. People who are giving direction to organizational effort must help nonparticipants understand that there is a *why* for every *what* and that the process is related to the goal. Process might be said to be a sort of kinesthetic experience that gives a sense of action that seems rewarding. The goal, or ideational experience, does not seem part of the desirable sense of achievement that people seek. A move toward avoidance of conflict between goal and process will gain a rational mix of goals and processes. Nonconflict strengthens management.

Examples of Strategy

1. *Develop a list of questions that, when answered, will reveal the thinking about the relationships of processes to goals. Test the effectiveness of these questions by asking a few staff members to analyze a recently completed plan of action.*

2. *Select one school district educational goal and ask teachers to define the goal as they understand it. Have the definitions submitted in writing and tabulate, indicating each different response and the number submitting each definition. Use copies of this summation as a stimulus for open discussion to focus and reach agreement on goal definition.*

3. *Select a new approach being suggested to implement a part of the instructional program and identify whether there are any assurances that the educational goals will be better met than by continuing existing approaches.*

4. *Organize a panel of administrators and teachers to discuss the question, "How do the present teacher supervision and evaluation instruments differentiate between goals and processes of the teaching act?"*

GOALS AS ACTION STIMULANTS

The position has been taken repeatedly that goals establish a guide to actions that can be most rewarding in goal achievement. Goals give purpose to action, and purpose is one of the best stimulants for participants. People are not enthusiastic about drifting or going through the motions. This problem has been exposed in many assembly-line analyses. Serious attention must be given to keeping enthusiasm alive and people stimulated in their tasks.

Goals help to identify the stages of progress. When people have a sense of movement toward an established goal, stimulation is gained in the realization that steps of progress can be observed. The steps or stages of progress must be clearly visible to all participants in an organizational action in order to stimulate them to do their best work.

Goals also tend to attract other people to the action or process. When goals are clearly stated, people can decide whether they want to become a part of that organization seeking to attain those goals. When the number of people in pursuit of a single goal increases, other people, as well as those already involved, are stimulated to participate. They are engaging in something that is attractive to many other people. Goals make limitless participation a possibility and provide a great source of stimulation to those engaged in the activity.

A similar phenomenon may be observed in participants in a group action who want to keep pace with associates. The marked exceptions are those who do not want to see any associates outdistance them and who develop deterrent·actions to hold back the high achievers. This, however, seems to be an exception to what one usually observes. Keeping pace with associates may provide a stimulation. Goals have been credited with stimulating goal associates.

Goals give clues to the ways of approaching the tasks at hand. The ways of doing (the processes by which people make progress toward goals) are determined in quality primarily by whether the outcomes of those actions lead to the accepted goal. At the same time, the goal provides the criteria to evaluate the action. As criteria are known, and as participants become aware that they are meeting the criteria, the assurance of progress becomes stimulation. Almost every person has a desire to win. This desire can be related to the individual's purposes or goals rather than to the organization's goals. In capitalizing on this innate desire to win, it is important that the organizational goals provide the stimulation to satisfy the desire for accomplishment and achievement.

Goals are for achieving. Everyone knows it and everyone can be stimulated, and most people are, by pursuing known goals.

Examples of Strategy

1. Ask teachers to query students about their goals and whether their school experiences seem relevant to their goals. Follow these summaries with a discussion of the extent to which teachers should provide a model to stimulate students to relate goals and their learning activities.

2. Review with each building administrator the goals of that building. In a work seminar, determine scope and sequence of those goals on a K–12 continuum.

3. Ask subject or department members to suggest steps or stages of progress in achieving a goal, with time lines submitted for administrative and board scrutiny. Results may eventually be released to inform the citizenry.

4. Create a large wall chart in a visible administrative area listing district goals that have been agreed to and department missions or target time-lines that can be noted when achieved.

VALUE IN CHOICE OF ALTERNATIVES

Previous sections indicated that the choices of process can be made more wisely providing goals guide that selection. As in the case of evaluations that lead to a choice of one goal, the choice of process will improve if alternative processes are identified and described. There is danger in the process of one-wayism. If you assume that each goal has one fixed process, the alternatives that might be chosen at the outset or along the way tend to be lost. The failure to identify and describe alternatives in the selection of process results in the loss of the optimum selection for that process. The fact that there are alternatives from which to select the process lends strength to all of the alternatives. This is particularly true for the process selected as best adapted to the needs of the participants in the organizational activity.

The fact that alternatives are identified and a selection made provides the basic ingredient for a continuous and progressive development of the processes involved in the organizational effort. Making a choice from alternatives establishes the belief that there is no one way to accomplish the task. As the group progresses with one chosen alternative of process, other alternatives stand ready to be brought into action and thus provide a continually improving operational development.

Alternatives identified in the selection of processes provide the initial step in the establishment of accountability, of which all workers in an organization must be aware. When the choice of process has been made carefully, and in the light of those criteria related to the selected goal, the ingredients of an accountability system exist and one can be readily designed. At the same time, this accountability system is related to goals rather than to process alone.

The fact that alternatives have been chosen and specific individuals have chosen a particular part of the process as their own, the need arises for analyses of the specializations that exist within a staff. The study of alternatives in the process selection provides criteria to determine whether progress toward the goal is being achieved. It also provides the basis for the best differentiation of assignments of specific tasks to participating individuals. The best creative and specialized abilities of each person are brought to the total action and greater assurance is given that the goal will be achieved.

A very important administrative function is to encourage and direct the analysis that leads to the identification of alternatives in the selection of process, and to keep these alternatives related to the organizational goals. Adminstrators who bring the best talent to the task, utilize the highest level of specializations. This increases the probability that the selected processes will contribute to the goal achievement. Flexibility in action is assured by the reserves established through the identification of process alternatives. This flexibility through a reserve system strengthens the organization and assures that the goals will be achieved.

Examples of Strategy

1. Retain a list of the alternatives from which an operational process has been chosen. Present the list periodically to the participants in the action and raise the question, "Does our choice still look best or should we re-evaluate?"

2. Use the list of alternatives as a periodic reminder to staff that a reserve power is always available. The opportunity to change processes is evidence that we are capable of abandoning the historic "positive results syndrome," where every process has to be employed successfully.

3. Periodically provide a list of moveable equipment and instructional aids, and their locations within the school district, as a way of stimulating thought regarding alternative processes that might be employed. The notion of sharing and caring could stimulate shared planning and group commitment to goal achievement.

4. In small group discussions, have teachers indicate various alternatives students can use to accomplish successfully the goals of a particular school course. Compare these alternatives with other school courses where the alternatives are limited in number.

5. Review course options available to students at the secondary level and determine if all of these options are viable alternatives to meeting the district's goals.

LEGISLATED MIX OF GOALS AND PROCESSES

Inflation and the increasing expectations of citizens for more and more services from units of government have caused local units of government, including school districts, to experience severe financial strain. One of the results of this pressure for increased service at the local level is to approach the state and federal governments for additional funds to help provide desired services. An interesting phenomenon of this approach is that people in the local district seem to feel that it is outside money rather than their own tax monies. At the same time, federal and state officials may regard monies being disbursed as new dollars for those local districts, rather than a return of local money. This varies greatly from community to community, but the attitude of federal and state governments toward local units of government causes some rather questionable and often undesirable things to occur at the local operating level.

Historically, legislative actions were limited to goals. As the amount of money granted to local units of government and local school districts increased, there was an increased inclination to monitor the use of those funds. Gradually, bills passed by the state and federal legislators began to include more than the establishment of goals or desired outcomes; they increased the amount of legislated process required at the local level and envisioned as essential to the achievement of the goals. Any casual observer of the legislated enactments can see that the number of bills passed into law has steadily increased. The goals envisioned by legislative groups do not require that much more detailed definition and explanation. The length of the laws results from the detailed description of the process the units of local government are to use to achieve the goals.

The intent here is not to criticize the selection of the goals as provided in legislative acts. They are proper and often needed. The problem is one of constraints for those who must implement these acts at the local level. These constraints limit almost all opportunity to explore alternative ways of achieving the goals. For instance, attention should be given to the education of the handicapped. The laws, however, requiring this service, both state and federal, detail how each teacher shall report on each child in the program. Those who are designing these processes, at such a distance from the scene of action, impose almost impossible and sometimes impractical expectations on those who are implementing programs at the local level. At various points in this book, the desirability of identifying alternative ways of doing has been stressed. Unfortunately, the benefits of alternatives are increasingly lost as increased amounts of money come from federal and state levels. Money is power. Those who disperse the funds feel this power and seem to get satisfaction in exercising it. The control process imposed by federal and state agencies in detailing the eligibility for fund grants becomes one of the most rigid constraints on those who apply for funds.

Legislative acts often have posited in some bureau the responsibility for establishing guidelines for fund grants. They seek to control the process for implementing the purpose of the fund grant. These controls are called guidelines but more often they operate as regulations. It would help to redefine the terms that are used. If there were guidelines, alternatives would be possible. But the administrative bureaus at federal and state levels apparently regard guidelines as rigid regulations and administer absolute control with rules that have the power of law. The monitoring system used by the federal and state governments, especially the federal government, represents a remote control accomplished primarily by paper reporting. Thus, the large grants of federal money made to local school districts engender a system of forms for reporting information that requires substantial personnel and time that could be better deployed at the local level.

The state departments of education usually are called on by the federal and state agencies to serve as intermediate agents for the collection, organization, and transmission of information from the local districts, the targets of monitoring the legislated process. This represents an unfortunate mix of legislated goals and processes. The effect on the state departments of education, which are staffed by people who were appointed because of their specialized abilities, is the loss of their original purpose of serving the local educational agencies. When specialists in many fields must devote their time to developing forms, collecting data, and transmitting data to the state and federal bureaucracies, a different kind of specialization displaces the one intended at the time of employment. The personnel in the state departments of education become information gatherers rather than information givers. Specialists in the state departments of education should not have their time and abilities diverted to data collection. They should be working in a much more creative way with individual staff members in each of the local school districts to provide leadership and service.

The effect on the relationship between the state departments of education and the school boards, administrators, and teachers in local school districts has been most unfortunate. With state and federal governments calling on the state departments of education to fulfill continuously their demands for information, the goodwill generated by professional assistance is being lost through regulatory policing demands. These increasing demands to regulate originate in the legislated acts at federal and state levels.

Would the actions of a local board of education constitute the same sort of problem to the administrative and teaching staffs of the local school systems? The difference is proximity. Local boards and staffs can get together and talk things over; federal and state agencies lack the proximity necessary for good working relationships.

Examples of Strategy

1. *Take a copy of a recent legislated act relating to some aspect of education for the handicapped. Underscore the stated goals and purposes with black ink and the stated operational requirements with red ink. Do the same thing for a bill passed 25 years ago. Compare the spaces used for stating goals and processes.*

2. *Review the administrative guidelines for recently enacted educational legislation and underline the "must do" aspects that represent regulatory rule language. List the district impositions or problems that impinge on necessary flexibility to achieve the desired ends in implementing the legislation.*

3. *Review the services rendered by your State Department of Education and determine if the goal has changed from information giver to information gatherer. Attempt to explain this goal change if it has occurred.*

UNMIXING THE MIX

The preceding section emphasized that legislative bodies at the federal and state levels increasingly legislate the process of action rather than the establishment of goals to be achieved. The determination and monitoring of processes should be delegated to local agencies, thus benefitting from the face-to-face interaction in determining the best alternatives for process. It may be difficult for legislators to reverse this trend of process control.

The tendency to increase the time spent in legislating and the legislative staff services does not show much promise of getting legislative bodies to consider goals, rather than goals and processes, in legislative acts. The proposal here might be called "unmixing the mixed" through the use of the five *D's*. These are: (1) *define purpose*, (2) *differentiate goals and purposes*, (3) *develop written plans of action*, (4) *disseminate plans to all affected and interested people involved*, and (5) *deliver on responsibilities*. The purpose of the five *D's* is to establish steps to determine goals and to develop processes. They also might clarify more productive relationships between legislative bodies and local agencies. If legislative bodies would spend more time on the first *D*, *defining purpose*, in conjunction with those who are the target of that purpose, the selected goals would be more global in nature, with specific processes properly allocated and contributing to the achievement of goals.

The second D, *differentiation of goals and purposes,* is very important. As indicated previously, goals are the general targets and purposes are the more immediate objectives that lead those responsible for the operational activities to the processes necessary for goal achievement.

The third D, *developing written plans of action,* would be better than embalming such plans of action in the laws themselves. Again, if action is not formally and restrictively stated in the legislation, provision can be made to involve people other than those who are limited to legislating. This constitutes just as much expertise in judgment at the local level as displayed at the state and federal legislative levels. This does not mean that people do not use good judgment in the election of representatives to their legislatures. The good judgment, however, that local people expressed in sending good people to the legislature is not lost when the election is completed. The easy assumption for those elected is that the people need the judgment of legislators to guide and control more and more of their lives. It is doubtful that the expertise residing in members of a legislating body needs to supplant the judgment of people at the local level.

The fourth D is that of *disseminating plans to all interested and affected people involved.* When plans that are developed are put into written form, they often are disseminated only to a limited group and not shared with the people specifically affected by the action. The judgment of people who will be affected by a legislative act should be part of the input sought by legislative bodies at the time of consideration. The mere fact of announcing a hearing on a bill does not provide the amount or quality of participation that is envisioned in the suggestions made here.

The fifth D is that of *delivering on responsibilities.* This usually falls to the local education agency. In order to make sure that things happen as legislated, the legislative body seems to feel that it must have detailed monitoring of the operational processes. People in local communities are no more honest or dishonest than their representatives in the legislative body. Ways of auditing can determine whether or not the responsibilities have been met. The biggest problem with managing an audit from the distance of the state or national capitol is that attention is directed primarily to the most visible part of the operation, the processes. The evaluation or auditing of the processes a local agency uses to accomplish the goals described in legislative acts does not necessarily prove that the goal has been achieved. There needs to be a differentiation between monitoring of processes and auditing of achievement. The manner of determining whether a goal has been achieved could be determined long before the audit impact or, even better, developed at the time the plans are made and declared in the legislated act.

The five *D*'s can be applied to the determination of goals and processes. The same five *D*'s can be applied to the identification and selection of process alternatives. If goals and purposes are carefully designed, they will lead to the kinds of processes that should be scrutinized in order to select those that can best accomplish the purpose. The selection of a process to achieve an immediate purpose must contribute to the ultimate goal. If not, the best alternatives of processes have not been selected and the operation is not going to accomplish the things envisioned in the original legislated act.

A consistent use of the five *D*'s, or any other system of steps, would be better than the total legislated act and its acceptance under the present system. This might lead to an unmixing of the legislative mix of goals and processes, making it possible for local educational agencies to accomplish the purposes more creatively and progressively. The present system calls for monitoring the degree to which the local agency follows the processes that were determined at a distance from the scene of action.

Examples of Strategy

1. Try using the 5 D's in establishing a new and voluntary program change. On completion of the program development, compare the experience with another development required by a legislative act.

2. Invite legislators to meet with the district staff to talk about areas of concern they feel will be addressed through future legislation. Utilize this future orientation to develop suggestions for auditing goal accomplishments that might be recommended to the legislator prior to developing final language in the bill.

3. It is common knowledge that many legislative conclusions are drawn very early, regardless of a public hearing and the expressions of those in attendance. The suggestion then is to discuss proposed bill language with legislators prior to the hearing stages. Create a legislative network, where a limited number of people in your legislative area have a system of organized input to legislators, and a telephone contact system to assemble people on short notice. Identify participant categories of responsibility such as those described in the following "Sharpened Concept of Participation." Managers coordinating such activity can see to it that an organized representative voice speaks to legislators. Legislators who develop confidence in this organized system will likely use it regularly to influence decision making.

4. In following the 5 D's review the courses of study in your building to determine if all of the components are present. In small group discussions, determine the processes used for each component.

5. Develop an in-service program for your staff whereby a legislator explains a recently passed educational law in terms of the 5 D's.

SHARPENED CONCEPT OF PARTICIPATION

Emphases were given in the preceding section to the need for increasing participation in the determination of goals and the selection of processes to achieve goals. Inferences were made that the participation increase would provide an additional amount of expertise that could be directed to the assignment of goals and the analysis of processes for improved selection. One way to approach participation is to look at the jobs that need to be done and then to identify the kinds of people who might do those jobs best. This would provide a select group of participants, each of whom can make unique contributions to the total operation. Seven categories of participants will be identified here to illustrate the kind of thinking that might improve the spread of participation in those operations involving federal, state, and local agencies.

The need, first of all, is for a data-based goal selection. Even though goals are determined on general or global bases at the federal or state level, there must be more than just a legislator's idea. There must be information relevant to the action the legislators have in mind, information that would provide a data-based goal selection. The participants who can make the greatest contribution to this data base can be identified as *fact finders*. Fact finders can perform the unique service of securing and analyzing data relevant to the general idea of the goal being considered for selection and legislation.

A second type of needed action is data interpretation. The accusation has been made many times that data are collected from all parts of the country and simply stored. Facilities are now available to acquire and manage massive data collections. These facilities also should be used for data interpretation by participants identified as *interpreters*. Here again, a unique contribution could be made to the total process of legislating goals and freeing intermediate and local agencies to develop processes to achieve goals.

The third area in the development of good goal and process selection is future application. Someone needs to develop the expertise to take collected data and determine the ways and extent the data would apply to a determination of the future. This calls for the participant category of *projectionist* to provide a unique expertise for the total pattern of goal determination and process selection. At the same time, with the participants in unique categories, a better selection of legislated mandates would be possible.

The fourth need is to develop the action plan. If goals are selected on a good data base, if data are interpreted well, and if projectionists can apply those data to future impacts, the action plan can evolve from a sound approach to development. The participants needed for the development of an action plan can be identified as *planners*. Here again, a unique type of contribution can be made by this category of participants. Another area can be described as the development or setting into motion of the action pattern previously developed. This calls for the fifth category of participants, the *implementers*. Most implementers probably would be found at the local level, but implementation can be applied to a soundly developed program of action that grew out of good goal selection processes, whether at the federal or state legislative level.

Provision should be made, at or prior to implementation, for evaluational action. This calls for participants identified as *auditors*. Also, the service of coordination is essential to the best use of all categories of participants. This requires a seventh category called *managers*. Managers are responsible for keeping the original goals and purposes in mind, to see that each of the unique categories of participants works to common goal and purpose and applies the expertise to accomplish the intent of the organization. Managing provides the necessary coordination so that the unique categories of participants make substantial contributions to the total action. This is better than letting each person determine what might, on the spur of the moment, be the most convenient thing to do and then set about doing it.

Participant distance from the scene of the action must be kept in mind when identifying participants as well as the expertise available in this country, whether at the local, state, or federal level. Certainly, an implementer must be on the scene of action continuously. Some of the other participants might be at a greater distance and yet make a substantial contribution to the total process. The important thing is that some attention be given to these considerations at the time the legislated intent becomes official. Goal and process differentiation can be achieved if more care is given to the matter of distance from the scene of action. A process dreamed up hundreds of miles away may not be applicable to the unique characteristics of the local school district. If attention is given to the importance of distance from the scene of action, the problem of centralization versus local control can be solved on a more rational basis.

The inclination has been that the source of money becomes the centralized focus of control. The local scene loses more and more autonomous action and feels imposed on. This is unhealthy for a local school district or municipality. Consideration of the participant distance from the scene of action also has great implications for the matter of flexibility versus rigidity. The farther the control from the scene of action, the more rigid the guidelines and regulations imposed on the local operation. Flexibility still has its virtues and does not mean that no pattern is needed. The analyses of alternatives becomes the strength of a local operation. It is hoped that consideration of the pattern of participation and the distance from the scene of action may provide a way to liberate local school districts from the increasing rigidity being imposed on them, with respect to goals as well as processes.

The emphasis on differentiating goals and processes led directly to a concern for keeping the process determination prerogative near the scene of action. This would increase the potential matching of talents and tasks—the best outcomes of the process of delegation. Delegation will be explored in detail in chapter 9.

SOME READING MIX

Hamilton, Norman K. *New Techniques for Effective School Administration.* West Nyack, New York: Parker Publishing Company, Inc., 1975.

Jensen, Gale Edward. *Problems and Principles of Human Organization in Educational Systems.* Ann Arbor, Michigan: Ann Arbor Publishers, 1969.

Owens, Robert G. *Organizational Behavior in Schools.* Englewood Cliffs, New Jersey: Prentice-Hall, Inc., 1970.

chapter

9

Delegation of Instructional Tasks

The management tasks of the school administrator are complex and often difficult. The historical and traditional practices of school administration are evolving through a steady merging of concise theory and operational demands. It still will take strategies of accommodation regarding research and development to come to agreeable and acceptable definitions of the roles and responsibilities of administrative positions.

The term, school administrator, as used in this chapter, is defined as a person having management responsibilities in the educational process. The major administrative thrust of this book is toward the instructional program. Theoretical concepts and practical applications found in this chapter are designed to be applicable in all areas of school management. The readers should consider their positions in the educational system when reviewing the procedures of the delegation process, in order to obtain maximum benefit from and comprehension of this chapter.

DISTRIBUTION OF RESPONSIBILITIES

The delegation process is a means to an end. It is a process whereby a complex array of obligations can be accomplished within an organized structure of a defined order of responsibilities. Specifically, *delegation* is defined as the commission to another person to apply expertise to a given task. The need for delegation does not grow out of a school administrator's desire to feel and act as an executive officer, but rather out of the realization that one person cannot accomplish all the expectations characteristic of such a position.

The complexities of school districts are multiplying because of the increase in tasks being allocated to them. With society's demands becoming more manifold, schools are being assigned obligations that increasingly place them in positions of even more importance to society; consequently, school personnel are being held increasingly accountable to society for the accomplishment of additional goals. Examples that amplify this point of increasing expectations are: career education, sex education, value clarification, self-realization, humaneness, individualization of instruction, leisure time activities, community involvement, and the responsibility of educating students, ages three to twenty-one, with special educational needs. More examples could be cited, but the case in point is that as an institution increases its responsibilities, the tasks multiply, the means to accomplish the tasks become more diversified, and the goals become more general. Thus, a sound approach to the delegating process is a management skill that must be mastered by all school administrators.

The school superintendent is responsible and accountable to the board of education for the management and operation of the school district. It is the incumbent in this position who directs the implementation of policies approved by the board of education. As districts become more complex, the need to delegate tasks and responsibilities becomes readily apparent. Delegation by the superintendent is the commissioning of others to act in place of the superintendent on the tasks specified. Delegation by the building principal is the commissioning of others to act in place of the principal on the tasks specified. Similar statements can be made for all who have been assigned to positions involving administrative responsibilities.

A flow of directive skill is put into action in the delegating process; action transfer is the basic framework of the delegation process. This flow of action results in a work-sharing sequence of responsibilities among individuals in the school system. The concept of work sharing is of paramount importance in the delegation process and is intertwined with the flow of action concept. Three key elements of delegation, namely, (1) flow of action, (2) work sharing, and (3) accountability, are useful means to accomplish the school's goals and objectives.

The existence of an organizational structure within the school system helps it to accomplish the goals and objectives that have been identified and defined. Without specified goals and objectives, an organizational structure need not exist for it would serve no purpose. The very existence of an organizational framework indicates, therefore, that a delegation process has taken place that presumes an accommodation of the three elements of flow of action, work sharing, and accountability.

School administration has been defined as involving many functions. Over the years, the terms used to define these functions have changed, but the basic job description of the position has remained fairly constant. These authors tend to use four categories of work process to identify the major functions of administrative action. These categories, presented in chapter 7, were: Managing, Influencing, Evaluating, and Planning.

The administrator must make many key decisions in the area of Managing in order to attain the goals of the school system. The authority to make decisions is an exercise of management responsibility. The authority to delegate some selected managing responsibilities to other people is also an exercise of the management function. The role of managing delegation must contain the element of support resources that flows from that individual to other individuals receiving and accepting the delegation.

Influencing, in educational administration, connotes the ability to stimulate the necessary energies that will result in implementation of an action program. Influencing requires the input of many resources from numerous sources. The ability to gather sufficient data depends on delegated activities from the delegator. As a result of delegation, support resources are transferred from one individual to another, or to several individuals.

Stimulating is the motivating or Influencing of other people in the desired direction. The influencer and stimulator is also a delegator. In order to motivate people to move in the desired direction, a certain amount of delegation must be exercised to provide the proper base of responsibility. This stimulation is a delegation of responsibilities to another individual or individuals, and in essence, a flow of influence from one source to other sources.

The coordinating aspect of educational administration also contains an inherent source of influence. The ability to coordinate activities implies that delegation has taken place through a rational use of Managing and Influencing administrative actions. The coordinating responsibilities of the administrator create a framework for communication in a two-way setting. This framework provides the necessary vehicle to transfer support resources from one person to another. Coordination is the subject of the next chapter.

The third aspect or category of work process is Evaluating. The basic purpose of evaluating is to determine the progress made toward, or the completion of, objectives associated with the goals of the school. The ability to evaluate contains the elements of expertise and support resources to fulfill the requirements of an evaluation system.

The fourth category of work process is Planning. This process is a logical follow-up of evaluation. Planning is the relating of facilities and personnel expertise to the accomplishment of desired outcomes. It is the ordering and sequencing of action so that support resources are used to maximum advantage. Planning is the first logical step in Managing, Influencing, and Evaluating. Planning anticipates the appropriate and rewarding delegation of human and physical resources.

The flow or transfer of support resources takes place in all categories of process. This flow results from delegation, in which areas of responsibilities are shared among many individuals rather than retained by one. This sharing aspect allows the school to meet its goal in a more expeditious manner.

The basic function of any educational system is to provide an instructional program. It is the reason for the existence of such an institution. Other functions, such as finance, personnel, maintenance, bus transportation, food service, and clerical, support the instructional aspect of the system. The task of delegating responsibilities is of the utmost importance to the instructional program. This does not negate the importance of the delegation process in supportive areas, but the major thrust of this chapter focuses on the delegation process of school administration as it relates to the instructional program.

The operational use of delegation can be viewed in three distinct but interrelated parts. Delegation operationally means (1) assigning responsibility, (2) granting authority, and (3) creating accountability. These three interlocking and interrelating parts properly define delegation in the operational sense. These actions constitute an operational translation of the key elements of delegation identified earlier.

The delegation process in education, in contrast to industry, is a relatively new phenomenon. In recent years, school systems have become increasingly complex, justifying a more sophisticated process of delegating responsibilities. In addition to the complexities of school management, other variables, both educational and noneducational, are coming to the forefront and are increasing pressures to develop a more sound theoretical basis for the delegation process.

Examples of Strategy

1. *Submit the school district's organizational chart to representative staff members for reaction concerning their perceptions of a smooth flow of responsibilities.*

2. *Promote a brain-storming session of all personnel identifiable on the organizational chart to determine if appropriate delegation, flow of support resources, and working-sharing responsibilities are achieving district goals and objectives.*

3. *Review the school district's job descriptions to determine any hindrances to individual responsibilities.*

4. *Differentiate the nearness and remoteness of various positions with respect to the end product — learning.*

ACCOUNTABILITY EMPHASIS

Accountability demands are being communicated through state and national assessment programs; through administrative evaluation (MBO, EBO, PPBS, PERT, LBO); through various groups organizing themselves for security within the school system (teacher associations, student's bill of rights, principal associations, paraprofessional associations); through many community reactions (bond referendums, teacher strikes, high school taxes); and through numerous other sources.

Accountability should be a positive word, but societal values are creating a negative image. Accountability is essentially an enumeration of those elements that determine the extent to which responsibilities have been met. Thus, as a process it is neither positive nor negative.

Accountability is inherent in the delegation process. Work sharing, as described earlier, is an important aspect of accountability. When an individual is delegated some tasks to perform, an implicit assumption is made that the work is now being shared and that the delegated tasks are being accomplished. Accountability sustains the attainment of organizational goals and leads to satisfaction, either from an individual's or a group's point of view.

The accountability process might also be termed a control system. Many people are annoyed by the need for any control system. This antipathy to control systems stems from the fact that most people view only the negative aspects of the word control. A control system includes both rewards and corrections. Thus, a control system is positive and normally accepted when rewards are in order. On the other hand, a control system is negative and normally rejected when corrections are demanded. It is interesting to note that in many school systems the formal control system procedures that exist seem to be applied primarily to the classroom teacher. A case in point is illustrated by the grievance procedures that are outlined very specifically in many master contracts that exist between teachers and boards of education. There seems to be a different attitude in applying a formal control system to positions in the administrative and supervisory spheres of influence. The trend toward more accountability at these levels tends to crystallize the formal control system.

A difference seems to exist in the accountability system between the superintendent and the second and third levels of management, than exists between the superintendent and the level of classroom teacher. A partial rationale could be that, in the basic design of educational administration, midmanagement receives superintendent delegated tasks of functions normally ascribed to the superintendent's position. The teaching functions, on the other hand, are performed as a school system service, rather than as a delegation of some of the superintendent's responsibilities. It has been assumed that the superintendent is responsible for the supervisory or management functions rather than the direct teaching-learning process within the classroom.

The superintendent in each school district develops many techniques of correctiveness or redirective control for the members of the administrative and supervisory staffs. When occasions call for redirection of some type, the correction method may not be the only method used by the superintendent. It is more important that, as feedback information provided to the superintendent indicates, when some staff member has not fulfilled delegations adequately, the superintendent assume the role of counselor, rather than judge and executioner. The superintendent presumably and intentionally exercises the best judgment in making appointments and in delegating tasks and functions. It appears reasonable, then, that the superintendent would want to be assured that the judgment was best by preserving the potential observed in the staff member and seeking to bring about improvements in performance. Rewards are proper and corrections are necessary, but of secondary importance relative to the superintendent's teaching and directing function. This transcends the means of establishing a negative control system.

Correctional imperatives must gain the attention of the superintendent, for the benefit of both the teacher who is committed primarily to the instructional function and the administrative and supervisory staffs who have a great variety of delegations. The superintendent must see the correctional imperatives of the office in terms of the delegations made, the means by which delegations can be fruitful for the purposes of the district, and the extent to which the influence of the office must be used in making delegations. The superintendent must maintain some contact with classroom teaching-learning situations in order to assure the board of education and the community that the best quality of education is being provided. The contact with classrooms depends on the system of delegations established and the precision with which the superintendent holds members of the staff accountable for delegated responsibilities. The assurances that delegations have been well made and that accountability systems prove adequate standing alone are insufficient. They constitute, however, the basic working tools for the superintendent to establish a sound delegating process. A more detailed discussion of the audit and accountability phenomena will be presented in chapters 12 and 13.

Examples of Strategy

1. *Develop and/or review a formal control system for school administrators that includes both rewards and corrective actions.*

2. *List all the subpublics of the school system and their usual means of advocating accountability.*

3. *Invite all staff members to list the ways they could satisfy the requirements of an accountability system.*

SENSITIVITY TO EXPECTATION SOURCES

The basic purpose of delegation is expediting the accomplishment of the institution's goals. Delegation is the means, not the end product. Without the means, the end is never accomplished.

The wise use of expertise is accomplished in delegating. The type of expertise needed to accomplish the various goals of a school system will vary from task to task; by developing sound delegation processes, the many varied tasks can be completed satisfactorily, thereby meeting the predetermined goals of the system.

The goals of any school district should reflect a sensitivity to community expectations. School district goals should be developed and designed after obtaining input from the many segments of the community. The various methods used in securing expectation data may range from simple means to sophisticated and complex strategies.

The district's goals should be a basis of commonality among contiguous school districts that form the basis for regional educational goals. Compiling the many regional goals results in an identification of state goals. It is readily apparent that the many state goals may be a resource for national goals.

An example of school district goals that reflect community expectations follows:

1. Each graduating student can show respect for self and for the rights of others. A student will have received:
   – –information about alternative value systems; their influence on individuals and society.
   – –the opportunity to develop a personal value system, or revise his present one.

2. Each graduating student may show evidence of possessing an inquiring attitude and the capability for self-development and self-direction in line with his native ability. A student:
   – –will have had opportunities to use varied resources for independent study.

— —will have received information which will help him develop independent decisions.

— —will have been encouraged to have a desire for continued learning and will understand the need for it.

— —will have acquired experiences in the effective use of his time.

— —will have been given opportunities to demonstrate his creative ability within the context of the curriculum.

3. Each student will foster the natural joy and enthusiasm for learning.

4. Each graduating student will be allowed to select courses that will help him/her acquire positive attitudes toward family relations and gain knowledge and skills necessary for home management and intelligent consumption of goods and services. A student:

— —will understand how members of a family work within different family patterns.

— —will have some understanding of how a child develops and what skills are necessary to care for a child.

— —will have had opportunities to acquire the knowledge and skills needed for managing personal and family finances.

— —will have had presented to him alternatives available to consumers, opportunities to understand the consequences of different actions and opportunities to make choices in regard to consumerism.

5. Each student graduating will be prepared to either continue his education or meet the requirements of the job market in a field consistent with his interests and ability. A student:

— —will have been informed of career opportunities and the job competencies needed for employment.

— —will know of the need to continue his education and improve his skills in order to meet the changing demands of employment.

6. Each graduating student will have a basic comprehension of the modern curriculum. A student:

— —will have the knowledge necessary for developing concepts in social studies, mathematics, science, fine arts, practical arts and human relations.

— —will have knowledge of his economic role in life as it relates to the production and consumption of goods and services, and to his political role as a full and involved citizen.

7. Each graduating student will have a command of the learning skills equal to his ability. Such skills relate to reading, mathematics, writing, listening, speaking, and physical fitness.

8. Each graduating student will have received information about safety concepts and physical and mental health so that he can practice sound personal health and safety habits. A student:
   — —will have heard about the personal and social consequences of health and safety problems.
   — —will have been alerted to personal safety, physical and mental health needs, and been advised of ways to meet these needs.

9. Each graduating student will have been informed of the problems of society; environment, race, human relations, food and shelter, etc.

10. Each graduating student may be able to apply appropriate knowledge, skills and attitudes to real and projected school and community government situations and concerns. A student:
    — —will have had opportunities to participate in decision-making in school affairs.
    — —will have received information pertaining to operating procedures of the school district, municipal, county, state and federal government.

11. Each graduating student will have opportunities to explore, and to participate in constructive leisure time activities for personal development and enjoyment.

12. Methods will be developed to identify more accurately and completely the potential of each learner.[1]

These district goals are broad and general in nature. The actual accomplishment of these goals is done through local buildings and within individual classrooms. District goals may stimulate the recognition of a need for regional goals, which provides the framework for state goals.

The broad local and state goals indicate that numerous means must be devised to accomplish them. The many means serve as a foundation to determine what tasks are to be delegated within the local district. These delegated tasks then serve as a foundation for the development of an organizational design that facilitates the process of accountability in meeting the goals.

Examples of Strategy

1. *Submit the school district's goals and objectives to the staff members to determine the kinds of expertise needed to carry out those tasks most promising for goal and objective achievement.*

---

1. From "The 12 goals of Neenah Joint School District—Board of Education, Neenah, Wisconsin. (An unpublished copy in mimeograph form.) Reprinted with permission.

2. *Review state goals of education in conjunction with district goals to determine parallel direction and purpose of education.*

3. *Promote a regional set of goals and objectives to reflect geographical community concerns that encompass local district goals and objectives, while maintaining the state's general purpose and direction.*

RATIONAL INCENTIVES

Some rational assumptions are imbedded in the purposes of delegation. These assumptions provide the foundation for delegation processes and serve as incentives to improve the administrative skills of delegation. Some rational assumptions are:

1. There is a person who has more expertise than you to do a particular task.
2. There is a person who can do a particular task at less expense than you.
3. There is better use of time if a person other than you accomplishes a particular task.
4. There is better total staff development throughout the district if delegation takes place.
5. There is greater opportunity for the district to accomplish its goals if delegation takes place.

These assumptions may constitute a rationale of the delegation process and the accrued benefits derived from their acceptance. The delegation process benefits by allowing the delegator more opportunities to administer the responsibilities assigned. A second benefit allows for better supervision of assignments and demands more acceptance of and accountability for the tasks. Another benefit of the delegation process is increased time for the administrator to develop strategies for continued improvements within the assigned tasks. This increased time allows for more efficient means to accomplish the ends. A fourth benefit of the delegation process is the development of the district staff. If a good staff development program is to accomplish its function properly, the delegation process must be properly designed, implemented, and continually evaluated. A fifth benefit of the delegation process is the creation of a sound organizational framework. This framework provides for a functioning district to work toward the fulfillment of its goals. It also permits an organization to be continually ready to accept the challenges constantly being presented. The final benefit of the delegation process is the development of a management team concept. This benefit is equally applicable at the district level or at the building level of operation.

Examples of Strategy

1. *Discuss the assumptions and/or principles of task responsibilities to determine if they are accepted in practice by all those involved.*
2. *Describe the probable benefits of the delegation process to representative groups within your district and list the actual relevant and observable outcomes.*

THE MANAGEMENT TEAM

The management team is a direct result of the delegation process and the benefit is increased administrative effectiveness for the district. Many desirable characteristics evolve as the management team gains in effectiveness. These characteristics result in identifiable leadership within the group, which consequently provides a more open climate for better delegation and communication among its members. The most important achievement of a management team is the concentrated and concerted effort expended to realize the defined goals.

The delegation process is a sequential series of steps leading to an outcome. It is a well-designed method of operation when certain guidelines are clearly understood and creatively observed. Some of these guidelines are discussed here.

Guideline One

Adhere to the knowledge of (1) why delegate, (2) what to delegate, (3) how to delegate, and (4) when delegation is accomplished. The understanding and comprehension of this guideline are mandatory in the beginning of successful and effective delegation.

Guideline Two

Make sure that delegated tasks are clearly understood by the delegatee as well as by the delegator. This essential guideline is often overlooked by one or both parties before the task assignment is made, and this oversight will almost guarantee the automatic failure of successfully completing tasks.

Guideline Three

Understand clearly and completely the expected outcome of the delegated task. If the task is that of completing a final report, forming a committee, developing new curriculum, or analyzing and recommending a new textbook, then the task is perfectly clear as to the expected outcome. In this way, the understanding of content and the understanding of process will not be confused. Too often, the terms content and process are not used in their proper context and the delegated task is not accomplished. The process (strategy) is designed to accomplish the content (goal). Therefore, the goal is the delegated task as defined by the delegator; the strategy is the process activated by the delegatee.

Guideline Four

Once the delegation assignment has been made, the delegator leaves the delegatee free to determine the means. Constant changing of the desired end results will lead to confusion in the strategy development process. The failure to follow this guideline results in the inability of the delegator to understand clearly the process of delegation. Leaving the person alone to complete the delegated task does not, however, preclude monitoring of the progress being made toward completion of the task assignment. The important differences of mingling and monitoring must be clear in the minds of both parties.

Guideline Five

The monitoring performance must be planned carefully. The difference between mingling and monitoring was suggested in the fourth guideline. This final guideline indicates that a monitoring performance design must be established and followed if the delegation process is to be effective and successful.

Examples of Strategy

1. *Analyze past delegation practices in terms of the five delegation guidelines. Were all five followed? Which guidelines were not followed? What rationale can be given for those guidelines not followed?*

2. *Review entire organizational chart to explore more efficient means of goal accomplishment.*

3. *Provide a district in-service training program to increase the possibilities for personnel to transfer to other positions.*

STEPS OF DELEGATION

The understanding and comprehension of the above five guidelines are essential to successful delegation and to effective administrative team action. Delegation is a series of sequential steps that guide the delegator. The steps within the delegation process are: (1) decision making, (2) communication, (3) implementation, and (4) evaluation.

Decision Making

The first step in the process is to determine who does what task. These decisions are crucial to the entire process and care must be used in matching the skills, knowledge, and capabilities of the delegatee with the demands of the task assignment.

The development of a frame of reference for the delegator is an extremely important first step. The decision maker must understand the procedures involved in arriving at a decision. Agreement by authorities indicates that individuals go through the following steps in making decisions: (1) recognize, define, and limit the decision target, (2) analyze and evaluate, (3) establish criteria or standards for alternate solutions, (4) collect data, (5) formulate and evaluate the alternatives for the solution, and (6) select the alternative. This sequence of steps illustrates the necessity of matching the expertise of the delegatee with the tasks to be performed. The assignment of tasks based on the criteria of seniority, friendship, persuasion, informal recommendations, or lack of knowledge of the individual negates the probability of goal attainment. This assignment decision requires the accumulation of data, which may come from formal as well as informal sources. The delegation of the task of curriculum development to someone lacking the theoretical aspects of curriculum building and/or lacking knowledge of the subject content is asking for an unsuccessful completion of the task assignment. A similar analogy is the delegation of the task of administering an innovative school to a principal who has not developed the type of philosophy compatible with the staff of the school. An immediate conflict of values within the building may result in open confrontation. A successful and intelligent decision-making procedure is basic and essential to the total delegation process if goal attainment is to be accomplished.

Communication

The communication procedure is the second step within the delegation process. Once the decision has been made regarding the task assignment, communication must take place between the involved parties. If this procedure does not clearly indicate the exact responsibilities being assigned and the expectations being specified, the entire process of delegation is disrupted. Communication may take place in a variety of media. The most common form is a verbal exchange between the parties, although this mode of operation should be followed by a written confirmation. The written form is primarily to record what transpired rather than to communicate initial information. Certain identifiable obstacles must be overcome if communication messages are to be comprehended clearly by both parties.

Obstacles such as the lack of openness and trust between communicators, of sincerity in relations between the parties, and of communications that are free-flowing will impede the proper understanding of the expected outcomes.

Berlo,[1] in his communications model, indicated a number of components that are involved in transmitting information from one person to another. These components range from the source to the receiver and back to the source. The sender places the ideas into some kind of code or special language before transmitting them to the receiver. The receiver must decode the ideas or information before proper meaning and interpretation can be made of the original message.

The delegation process, by its very nature of having one individual act in lieu of another, creates an obligation on the part of the receiver of the communication. This duty is an expectation that must be transmitted clearly to the delegatee. This atmosphere of obligatory responses will not exist without a clear communication system. The importance of clear communications, as related to the delegation process, must be internalized thoroughly by the delegator as well as the delegatee.

Implementation

The third step in the delegation process is the implementation of action, putting the delegated tasks into meaningful operation. The creation of the necessary resources must be completed prior to any outcome expectations. Basically, these resources that are to be created for the delegatee can be divided into the task assignments that include the authority and time necessary to fulfill the required expectations. To do otherwise is an exercise in futility. A case in point is where the principal is held responsible for the instructional program of the school, which must include evaluation of the teachers. It is an extremely difficult situation if teachers are assigned to the building without principal involvement in the decision-placement process and the principal is then held accountable for the instructional program. In order for the concept of accountability to be operational, the principle of authority must be considered.

Another resource is time. Often time is neither considered a resource nor used as a resource in the delegation process. The appropriate amount of time must be considered if the entire delegation process is ultimately to meet the goals of the institution. To assign tasks to administrators, either at the district or building level, without

---

1. David Berlo. *The Process of Communication: An Introduction to Theory and Practice,* (New York: Holt, Rinehart, and Winston, 1960) p. 23.

regard to a consideration of the time resource, is to introduce a substantial risk factor.

The next resource is the necessary human and material resources deemed appropriate to the task assignment. Attempts to accomplish general or specific goals and/or objectives without considering the necessary human or material resources may occur because of improper analysis and expectation of the tasks to be completed. Too often assignments are made with the primary emphasis on an economic rationale that could predispose outcome expectations. Classic examples of violations of this resource are: (1) a second-grade teacher responsible for the teaching of all disciplines to a class of students that is exceptionally large; (2) a supervisor who is to maintain a close working relationship with teachers for curriculum improvement but does not have an adequate budget to support the purchase of essential items; (3) a principal who is responsible for the instructional program within the building but does not have adequate materials to accomplish the objective; or, (4) a superintendent who is expected to raise achievement levels to state or national norms but has the budget continually reduced.

The next resource is the functioning facilities appropriate to the task assignment. The delegator must recognize that facilities may enhance or destroy the successful completion of the responsibilities assigned to the delegatee. Situations can arise in which assigned tasks have no measurable chance of success because of improperly defined facilities. The supervisor of a special education program, who must diagnose individual students for placement but does not have the type of facility that is conducive to individualized testing, surely will fail to accomplish the responsibilities assigned. The building principal who has responsibilities for providing a sound instructional program and has the adequate square footage of facilities, but not the specific arrangements, surely will fail to meet the goals of the assignment. The resource of facilities must be considered in determining the congruency of the task assignment and the expected successful completion of that task.

The final resource is the availability and adequacy of measuring devices. The assignment of tasks to be completed successfully must include the type of measuring devices that are to be used to assess the completion of the task. This area must be understood thoroughly by all participants if any measure of effectiveness is to be documented. Measuring devices can assist the many media, such as observations, written and oral reports, informal and formal surveys, standardized testing, and written and oral feedbacks. The concept involved is to understand the importance of predetermining the framework in which tasks are to be completed effectively.

Evaluation

The fourth and final step within the delegation process is the evaluation procedure. This procedure is of equal importance and weight to the other three steps and must be developed carefully if the entire process of delegation is to be effective. The ultimate objective of the delegation process is to achieve goals. The first concept in the evaluation step is the continuous monitoring or auditing of the strategies used by the delegatee in completing the task. This monitoring design does not imply a continuous mingling of tasks assigned by the delegator in unbroken influence of the process used by the delegatee. It does imply that authority has been granted to determine strategies used to complete stabilized tasks. Thus, a continuous monitoring or auditing design indicates a close working relationship between the delegator and the delegatee to provide benchmarks for evaluating the task assignment. The design must include frequent meetings between the parties, written and/or oral reports by the delegatee, and on-site visitations by the delegator. Only through such continuity can the evaluation procedure be truly effective and meaningful.

The second concept in the evaluating process is that predetermined objectives must be assessed if proper evaluation procedures are to be realized. A basic and simple statement, such as "Was there a statement of objectives and was it met?", is an instrumental part of the evaluating process. Without clear objectives, the evaluation of delegated tasks will not be valid and/or reliable.

The next concept in the evaluating process is that the strategies used by the delegatee were either acceptable or unacceptable. This area is of crucial importance in the evaluating process because it determines the possible success or failure of the task assignment. Caution must be taken, however, since even unacceptable strategies may accomplish the assigned tasks. Assumptions cannot be made that unacceptable strategies are automatic failures to successfully completed tasks. The unacceptable strategies may have been illegal, unethical, or in violation of a negotiated agreement. The intent of determining acceptable strategies is a valid part of the evaluating process.

The final concept in the evaluating process is that the evidence used by the delegator and delegatee were valid and reliable. The strategies used in the evaluating process must have been above reproach. The end product, as well as the means to that end product, must be acceptable. The type of evidence used in the determination of completed tasks suggests the criteria for judging the success of delegation. (Evaluation as a category of work process was discussed in chapter 7 and the application here is consistent with that discussion.)

Great emphasis has been placed on the comprehension of the four steps of the delegation process. Each step is of equal value within the total and must be viewed and accepted as such. The intent and purpose of delegation is to provide means to accomplish the stated ends. Delegation is merely the means to the end, and must not be construed as the end in itself. The end product is the accomplishment of stated goals of the school system, either at the classroom level, building level, or district level.

Examples of Strategy

1. Submit the school district's job descriptions to staff to determine accuracy and accountability.

2. Evaluate communication procedures in terms of whether they permit clear accountability throughout the organization.

3. Review a representative sample of delegated tasks to determine what resources have been made available to the delegatees.

4. Ask selected staff members to review the evaluation procedures to determine if delegated tasks were achieved as planned.

KEY ELEMENTS OF SUCCESS

The basic purpose underlying the delegation process is to meet the instructional goals of the school system more adequately and effectively. If the organization is relatively simple in design or relatively complex because of size, the delegation process must be adapted correspondingly. The delegation process is designed to function regardless of the degree of complexity.

Once the delegation steps have been followed, certain key elements manifest themselves that support success. The delegation of task responsibilities allows for a better utilization of time resources by those responsible for management. This action frees the delegator from many disparate routine tasks and permits more effective leadership. The skills of leadership are correlated directly with the time resource. Leadership increases with maximum utilization of time. Once the time resource is managed, the delegator is able to communicate with the various publics. The communication procedure is instrumental in meeting the goals of the institution and includes the many publics that are involved as variables in contributing to the completion of the goals. Management of the time resource, in addition to allowing for leadership opportunities, allows for more creative leadership. Leadership skills, alone, are inadequate without creative talents that surface in conjunction with these skills. The wise utilization of the time resource benefits the administrator by allowing for more effective leadership, better communication, and more creative talents to emerge.

A second key element that manifests itself is furthering the growth and development of individual staff members. This aspect is positively correlated to the amount of delegation present and the number of delegatees involved.

The third key element evidenced in the delegation process is the creation of a management team concept. The magnitude of the delegation process enhances the mind-set of individuals concerning cooperation and completion of task assignment. The team orientation contributes to individuals as well as to the institution; both satisfy their respective goals.

Examples of Strategy

1. *Keep a daily log of your task responsibilities to survey the percentage of time spent on each task.*

2. *Analyze the internal promotion practices for the past several years. State and explain your results.*

3. *Describe your district's concept of a management team and ask for a critique by all team members.*

OBSTACLES TO SUCCESS

Successful delegation hinges on the completion of the tasks assigned to staff members. Certain benchmarks can be ascertained to measure progress toward the attainment of goals. These benchmarks may include merit adjustments, promotions, increased revenue, decreased costs, and observations. The final benchmark is the achievement of the goals of the school. Many obstacles, however, stand in the way of attainment of these goals. These obstacles manifest themselves in many forms but the most critical, yet not the most obvious, is the failure to follow the delegation process. As mentioned earlier, the process is sequential and failure to maintain this order and to provide a framework of methodology will result in obstacles to the total process.

Several general areas lend themselves to stonewalling the process. Failure to select the right person for the right task often results in unaccomplished tasks. The result is frustration and disappointment for both parties, as well as for the organization.

Another common obstacle to successful delegation is the misunderstanding of adequate resources, which results in personal blame for failure to accomplish assigned tasks. The various resources of time, authority, and personnel facilities or finances can easily be overlooked or underestimated in the delegation process. To hold a person responsible for certain task outcomes, who has no authority to act, places that person in an impossible situation. There are many other examples in resource areas that illustrate this type of obstacle.

Assigning the proper person to the proper task may be excellent if adequate resources are made available, but there still may exist a power struggle between the delegator and the delegatee. This type of conflict is often covert in nature and difficult to pinpoint as a stonewall in the delegation process. Power struggles can be rooted and nurtured in numerous sources. The upwardly mobile individual may be subverting the system for personal, rather than institutional, gain. The administrator who cannot delegate because of the imagined loss of ego position and authority, contributes to this basic conflict in personalities, values, and philosophy that often results in ineffective delegation and nonattainment of goals.

Decentralization or centralization of the organizational structure also may have definite impact on the success of the delegation process. Geographical distance often is a contributing factor to a poorly functioning process. Some factors that can be attributed to obstacles because of decentralization are: (1) lack of monitoring and feedback, (2) misappropriation of adequate resources, (3) improper decision making in the task assignment, and (4) an ineffective communication system. This does not imply that decentralization is arbitrarily an obstacle to successful delegation and goal attainment, but it is a variable that should be considered. Centralization of the organizational structure also may provide a stonewalling effect in the delegation process. The delegator may be too close to the methods of the processes used by the delegatee, which could result in lack of authority and freedom to act. The power struggle that may exist could contribute to the environment in which it ferments. The communication design may not be clearly thought out because of the close proximity of the parties.

The stress on organizational power by teachers, administrators, and noncertified staff can be an obstacle to successful delegation. As explained earlier in this chapter, the delegation process must remain open and clear to allow for communication exchange, monitoring and feedback, and the right person for the right task. These characteristics are at times contrary to the basic philosophy and purpose of organizational groups. If all roles and responsibilities must be painstakingly detailed and outlined regarding both parties' obligations and functions, the process of delegation loses its meaning, impact, and purpose. Delegation implies accountability; lack of delegation implies diffusion of accountability and promotes an atmosphere of impossible goal attainment.

Examples of Strategy

1. *Analyze the successful or unsuccessful achievement of meeting the district's goals and objectives. List the means that allowed or prevented this achievement in terms of curriculum, personnel, finance, etc.*

2. *Structure the district's organizational chart to indicate a centralized means and a decentralized means designed to achieve the goals and objectives. Submit both designs to staff members for their reaction.*

PUTTING IT ALL TOGETHER

The district administrator is responsible for goal attainment. The organizational framework is a facilitator, the means to accomplish this end. Within the organizational framework exists the delegation process. Sound and successful procedures used in the delegating processes depend on a clear and concise understanding of the expertise demands of delegation.

Delegating responsibilities alone will not attain the goals of the school. Each delegating process is a unique situation and cannot be explained or treated en masse. The key to goal attainment is functioning delegation combined with the coordination of these steps by the administrator. Delegation is only one process; another is the coordination of efforts as discussed in the next chapter.

HELP FROM OTHER AUTHORS

Beckett, John A. *Management Dynamics: The New Synthesis.* New York: McGraw-Hill Book Company, 1971.

Carnegie, Dale, and Associates. *Managing Through People.* New York: Simon and Schuster, 1975.

Drucker, Peter F. *Management, Tasks — Responsibilities — Practices.* New York: Harper & Row, 1973.

Heyel, Carl (ed.). *The Encyclopedia of Management,* 2d ed. New York: Van Nostrand Reinhold Company, 1973.

Maxson, Robert, and Walter Sistrunch (eds.). *The Administrative Team Concept,* "A Systems Approach to Educational Administration," Dubuque, Iowa: William C. Brown Co., 1973, pp. 76–106.

McConkey, Dale. *No-Nonsense Delegation.* New York: American Management Association, 1974.

Coordination of Instructional Tasks

Chapter 9 emphasized the use of the delegation process as one mode of operation the school administrator uses to accomplish the expectations of the position. The school administrator must be the performer of some tasks; in others, the school administrator must cause someone else to perform tasks. Delegation of task assignments is a means to accomplish the goals of the institution. A wise and discretionary use of the process results in more effective and efficient accomplishments.

Delegation of tasks and responsibilities involved in working toward accomplishing institutional goals is not necessarily a difficult charge. The process guiding the delegator through the theoretical and operational framework of task assignment was examined in detail in the previous chapter. Task assignment can be as simple or as complex as the delegator chooses, but the risk factors of success and failure are in direct correlation with the procedures used. The delegation process needs constant attention if the outcomes are to be predictable and successful.

The process of task distribution is only part of good management practice by the school administrator. Merely to develop and implement sound delegation practices will not assure the success of institutional goal attainment. The administrator who follows the entire gamut of decision making, communicating, implementing, and evaluating in the delegation process, now must consider the processes of coordinating the delegated tasks. Delegation achieves a differentiation of task assignment; coordination assembles the separate elements into harmonious and purposeful total activity. Another part of good management practice is a sound theoretical and operational framework of task coordination.

SYNCHRONIZED ACTION

The importance and the relevance of the term coordination, as it relates to the attainment of school system goals, is revealed in its definition. Eye, Netzer, and Krey offered a diagrammatic comparison of cooperation, coordination, and compromise, as well as these descriptive statements:

> The rule of interpersonal relationships in coordination is that each may proceed to his own short-term goal so long as he does not interfere with the other's opportunity to pursue those behaviors which lead him to his short-term goal. In the case of coordination, the short-term goals may not be held in common but may contribute to the common general purpose of the school system.[1]

The term coordination must depend on some central thought, theme, or purpose as a part of its definition. Inherent to acts of coordination is the implication that many forces, activities, or persons are involved. These multivariants are committed, all or in part, to some singleness of purpose. The act of coordination occurs when all similarly goal-directed forces combine and mesh energies harmoniously toward the clearly defined result. A successfully coordinated effort is somewhat analogous to a machine comprised of many components, each having an identifiable function of its own yet contributing critically to the output of the total   mechanism. Coordination is an orderly plan for group action and promotes solidarity of effort in the accomplishment of institutional goals.

Coordination in most lists of major processes of administration is prominent and persistent. Any student or practitioner of administration should value the word, the concept, and the related behaviors of coordination. It is well, however, to back off for an opportunity to gain a perspective of the process. There is a personal attraction to primary outcomes, no matter what position is held or in what segment of the organization an individual performs work. This attraction must not dominate either the use, the importance, the impact, or the probable outcomes of efforts leading to coordination. If the attraction to primary outcomes, that is, visible behaviors that can be labeled coordination, becomes excessive, then coordination is an end rather than a

---

1. Glen G. Eye, Lanore A. Netzer, and Robert D. Krey. *Supervision of Instruction,* 2nd ed. (New York: Harper and Row, 1971) p. 201.

means. Coordination as an end induces administrative behavior that demands that all participants give greater priority to the characteristics of behavioral process than to the personal, professional, and organizational goals.

The complexities of educational programs have increased tremendously in past years. The educational process of past generations appears now as very simplistic in nature compared to many types of programs existing today. The many innovations and trends on the cutting edge of today's programs will add to the complexities of future coordination processes. Different approaches in school organizational structure, such as, individually guided instruction, community based programs, and total immersion projects, are but a few trends that may be commonplace in tomorrow's organizational schemes. The instructional process of the past must change to meet future organizational designs.

The concepts of mechanized methods of instruction, independent learning, concentrated exposure, and massive audiences will dictate new means and methods of coordination efforts. The more diffused the delegated tasks become, the more complex the coordination efforts. Negotiated agreements between teachers and boards of education will continue to add to the complexities of coordination. Titles beyond that of teacher will increase the types of job descriptions within the instructional staff. Any new job description entails different duties and responsibilities that necessitate additional delegated tasks followed by additional coordination efforts. The administrator of tomorrow's educational system must have a sound theoretical philosophy counterbalanced with a sound operational approach to a coordination system.

Coordination as a process was never intended to be an end in itself, insofar as the theory and the philosophy of administration is concerned. When it becomes a means to an end, it is evident that the individual practitioner has used the proper intent of the process. If coordination is the means to the administrator's personal satisfaction, rather than to the instructional purpose, the process of coordination is serving the primary purpose of the major power figure. Administrators need to learn to find satisfaction in the secondary outcomes of their positions, that is, the school's teaching-learning products.

The secondary outcome for the administrator is the primary outcome of the school as an organization of effort. The main target for administrators is that primary efforts at coordination relate directly to, and contribute to, the school's ultimate product. This calls for readjustments on the part of many administrators with respect to their appreciation for and application of the process of coordination.

The administrator properly should find satisfaction in the visibility of the work, provided that the focus on visibility does not dominate the evaluation of the outcomes of the school. Such emphasis may indicate that the administrator considers the observable part of coordination as an end, rather than a means to achieving the school's purposes. Administrators can, while emphasizing the smooth running machine for which the administrator is responsible, relate this smoothness to the major objectives and products of the school. With this type of perspective, the means-end problem of coordination need not constitute a hazard for administrators, but rather a vehicle by which the tasks can be accomplished. Giving visibility to coordination as an administrative means to the development of instructional quality may enlist the support of the public. This creates the environment in which coordination can accomplish quality as a goal.

The authority inherent in the coordination function results from the authority vested in the delegation function. To delegate with no ability to coordinate is an exercise in futility. One process must follow the other, with appropriate authority eventually vested in the individual held accountable for a specified element of goal attainment.

A term synonymous with the responsibility to coordinate is supervision. This function also implies inherent authority to delegate and coordinate task assignments. The Taft-Hartley Act of 1947 defined the supervisor as,

> any individual having authority, in the interests of the employer, to hire, transfer, suspend, lay off, recall, promote, discharge, assign, reward or discipline other employees, or responsibility to direct them, or to adjust their grievances, or effectively to recommend such action, if in connection with the foregoing the exercise of such authority is not merely routine or clerical in nature, but requires the use of independent judgment.

This definition of a supervisor can be transposed easily to a definition of a person who delegates and coordinates. It can be stated, then, that a delegator/coordinator is an individual who (1) has the appropriate knowledge of the tasks to be performed, (2) receives appropriate recognition for that knowledge, and (3) is in a position committed to decision making.

The delegator/coordinator must be effective in both competencies or the processes fail to mesh and function properly. The necessary skills are interrelated and interlocked to form a perfect sequence. The old adage, "I must be effective for them to be effective" is extremely appropriate in the fulfillment of instructional goals.

Examples of Strategy

1. Subject the coordinating practices in your school district to close scrutiny and determine if they are means to an end or ends in themselves. Attempt to rationalize each practice.

2. *Review current job descriptions to determine if appropriate supervisory coordination and authority are vested in each description to allow the position to be successful.*

3. *Review the district's organizational chart and trace the coordination and authority line from a specific goal in a course of study to a specific goal of the district. Make recommendations for corrections in the organizational chart if the line is not continuous.*

REINFORCEMENT POTENTIAL

Various strategies to be used in managing the many aspects of instruction have been presented throughout these chapters. Considerable discussion was directed in the previous chapter to the delegation process as a means of accomplishing the end product. Numerous books, pamphlets, study guides, seminars, workshops, and college courses spend extensive amounts of time and effort on the promotion and understanding of the delegation process. A careful review of these sources indicates that the promotion and understanding of the coordination process is missing or undeveloped in any theoretical or operational manner. Coordination is a mandatory part of the whole program. To delegate and not coordinate is an ineffective procedure. Coordination is a means of successfully achieving the delegated tasks.

The only proper aim of an institution is to accomplish a purpose or purposes. Within the institutional framework, an organization is created in which various work-sharing responsibilities are distributed in order to develop efficient mechanisms that ultimately result in the accomplishment of goals or purposes. The organization is a means to the end product. When the work-sharing responsibilities have been assigned and/or distributed according to the organizational chart, each of the structured personnel delegates various aspects of major task assignments, in order to accomplish these assignments. The successful completion of task assignment, however, cannot be evaluated in terms of success or failure unless some aspect of the coordination process is followed. Coordination is the feedback system of a task completion monitoring process. It is a feedback procedure that allows the delegator to measure the degree of task progress accomplishment. The organization, although a means to an end, also has its own internal goals to accomplish. One necessary organizational goal is effectiveness. If an organization is ineffective, the institution does not realize its intent and purpose. All segments of the organization must demonstrate coordination efforts to ensure effectiveness. School districts that practice program-planning-budget-system (PPBS) concepts must rely on effective communication and coordination network of the many delegated tasks. The same is true of a school district that undertakes management by objectives (MBO) for any part of their system. Many areas within the MBO plan demand coordinated efforts orchestrated by the delegator of the initial tasks.

Individuals within the organization also have personal needs to fulfill. One need is to accomplish the task assignments delegated by another member of the organization. The position held by the individual is a debatable point, except to the degree of task assignment. The superintendent of a school system has individual expectations to fulfill and must coordinate the delegated tasks. The building administrator has job expectations to be accomplished and must coordinate the delegated efforts of the staff within the building. An athletic coach must accomplish the instruction of the necessary drills and plays in order to fulfill successfully the job expectations, and this requires coordinated efforts from the assistant coaches, players, managers, and parents. Any person within an institution must delegate and coordinate the efforts extended for task achievement.

Examples of Strategy

1. *Review current literature, seminars, and college courses for units on the comprehensiveness of theoretical and practical aspects of the coordination process.*

2. *In small group discussions, list separately the goals and objectives of the institution and the organization. Review each list for duplication, overlap, and continuity. Make any necessary corrections for maximum understanding and clarity.*

3. *Analyze any specific planned and structured program to support the integration of personnel, instruction, finance, materials, etc. Determine the effectiveness of the coordination process in order for the district to accomplish its goal successfully.*

PRINCIPLES OF COORDINATION

The principles of coordination must be defined clearly and understood by the delegator if the coordination process is to succeed. For purposes of this discussion, a principle is defined as, "a general statement describing a persisting relationship between two or more phenomena which gives direction to action."[2] The principles presented on the following pages are of equal priority and are sequential in nature.

The first principle of coordination concerns *goal acknowledgement.* In order for an institution to be successful, it must achieve its goals. The basic principle underlying the coordination process is that

---

2. Ibid., p. 56.

each involved member of the institution knows and understands the goals that the institution is striving to accomplish. An indepth understanding of all of the goals of the institution is not mandatory for all employees, but goals relating directly to the task assignment of the particular individual must be understood. The delegator, as well as the delegatee, must agree completely on the outcomes of the institution's goal attainment. The delegation of tasks and responsibilities without futuristic direction is similar to a pilot without a flight plan. Too often, delegated tasks and responsibilities do not indicate long-range objectives, resulting in a lack of proper strategies designed or implemented for long-range accomplishments. The importance of goal acknowledgement is that task assignment be an integral part of meeting the institutional outcomes.

The second principle of coordination relates to *clarity of task assignment.* Delegating tasks and responsibilities without a total comprehension of the task is asking for ultimate failure. The principle of clarity is defined as an *understanding and mutual agreement of what is to be achieved by the delegation and the delegatee, and parameters of authority involved in (1) strategy development, (2) resource availability, (3) time allotment, (4) facilities appropriateness, and (5) evaluative means for determining task completion.* These five aspects constituting the clarity of task assignment provide a mandated principle of coordination.

The coordinator must not assume that the delegatee develops a clarity of task assignment without input, guidance, and direction in a mutual environment of the supervisor and delegatee. The coordinator should indicate, preferably in writing, the details of each aspect for future reference during the succeeding principles of coordination. Written records allow for positive reinforcement of the task assignment and for eventual evaluation of the task accomplishment.

The third principle of coordination concerns the basic understanding of *individual differences.* The coordinator or the delegator must have *a theoretical framework of human development and psychology of human behavior to allow for individual differences among the many people assigned tasks for fulfillment and completion.*

Research has indicated that individuals have differences and that, with proper training, coordinators can differentiate varying needs, interests, and desires among individuals. Maslow,[3] in his work in determining individual differences, listed the basic needs of all individuals. The degree of satisfaction of these needs varies among individuals; no two people have identical makeups concerning the satisfaction of any or all of these needs. He indicated that all individuals

---

3. Abraham H. Maslow. *Toward a Psychology of Being,* 2nd ed. (New York: D. Van Nostrand Co., 1968) pp. 21–43.

have (1) physiological needs—hunger, shelter, sexual gratification, (2) safety needs—protection against dangers, that is, threats from either the environment or from other people, (3) social needs—love, affection, and belongingness, (4) esteem needs—the need for self-respect and the good opinion of others, and (5) self-fulfillment needs— value and satisfaction of the work and the good of self-actualization. Each individual satisfies these needs in varying stages of life and each individual has varying standards of need fulfillment. The satisfaction of one individual in the social area will not be identical to that of another. No two people will have the same profile of need satisfaction in all five areas. The coordinator must utilize the understanding of human psychology in allowing for task completion by differing individuals. These varying need satisfactions directly influence the productivity of each individual.

The fourth principle of coordination is the establishment of a *communication feedback system*. Without proper means to receive information from the many delegated sources, the entire function fails to be achieved. The feedback system must be *designed carefully before the task assignments are made so that the system will be understood thoroughly by the delegator and delegatee*. The most successful systems include reporting periods (daily, monthly, or yearly), means of reporting (verbal, written, or a combination), and methods of reporting (forms, narration, or a combination). These strategies should be discussed, agreed on, and recorded prior to the performance of task assignment. The ability of the coordinator to differentiate between types of feedback systems needed for successful accomplishment of the delegated tasks is of the utmost importance. For some purposes, only a very simple feedback system is necessary because the task assignment may be of short duration and the delegator and delegatee may be next door to each other. In other situations, the feedback system must be complex as the task assignment may involve huge responsibilities with variable geographic, budgetary, or long-range implications. Each task assignment must have an individually designed feedback system.

The fifth and final principle of coordination encompasses the *evaluation phase*. The basic question to be answered by the coordinator is "How do you know you have accomplished your task assignment?" The evaluation design must *identify the evidence to be used, determine the ways information is to be secured, describe the procedures for processing the data, and establish the criteria appropriate for translating the data into judgments*. A busy administrator, who delegates many responsibilities, is still held accountable for the job expectation. The administrator may have followed the first four principles of coordination in elaborate and sophisticated design, but if the administrator cannot formalize the other designs into the fifth principle, effective coordination will not take place. Every delegated task may have been accomplished successfully, but without the individual principles orchestrated into a symphony, the final goals cannot be realized. For example, the building administrator wants to improve the students' ability to read. Many tasks are delegated, that is, reading consultants work with teachers, counselors work with students and parents, committees select appropriate instructional materials, and appropriate tests are researched to measure progress and results. If the building administrator cannot, or does not, adequately allow for final interpretations of the delegated tasks, the basic goal of student improvement in reading will not be realized. The coordinator of the delegated tasks must understand and follow the five principles of the coordination process.

Examples of Strategy

1. Review with staff the goals and objectives of the school district to ensure that all personnel understand the purpose and direction of the instructional program.

2. Review the educational training of the staff members who have coordination responsibilities to determine the extensiveness of preparation and training for the task assignment.

3. Construct a matrix using the types of communication strategies and reporting periods of time for the two major axes. Complete the cells and analyze the matrix notations for efficiency and effectiveness.

4. Conduct a brain-storming session with personnel assigned coordination responsibilities to discover appropriate methods to use as evaluation designs for determining task completion.

KEY ELEMENTS OF SUCCESS

How do we know when we are successful? How do we know when we have achieved a fully functioning coordinating system? What are the criteria for success? The obvious answer will be found in the degree to which the institution meets the goals and objectives previously determined.

Factors other than coordination contribute to the successful conclusions of delegated tasks of instructional management. The factor of morale among employees is a key element in successful coordination. It may appear that there is only a distant relationship between successful coordination and employee morale but, on closer scrutiny, it becomes apparent that goal and objective attainment by the institution is the result of the contributions of all employees. All employees, regardless of the degree of individual responsibility, should have worked toward that success.

Successful coordination includes a sound communication system. Communication keeps everyone informed as to the progress the institution is making toward its goals and objectives. Administrators delegate many tasks to be accomplished and these tasks are often interrelated and interdependent among a number of people. It is imperative that people be kept informed of the status of other's progress through the administrator's effort to coordinate.

Communication is a skill that can be acquired through a thorough and indepth understanding of the communication process. The communicator must be aware of the following concepts of good communication skills.

1. Look ahead before you communicate. It is important that you plan what you want to say to the person with whom you are communicating. Is it to be verbal, written, or both? All media have their important aspects as well as their disadvantages. How will you state your message? Will it be direct or indirect, narrative or graphic, or a combination of others?

2. Clarity of your message may appear to be similar to the skill mentioned above, but this skill is the actual message. Regardless of the planning you have done, the message must reflect your planning. If you plan to be direct and use figures in your written communication, and your letter ended with pages of narrative interspaced with a few tables or figures, then the clarity of your message to the receiver may not be guaranteed. Make sure you say what you mean and mean what you say.

3. Each message must state its purpose. It is very important to state at the beginning that your message is for action, information, discussion, reaction, etc. When a receiver reads or listens to your message, the entire purpose may be lost if a number of pages have to be read or a fifteen minute speech listened to before the receiver knows what is expected as the result of the message. A receiver will direct the necessary train of thought if the purpose is stated at the beginning.

4. Include supportable and/or supplementary action in your message. Regardless of whether your message is for information, reaction, action, etc., it must contain some type of action on your part. The willingness to provide additional data, finances, time, personnel, or other resources makes your message practical and realistic to the receiver.

5. Appropriate timing of your message—the timing of the arrival of your message is extremely important to convey the true intent and meaning. A message requiring action, which arrives on the same day or even the day after a deadline is stated, indicates that either the sender is poorly organized or that the

sender does not have much confidence in the abilities of the receiver. The appropriate timing of the message varies with the purpose of the message and must be considered carefully in every instance.

6. Message overtones—messages may contain hidden agenda. The sender possibly does not convey the many overtones that can be associated in communicating with other people. In a verbal communication, the tone of voice, the length of the conversation, the questions asked or not asked, are all part of message overtones. In a written communication, the use of certain words, the formal or informal style, the length of the message, are but a few examples of overtones.

7. Approaches of communications—it might appear that the message overtones mentioned above and approaches of communications are the same, but the approach that is used can either be positive or negative. A positive approach usually brings the best results. The concept of encouragement tends to foster better relationships within the communication network; especially if the purpose of the communication is for action, discussion, or reaction. A negative approach may be necessary in some communications designed for specific reasons, such as, a reprimand, a legal answer, or a contrary decision. The approach used in communicating is an important aspect to the sender as well as to the receiver.

8. Communication feedback network—a design must exist that allows for two-way communications. One-way communication is not a skill, but merely a style or technique. The purpose of any communication is to convey thoughts and, depending on that purpose, communication feedback is generally necessary. The means and procedure of this feedback network must be carefully thought out in advance. Is the feedback to be verbal, written, or both? Is the type of feedback clear? Is the time element considered? These, and many other variables, must be designed into the feedback loop.

9. Understood and understanding—in summary, the necessity of communication skills rests on the statement, "Be sure you are understood as well as understand." The communication skills developed by the delegator are a vital element of success. The ability to coordinate is dependent on the degree of skill in conveying information to superordinates, other delegators, or to subordinates. One measure to determine successful coordination practices is the development of communication skills.

The nine skills listed above serve as the framework for judging the success of coordination. Another factor in successful coordination is the internal advancement opportunities for the institution's employees. Successful coordination depends on successful delegation, which depends on choosing the right person for the task assignment. The right person in the right responsibility at the appropriate time provides an excellent training ground for promotions to higher levels of responsibilities.

Examples of Strategy

1. Develop and implement a morale inventory among staff and interpret the results in conjunction with current coordination practices.
2. Develop an in-service program concerning the concepts of good communication skills. Evaluate the results using a pre-post-technique consisting of knowledge and demonstration.

OBSTACLES TO SUCCESS

An obstacle is a hindrance to a goal or objective achievement. It may be insurmountable or it may be removed in order to progress toward the successful accomplishment of the expected outcome. Failure to achieve the anticipated goal or objective generally results from obstacles that were not identified, analyzed, or described during the process of movement toward goal and achievement. There are certain areas of obstacles in any coordination process that can be identified, analyzed, and corrected. Although there may be specific situations that will result in specific obstacles, the basic areas are mentioned below.

The element of *time allocation* is one of the major resources available to administrators. The wise use of time becomes the greatest factor in successful goal achievement. The coordination process must allow for the maximum utilization of time. Building or district administrators who budget the time resource to allow for an effective coordination process will achieve previously determined goals or objectives. The well-established statements that time is money, time waits for no one, and time is precious, indicate the wisdom of maximum utilization of the time resource. Administrators must recognize the proper budgeting of time for coordination efforts, and also must impress on other people that coordination efforts require time allocations. Failure to do so may create a serious obstacle to success.

Another obstacle to effective and successful coordination is the inability of the coordinator to adjust to the different *behavioral characteristics* of the work participants. In any interaction between people, individual characteristics must be recognized and respected for what they are—individual characteristics. Administrators who do not consider the probability that other people have different characteristics from those of the administrators soon find that coordination efforts are unsuccessful. An administrator who attempts to involve four other people in a group effort to accomplish a specified task, and who routinely has debriefing meetings as part of the communication feedback design, must recognize and deal with the individual characteristics of the total group of five people. If several members of the group are sensitive to criticism and the administrator is a hard-nosed, insensitive individual, conflict will occur and progress toward the initial goal will be hindered if not totally stopped.

The institution, through its *organizational design*, may provide obstacles to successful coordination efforts. The expectations placed on an administrator by an unrealistic job description may not have the necessary relationship to other individuals involved in the specified goal achievement. The organizational design depicting an appropriate line and staff relationship is a built-in obstacle to effective coordination. Successful coordination practices demand realistic job expectations, as well as appropriate authority over those who are delegated task assignments, that have a direct impact on the coordinator's goal or objective. A midmanagement person with many responsibilities may never succeed if the organizational design does not permit a clear and accurate relationship among the personnel who are delegated tasks. The building principal who is held accountable for the development of special education programs, but is not involved in teacher selection, curriculum development, or student selection, is destined to fail because the organizational design did not permit involvement in these critical areas. Another illustration of organizational malpractice can be observed when a district administrator is held accountable for improvements in certain areas of the curriculum but is deprived of appropriate input for supporting budget determinations.

The coordinator must be cognizant of the numbers of people and tasks involved at any one time in the delegation process. There are practical limits to one person's span of attention. There are many situations, however, where substantial numbers of staff members can have their tasks coordinated, but it depends on the degree of complexity of task assignments. A span of attention and control can be quite large if tasks are simple to achieve. A district administrator may coordinate only a very limited number of people, if each of those persons is responsible for a wide range of tasks such as school finance, district operation and maintenance, personnel management, and district curriculum.

The attention and control should encompass personnel who have interrelating task assignments. This concept allows for more meaningful and purposeful coordination. To coordinate task completion among several staff members who must communicate between and among themselves provides for ease of management, better communication, and efficiency of goal attainment.

Examples of Strategy

1. *Develop a time allocation distribution by using the major areas of your position description. Maintain a daily log of actual practice for one month. Subject the results to your earlier decision of time allocation.*

2. *Review the organizational framework and areas of responsibilities in the descriptions of staff positions. Invite staff judgments as to whether they are realistic in terms of authority, facilities, resources, time, function, and span of attention.*

3. *In small group discussions of administrators, discuss additional obstacles to successful coordination that are specific to your district. Attempt to develop strategies that will eliminate the obstacles.*

PUTTING IT ALL TOGETHER

Coordination of instructional tasks has been discussed in the previous pages from the viewpoints of synchronization, reinforcement potentials, the principles of coordination, key elements of success, and obstacles to success. Each section has dealt with an understanding of the overall concept of coordination of instructional tasks.

The nature of coordination was defined as the harmonious effort of a number of participants working toward a common end. It is an orderly arrangement for group action and a solidarity of effort toward task accomplishment. The nature of coordination also inherently includes supervisory responsibilities. To coordinate explicitly indicates responsibility of delegated tasks. There cannot be successful delegation without coordination and there cannot be successful coordination without delegation. The two assigned functions are sympathetic to each other and are in similar cycles. Delegation and coordination are means to ends — not ends in themselves.

The need for coordination is obvious if institutions are to accomplish their goals and objectives. The organizational framework is designed for the institution primarily and predominantly for institutional goal attainment. To reiterate, delegation can exist if goal attainment is unnecessary, but coordination of delegation must exist if goal attainment is necessary.

The five basic principles of coordination must be understood and accepted if coordination strategies are to be successful. These five principles constitute the entire process of coordination. The understanding and acceptance of the institutional goals is the starting benchmark of the coordination phase. This information must be mutually acceptable to all personnel within the organized effort. Once the understanding and acceptance of goals is accomplished, the clarity of tasks must be agreed on between the delegator and delegatee. The means to the end cannot be subject to misinterpretation by either party. A consensus of agreement must be achieved prior to the initiation of the means. In following through with the clarity of task assignments, the need to understand individual differences among and between the delegatees must be clear in the mind of the coordinator. Each task assignment will be operationally different because of the individual differences among and between people. Good coordination also allows for constant feedback between the delegator and delegatee. Two-way communication must exist if positive monitoring is to take place. This communication network must be open and free for proper interfacing between individuals. The final principle of coordination is to evaluate the attainment of the goal or objective. How do you know you have arrived where you wanted to go? This end result is crucial to coordination. Successful coordination is realized when the original task assignment is accomplished and the fact can be documented.

The benchmarks for success are easy to determine but may be difficult to measure for achievement. Goals and objectives should be easily measured for attainment. Hard data, such as reading scores, job placement services, mathematical scores, and other cognitive achievements, are but a few areas that can be measured to determine success. The factor of morale is more difficult to measure for successful coordination. Fostering creativity in task assignments may develop competition among individuals which is healthy within the constraints of employee morale. The opposite will destroy the organization and goals will never be achieved. The many factors of communications are vital to effective coordination. The value of communication cannot be underestimated in the coordination process. It is a mandatory skill of effective coordinators.

Another measure of successful coordination is the development of potential coordinators within the institution. Advancement in the institution proves that effective coordination is taking place, allowing potential coordinators to learn the skills necessary for goal attainment. A poor internal advancement statistic is indicative of a number of variables, one of which is ineffective coordination of task assignments.

The final segment of coordination skills is a thorough knowledge of the obstacles that hinder successful coordination efforts. Proper utilization of the time resource is necessary. Time is valuable and can be controlled just like other resources available to the individual. The coordinator must control the time element; time must not control the coordinator. The understanding of behavioral characteristics is a necessity for effective coordination. Assuming that all individuals can be grouped as though one person, leads to disastrous results. Each person is an individual and must be dealt with as an individual. To assume any other position is ludicrous and results in an exercise of futility in goal attainment. Organizational demands can be a hindrance to institutional goal attainment. The organization is only a facilitator. Conversely, the organizational framework can be a total hindrance to task accomplishment. Careful analysis of organizational structure will determine its effectiveness. Meaningful and effective coordination depends on the span of attention of the coordinator. This span of attention is of crucial importance and logical when the primary purpose of coordination is goal accomplishment. The larger the attention demands, the more difficult the other management variables become.

In summary, *the coordinator is a planner.* The proper planning of any coordination effort must be done with precision. This type of advance work illustrates the importance attached to the coordination skills needed by administrators to meet the goals and objectives of the school. To plan is to organize strategies and means, from the initial effort to the end product. Regardless of sophisticated techniques, such as PPBS, PERT, MBO, an effective planner is an effective coordinator.

The coordinator is an organizer. The organizational skills are the actual developments of the plan. Organizational skills are observed through sound and logical procedures that accomplish the end product. Logical and sequential methods of accomplishment, from the planning stage through the evaluation stages to the goal accomplishment, is the artistry of a good organizer.

The coordinator is a decision maker. The ability to make sound and prompt decisions is a mark of an effective and efficient coordinator. Throughout the process of coordination, certain decisions must be made if progress toward goal attainment is to be maintained. Decisions in goal acknowledgement, task clarity, types of means and procedures, systems of communication network, and designs of evaluation procedures are all benchmarks. Any of these checkpoints that fail to produce a decision will hinder the mechanism designed to produce an end product. Decision making is a skill of absolute necessity for coordinators.

The coordinator is a communicator. The stress on communication skills has been explicitly indicated throughout this chapter. Communications take many media, and all media must be understood and utilized in effective coordination. The many and intricate steps in communication skills are all viable and important to the entire process of relaying information between people.

The coordinator is an administrator. To administer is to manage. The coordinator manages the coordination events that take place in a well-planned, implemented, and evaluated pattern designed to meet the goals and objectives of the institution, as determined by the community within the larger framework of society. The administrative skills necessary for successful coordination encompass the many other skills that are subsets of the overall definition of administration. These skills are put to the test when an administrator implements direction through indirection, as discussed in chapter 14.

This chapter has emphasized the conditions and unique expertise involved in the coordination of the efforts of a wide variety of persons. Before behaviorial energies are released, pause and consider the staging prerequisites of that action. Chapter 11 provides an exploration of these staging conditions and expectations.

COORDINATE READINGS

AASA. (Stephen J. Knezevich). *Management by Objectives and Results,* American Association of School Administrators, Arlington, Virginia, 1973.

Levinson, Harry. *The Great Jackass Fallacy,* Harvard University: Division of Research — Graduate School of Business Administration, 1973.

Meares, Ainslie. *How To Be A Boss,* New York: Coward, McCann and Geoghegan, Inc., 1970.

Vance, Charles C. *Manager Today, Executive Tomorrow,* New York: McGraw-Hill Book Company, Inc., 1974.

The Antecedents to Action

A rather caustic observer once described an acquaintance as "A person who puts the mouth in gear before the mind is revved up." Even though caustic in inference, perhaps this statement is worth some thought for persons who approach action that will affect them or the institution they serve. Thoughts of this type caused these authors to pause in the discussion of those actions that seem essential to the management of instruction. This pause is symbolic of what always should be done before launching into an action program. Thought should be given to the conditions that affect action. These are the antecedents to action, some of which are presented in this chapter.

Declarations and actions must have purpose, and purpose results from careful thought rather than abrupt beginnings. Purpose, as indicated in an earlier chapter, is a product of the intellect. It is the result of studying what is wanted in relationship to the capacity to achieve what is wanted. The study of purpose is the "revving up" of the mind and should precede any action designed to achieve that purpose.

The action designed to achieve a purpose is process. Process, also a product of the intellect, is the planning of ways to pursue the accomplishment of the purpose. Perhaps it can be summarized as a case for deliberativeness. Those who identify a target and institute immediate action probably will not spend enough time selecting among the alternative behaviors best designed to achieve the purpose. Deliberativeness is not an avoidance of action or of work. It indicates one of the antecedents to action, that of giving thought to what is wanted and to the ways of achieving it.

Action is for accomplishment. It is for the accomplishment of the purposes chosen by individuals or by the organization to which they belong and for which they direct their efforts.

PACING CHOICES

The seeming abruptness of action indicated above is not necessarily the way to determine whether that action promises to be effective in terms of accomplishing the chosen purposes. There are many misapplications of the concept of efficiency. Efficiency often is viewed as the evidence of energy that moves. Unless the energies move in the direction of the purpose, however, efficiency cannot be achieved. Efficiency is the best application of the facilities possessed by individuals and supported in the organizational purposes.

The misapplication of efficiency places a higher appraisal on momentum than deserved. There are at least two faces to momentum. Certainly it is fine to have the feeling to move vigorously in the direction of chosen purposes. On the other hand, momentum can be worshipped to the point that it by-passes the need for the occasional pause that provides an opportunity to assess whether the action has been appropriate and whether it really is leading in the direction of the chosen purposes. When there is assurance that momentum is moving in the right direction, there is an advantage in not losing that momentum since it might mean having to start all over again.

Pacing is a concept of the use of momentum and it becomes an important consideration in preparing for a specific action. A part of the *pacing choices* that can be made are evidenced in a schedule of action or checkpoints in accomplishment. A time to start, a time to pause, and a time to arrive are all part of the schedule. There is discipline in this kind of schedule, particularly if the support facilities and the coordinated efforts of all participants have been carefully planned. This constitutes a total coordination that promises great efficiency and effectiveness. There are some determiners of pace, such as: (1) deadlines, (2) availability of resources, (3) client preferences, and (4) quality of product. Many more determiners might be identified and listed, but these four are easily used and normally effective in helping to pace the activities and resources designed to help achieve a specified purpose. Some may assume that pace should be steady. There are many who would attest to the fact that, once movement is started, a steady pace should be maintained until arriving at the desired location or achievement. This is not always realistic. There are times when a rapid pace is beneficial and gives assurance to all people involved that progress is being made. On the other hand, there are times when plans take participants through those trouble spots in which one mistake might destroy the entire enterprise. In this instance, the pace should be slowed so that deliberativeness can be achieved. Thus, pace variability becomes a pacing choice that is important in the preludes or antecedents to action.

The variability indicated above raises the issue as to whether there needs to be a comparison between the continuous and the inter-mittent attack of action. The philosophy holds that, as long as a pattern provides for the deliberativeness of evaluating the action at a specific point, the choice of continuous or intermittent attack becomes a rational decision. Variability can be seen as a modification of or variation in the continuous or intermittent attack. Pacing is worth much attention in planning the stages of action that are designed by the individuals in an organization.

Examples of Strategy

1. *Distribute to participants a list of periodic achievements that might be called a schedule of activity in the pursuit of a specified purpose. Use some insignia, such as a warning flag, to indicate at various points whether it is time to stop and look at what has been accomplished and whether the plans for the action are adequate to the hopes developed at the time of planning the action.*

2. *Distribute a brief questionnaire to all participants inviting their judgments as to whether the checkpoints have been achieved satisfactorily and, if not, to indicate the nature of the deficiencies observed at that particular time.*

3. *Create a matrix with stages of mission achievement listed on the horizontal axis and time frames on the vertical axis. Monitor, with suggestions from the administrative team, the arrival at various stages and develop adjusted pacing patterns at predetermined points.*

4. *List known factors affecting momentum. Determine, with the help of others, how these factors might be put to constructive use in setting the pace.*

SUMMIT IMAGERY

Images that the so-called persons at the top have of themselves and of those with whom they must relate are referred to as *summit imagery*. The images that exist in the minds of these persons tend to affect their ways of behaving, which in turn has a profound influence on the organization members and their productivity. Some aspects of this antecedent to action are discussed in this section.

Persons who occupy roles of administrative leadership in an organization may develop a sense of isolation. This isolation results perhaps from the individual's uncertainty as to whether the leadership design is adequate and whether the proper kind of influence is being realized by others in the organization. This sense of isolation also may result from the involvement of increasing numbers of people and inadequate time to maintain a satisfactory contact.

The communication system between the administrative leaders and those in the organization responsible for action is a critical factor in attitude status. This communication system is often the non-face-to-face type, making it difficult for those initiating the communication to determine whether understanding and acceptance have been achieved. This nonpersonalized communication may bring about the sense of isolation on the part of administrative leaders.

As the sense of isolation increases, it may acquire the appearances and effect of a psychosis. It is difficult to prescribe any therapy for those who have permitted themselves to slip into such a state, which really describes the lack of contact with others in the organizational effort. Self-developed therapy often approaches the nature of an idealized response image. In other words, as administrative leaders issue the communication, by whatever means, there is a tendency to maintain a sense of worth and happiness by assuming that everyone who receives it will respond in precisely the way the communicator envisioned. Variability among people makes this most unlikely but, nonetheless, the leader may still be inclined to this type of idealized response.

A more personalized communication system, such as, a small group conference, a one-to-one conversation, or even a large group face-to-face exchange, provides an opportunity to benefit from challenge. In other words, if some people do not understand, or if they differ in concept from what is stated, there is an opportunity for the differences to be presented to the administrative leader. In this way, the leader will get some sense of the extent to which the idealized response is characteristic of the group interaction. When there is little or no opportunity for challenge between the administrative leader and the members of the organization, members often ascribe inflexibility to that administrative leader. This type of mental reaction on the part of the members of the organization resembles the idealized response reaction of the administrator. In either case, the administrator's idealized response image or the participants' ascribed inflexibility to the administrator stimulates *directional blamability*. People seldom blame themselves for any of the inadequacies in the operation. It is much easier to blame either the administrative leader or vice versa; both are unsatisfactory to the organizational purposes.

Each person, regardless of status, role, and function within an organization, probably has a built-in capability to see oneself in a most complex type of operational state. At the same time, each person may assume that others are enjoying the simplest of responsibilities and actions. This does not happen from the top down or from the bottom up, but from the standpoint of how people assess their own problems in comparison to the problems of others in the organization.

There is need for interaction therapy to increase the personalization of communication and to increase the opportunities for face-to-face challenge as a means of avoiding some problems that derive from the phenomenon of summit imagery.

Examples of Strategy

1. *Issue a bulletin detailing some major plan that will involve many members of the staff and at the same time give a two or three point response form that would provide some test of whether those who receive the communication view it as feasible, desirable, and supportable.*

2. *Enlist from staff members, who have revealed informal grievances, the names of other members who might meet on an ad hoc basis to discuss concerns, review the action or situation that might bear on the issue, and arrive at some reasonable understanding and resolution.*

3. *Draft an agenda for meetings where teachers may discuss and react to plans for program changes. Create ad hoc review committees among those attending to itemize positive recommendations to help achieve the desired program outcomes.*

TARGET SCRUTINY

Another antecedent to action is *target scrutiny*. Every action must have a need and a purpose or it cannot be justified for inclusion in the organizational efforts or considered a proper target for the joint efforts of organization members. Frequent references have been made in the preceding chapters to the use of purpose and goals, and the identification of strategies to achieve them.

A complete plan may be designed, but stop at the point of beginning action to make sure that there is a differentiation between assumptions and knowledge about the purpose or target. It is easy to build a set of assumptions that can substitute for specific knowledge regarding the direction to be pursued. Chapter 7 presented, in Matrices 1 through 6, three management action targets with a number of related elements. The intent was to make certain that a differentiation was made between assumptions and knowledge. As action approaches, a review of these differentiations should be initiated.

A final test should be made of whether there has been an accurate definition or description of the selected target. This necessitates looking at the specific process as planned in order to make sure that the proper design has been chosen with the target or purpose in mind. A last minute check also should be made as to whether the purpose or target has an accessibility to attack. If it is too far away, too involved, or if it lacks time and support facilities, one must decide whether the target is accessible and whether something can be done about it. It is better to select realistic targets that are achievable than to dissipate valuable energy on goals destined to fail or likely not to be met.

A determination should be made of the extent of acceptance of the target by all who are to be involved in the action. At the same time, there should be a determination of the priority level that the particular target has as compared to other on-going responsibilities of the organization. This is the commitment that must be determined both by the administrative leaders and those who participate in carrying out the action.

Examples of Strategy

1. *Develop a standardized target checklist to serve as a guide for anyone in the school system who is about to begin work on a new task.*

2. *Ask potential participants in an action to indicate why they would be willing to devote time and effort to it.*

3. *Have the professional staff list items in order of importance to the educational welfare of students and list the obstructions in the path of success and the probability of achieving the targets. List by a numerical weighting, as devised locally, depending on the number of targeted issues.*

INVENTORY OF ASSETS

The emphasis on the need for a target or purpose is of first importance in initiating action that will accomplish individual or organizational goals. Prior to initiating the specific action, make a complete *inventory of assets*. It is necessary to know whether the powers, the materials, and the people are available in the right amounts to support the action envisioned in accomplishing the purpose.

One of the first assets to be checked is the attitude of the people involved toward the target for action. If the attitude is favorable and strong, creativity and energy will be focused on the tasks at hand. Without this creativity that is so latently controlled by attitude, there is little doubt that, regardless of the strength of the plan or the quality of the leadership, the outcomes will be inferior.

One of the determiners of attitude could be the legal authenticity of the target effort. Legal authenticity does not mean only that the proposed action conforms to the laws of the land and the decisions of the court. It also means that it has the support of those official and unofficial people in the community who would influence the effort. People must want the outcomes if they are going to support the processes that guarantee those outcomes.

Few targets or purposes can be achieved without a wide range of specialized knowledge and skills on the part of many people involved in the action. Unless the specialized skills and knowledge, as detailed in chapters 4 and 5 are available, there is little hope that the outcome can be as good as anticipated at the time the target was selected and the processes designed. This calls for a careful assessment of the unique contributions that each person in the organization can make to the effort. Too often, however, this assessment has been invalidated because not enough time and thought were given to the time availability of all those involved. If the action process constitutes an increasing overload on some of those involved in the action, the quality and scheduling of results are in jeopardy. The amount of time, while it is impossible to judge it with great precision, needs to be given some thought not only by the administrative leader designing the action and process, but by all of those who will become involved through the application of their specialized knowledge and skills.

Financial practicality is a main concern in many of the actions designed by school organizations. There are so many checkpoints and control facilities placed on the use of financial resources that it is almost impossible to make just one decision at the local level and proceed as though practicality had been achieved. Careful thought must be given to the extent of financial support available to carry on the activity; and, where space is required, make sure that that space is available.

The inventory of assets also must include the various environmental states. The conflict between special interest groups in a community could be anticipated at the outset and some arrangements made to assure that such conflict would not result in a major effort to thwart the entire process of action in seeking a declared target. The final item in this inventory is adequacy of control. This is related to the environmental state, but usually is applied primarily to those who work within the organization. Coordination takes direct effort. The involvement of many people requires coordination. Sufficient controls must be available, not only to enforce coordination but to encourage it through the provision of conditions that make coordination desirable and effective.

Examples of Strategy

1. Share with all task participants a list of assets required for a successful action as you perceive it. Invite reactions and suggestions.

2. Utilize a local needs assessment report to stimulate the identification of community assets available to achieve high priorities, needs, and goals.

3. Poll community members to determine volunteer or human assets available to assist in custom resolutions of issues or in fulfilling school missions.

REVIEW OF LIABILITIES

The inventory of assets presented one side of the coin, but the *review of liabilities* presents the other. The very first liability that can create great concern on the part of those involved in an action is the limitation of assets. This can be envisioned by reviewing the previous section and raising the question as to what would happen if one or more of these assets were absent or ineffective. The liabilities inferred in the environmental state in the previous section raises the problem of special interest biases that may exist in the community. All special interests do not have to be consigned to oblivion, but some limits must be envisioned on the extent to which special interests can influence the on-going process of the organization.

Possible liabilities may be found in errors of judgment. It was suggested earlier that there should be frequent stops in the process to provide opportunities to review what is happening and whether it is still on target. It may be that unexpected problems will emerge in the process. These can be due to errors of judgment—not just by the leadership but by all those who are participating in the activities.

No one has been able to design a process of action leading to any sort of target in which no unanticipated variables appear. For instance, it is impossible for a local school system to determine when some dramatic or critical situation might develop elsewhere in the country or in the world. At the time of the first Sputnik, many people in the country thought that the schools should have anticipated what the Russians were doing in order to keep our school systems geared to support that kind of progress in space. There is no way a school organization could have anticipated what the Central Intelligence Agency had not discovered.

The school organization cannot anticipate variations in the economic status of the country. Many officials, with vast resources of research, seem to have difficulty in agreeing on what can be anticipated in an ensuing decade or other period of time.

Another of the liabilities that should be assessed is called *shifting criteria*. It is possible that a project could be authorized by all of the officials involved in a community and in a school organization yet, when some aspect of the situation changes in the process, the same people might suddenly decide to base their judgment on criteria other than those used originally. Control of shifting criteria is practically impossible. The suggestion here is that, if there is a record of shifting criteria on the part of many people associated in the organization, this should be viewed as a liability.

Intercepting priorities can occur at any time in the process of pursuing the achievement of a target. Just as there are unanticipated variables, likewise there are changes due to steady or shifting criteria that make the priority choice quite different.

Another liability is that when something new is introduced, something else may be displaced. It is important to know how these displacements will affect the program and the people in the organization.

Examples of Strategy

1. *Invite suggestions as to the "worst things that can happen" as a new program of action is determined. Use this list as a basis for interpreting reality.*

2. *Seek the names of people who might form a temporary neutral impact team to review and suggest ways of dealing with liabilities that conceivably could emerge.*

3. *Invite suggestions of controllable and uncontrollable liability variables that could impact on the completion of the goal or success of the mission. List the identifiable liabilities that could be controlled or dealt with to improve the odds of reaching optimum success.*

PLANNING AN ACTION BALANCE

An earlier section of this chapter dealt with pacing choices. The concern was to review some of the different speeds by which processes would be directed toward the target or goal. The concern here is with the variety of actions available to those participating in the action. Pacing, as related to the variety of actions, means that variations can occur at the speed with which the chosen actions are carried forward.

Consideration now is directed to the different kinds of actions that are involved in the processes by which people proceed toward their goals. It is not so much a matter of pacing only, but also the choice of those actions that can be categorized in the processes indicated in chapter 7, namely, Managing, Influencing, Evaluating, and Planning. Each of these processes can be accomplished in a number of different ways. Managing, for instance, might be accomplished by a directive from the responsible leader, or it might be a matter of all participants agreeing on certain coordinating requirements that would make the organized effort a success. There are varieties of action that might proceed quietly or bombastically. There are other varieties that are related to communication patterns and media. There is an infinite number of ways an individual can display unique characteristics in going about the tasks at hand. It is extremely important that, with this vast array of action types or patterns, the differing kinds be kept in balance.

Balance indicates that no one type shall become the standard pattern for any person or persons involved in the action. Reference continuously is made to people and their ways of doing. There must be people involvement in any action. Thus, the problem of balance is one of variety of action as well as variety of persons involved in the operation. People often become highly enthusiastic about a particular task and a particular way of doing it, to the neglect of all other tasks and ways of accomplishing them. There are areas of potential neglect in the use of the variety of actions that are available. A potential neglect grows primarily out of the failure of involved individuals to review occasionally the varieties of action and to make new determinations as to which one is appropriate to the immediate tasks. In order to accomplish this kind of balance, there must be continuing assessment, not only of the kind of action used but also of the progress being made toward the selected purpose or goal.

Continuing assessment means that evaluation is not just one process of action. Rather, it is the procedure of intermingling with all the other processes used in the categories of action. As the processes are scrutinized on the way to achieving goals, it is necessary to make frequent adjustments in the amount of Managing, Influencing, Evaluating, and Planning that would be most appropriate at any one point. Adjustments can be made when it is observed that one process is being used, perhaps to the exclusion of others, when a better balance might get better results.

One of the serious problems involved in the overuse of any one type of action or process is the possibility of monotony. People need a change of pace from time to time in order to maintain the enthusiasm and the satisfaction that must go with creative and aggressive task accomplishment. Monotony can be a cause of fatigue, perhaps more so than the strong activity that might be applied to any of the processes of action.

Planning a balance in the actions or action types assures that the whole operation will move forward with precision. It also gains some insurance against the possibility that boredom, fatigue, and discouragement will set in and cause a lag in the progress toward the goals. A *well-planned action balance* can avoid pitfalls such as monotony and fatigue and give greater assurance that those involved in the activity will find excitement and satisfaction. Excitement and satisfaction, well-directed, can maximize the creative potential of all persons involved in an action.

Examples of Strategy

1. *Establish a communication procedure by which changing levels of boredom and fatigue can be reported without any inference of sanctions.*

2. Create a social setting (perhaps a breakfast or tea) for monitoring informally the level of personal fatigue and enthusiasm prevailing. Overtly support the quest for balance and the different action types or patterns as a goal is pursued. This may prevent the staff from concluding that the administrators have their "feet planted firmly in the air."

COUNTDOWN TO LAUNCH TIME

The primary concern of this chapter is to review the antecedents to action. Many of the kinds of precautions that wisely could be taken have been enumerated and discussed in previous sections. The concern here is to make sure that, as the time to start the plan of organized action grows near, some final precautions are observed.

A most important item in the countdown to launch time is a review of the plan's completeness. Such concern relates to whether the target or goal is clear, and whether it is clearly understood by all involved. Concern is appropriate as to whether the many variables that might influence the progress toward the goal have been reviewed, evaluated, and controlled. Obviously, there always may be some unexpected or emerging variables, but a part of the countdown is to exert every effort to make sure that the plan is complete in every aspect.

When a plan has been completed and people have become involved, there should be a final check on whether the schedules of all those involved have been cleared. It is unreasonable to assume that, just because the administrative leader is ready at a particular time to initiate action, all other people have their schedules cleared for that same purpose. Consequently, it is important that each involved person be given the opportunity to check the schedule and the future time involvements so that there will be no impediments due to overloads or conflicting loads in the action process.

A final check on the support facilities is always appropriate. Many types of action have fallen short of their anticipated outcome simply because a place to meet was not provided, the kinds of facilities needed for the action were not assured, and other types of support facilities were not available. A check-out of all items is always important before the final launch time.

An important final check is a test of communication adequacy. Are all people able to communicate with each other easily and effectively? One-way communication is not enough; a two-way communication must exist, with two-way understanding a result of the process. At this point, announcement of the anticipations with respect to progress reports would be helpful. A schedule of periodic reports would be very appropriate as one of the countdown concerns. When these types of things are assured and "all systems are go," then perhaps progress can be initiated with a greater promise of potential effectiveness.

Examples of Strategy

1. *Distribute a list of readiness factors and ask each staff member to report personal readiness to start the action program.*
2. *Arrange an informal "launch meeting" with participants to review final precautions, such as, communication system adequacy, support facility capacity, and personal schedule reasonableness.*

KNOWING WHEN YOU ARE THERE

Possibilities always exist for people to become tied to a program of action and thus be guided by that program more than by the realization of the target or goal selected. A time schedule often does not work as anticipated, sometimes moving toward the goal more slowly and sometimes more rapidly than anticipated. Overconcern with the details of the plan can become a burden; if the goal is achieved prior to the completion of every element in the action plan, it is easy to overlook this fact.

An important element in the continuing evaluation referred to in a previous section is that it continuously relates the plan to the result. When that result is the target or goal, the plan has been completed regardless of any items left in the schedule. Conversely important is the fact that all items in the plan may have been completed and the goal still not achieved. In this case, certain adjustments to the plan need to be made.

Intermediate evaluations keep all involved aware of the status of the plan with respect to the goal. This type of intermediate and continuing evaluation is essential to the orderly procedure of any process or action. When it becomes necessary to reduce the time anticipated in the schedule, reduce it. When it appears that the time schedule must be expanded in order to continue the processes toward the goal, expand it. These are the types of on-going observations, concerns, and adjustments that alert all persons to the relationship between the process and the product.

The judgment as to the extent to which the action plan is achieving its goal should be a judgment of all participants in the action. Each one has a different view of the relationship of the procedures or processes to the goal, and these views should be pooled, coordinated, and used as a basis for making judgments. The outcome, when realized, should be somewhat or greatly related to the vision of it that existed in the minds of the participants at the time the action plan was made and initiated. It is not considered an element of poor planning or bad handling of the processes if there have to be adjustments as inadequacies appear in the progress toward the goal.

Having achieved the goal and having been freed from the commitment to a schedule, it is important to avoid overkill in the pursuit of the product. Achievement is dignified and should not be the cause of any exuberant action that would lead people to continue the processes. When the processes have been successful and effective in achieving the goal, the temptation to continue them as a means of emotional satisfaction must be thwarted until a new goal provides reason for continuance.

Examples of Strategy

1. *Invite reactions to the scheduled progress reports in terms of state of progress toward goal.*

2. *Establish a meeting or series of meetings to monitor goal achievement. One such session could relate to participant's previously identified visions at the time the action plan was developed and initiated. Although the particular processes employed are not to be the essence of the endeavor, this procedure might reinforce through personal testimony the usefulness of systematic planning. This activity also might avoid participant oversight of the need for developmental planning to achieve optimum ends. It is to assure all that haphazard and accidental goal achievement is not the manner in which the district operates.*

THE MODEL REVISITED

The Purpose-Effort Strategy Model was presented in chapter 3. In the discussion of the Model, reference was made to the antecedents to action that would be presented in chapter 11. Some of these antecedents have been discussed already. It is appropriate, at this point, to review the Model in order to continue its relevance to the patterns of action presented and suggested throughout this book.

The assessment of instructional impacts were shown in the Model as being channeled through three sources of purpose, namely, the people and forces in the environment, the school as an institution, and the people in the school organization. The section titles in this chapter identify the kinds of statuses and relationships that condition the potentialities of action. The review, evaluation, and judgments involved in a study of antecedents to action lead directly into Process Planning, area 4 in the Model. The antecedents to action thus become the foundation for the selection of management strategies.

The Model will be reviewed in subsequent chapters until the Purpose-Effort Synthesis (area 9 of the Model) has been realized.

AND NOW TO CHAPTER 12

This chapter on antecedents to action has dealt with many of the planning and directing processes required in establishing a goal and developing the procedures to achieve it. Frequent reference was made to the need for continuing assessment or evaluation. This facet of the administrative process will be dealt with much more specifically in chapter 12, "Auditing as Continuous Evaluation," which will focus on the effectiveness of people involved in the action rather than on the evaluation the action plan itself. This will lead, eventually, through auditing and accountability, to chapter 15, which deals with directed self-management as a way of responding to those items that are revealed in the auditing and evaluating process.

READING ACTION

Boles, Harold W., and James A. Davenport. *Introduction to Educational Leadership.* New York: Harper and Row Publishers, 1975.

Dailey, Charles A. *Assessment of Lives.* San Francisco: Jossey-Bass, 1971.

Joseph, Ellis A. *The Predecisional Process in Educational Administration.* Homewood, Illinois: ETC Publications, 1975.

Sergiovanni, Thomas J., and David L. Elliott. *Educational and Organizational Leadership in Elementary Schools.* Englewood Cliffs, New Jersey: Prentice-Hall, 1975.

Wilson, John A. *Banneker: A Case Study of Educational Change.* Homewood, Illinois: ETC Publications, 1973.

Auditing as
Continuous Evaluation

The emphasis in chapter 11 was directed to the concerns for setting the stage for action so that continuity of progress might ensue. Checkpoints were suggested as a means for determining whether conditions for action were really supportive. This concept of periodic checking is expanded in this chapter as a continuous auditing process, conceived of as continuous evaluation.

Action balance and pacing assumes a continuity of action. This continuity of action does not assume that the concepts of balance and pacing change; rather, it is a concept of keeping the target in sight and of reassessing the action at many points in order to make sure that it is leading to the selected goal. The continuity of auditing must follow the action balance and pacing of actions. Continuity, however, indicates continuing attention to the responsibilities for making judgments about how far and how well the work has progressed at any point in time. This is the concept of auditing as continuous evaluation.

Auditing of any type calls for a high level of personal integrity on the part of the person auditing and on the part of the person being audited. Integrity in this instance, as in any other aspect of living, has its own price. The price of integrity in auditing is that of being able or compelled to strike down the biases that have existed in the minds of people for long periods of time. It means an openness of view and of thinking that leaves no time for biases. Biases are comfortable, as a rule, because they may have tempered the approach to life's responsibilities over a long period of time. Surrendering these biases can create a sense of insecurity since something new must be found on which to base judgments and actions. Another price of integrity is that of giving up the tendency to a life of simplicity; life is less complex if a decision is approached directly. Perhaps more difficult will be giving up the serious concern for devotees of simplicity who have a one-act remedy for almost anything that occurs. Life and certainly education are much more complex than that and the luxury of one-style correction or one-fact conclusion is wholly inadequate and cannot be honored.

A certain discipline comes in the price of integrity and that is the necessity for delayed judgments. The purpose in delaying a judgment is not to avoid making the judgment, but rather to have time to make the determination whether adequate information is available and appraised so that the judgment can be based on legitimate reasons and evidence. The price of integrity, with respect to delayed judgments and the reason for that delay, is a time demand on the person engaged in the audit. Facts must be had and they must be validated, but facts take time to get.

Those who want to hasten the conclusion of an audit and an audit-based judgment will find no luxury in the price of integrity. Time must be available and time must be spent. This chapter, "Auditing as Continuous Evaluation," is related to the Model presented in chapter 3. It is in the culminating cell of the Model, number 9, Purpose-Efforts Synthesis.

The audit with respect to purpose and effort is a test of reality. Was everything used that was required to accomplish the goal or task set? Did the people involved find ways of applying their own expertise to the particular task or challenge? In essence, a question that needs to be raised at all times is, "Did we get there?" In the educational world, this is one of the final and most difficult questions to resolve. Auditing, conceived as continuing evaluation, can serve that purpose.

NONALLERGENIC CONCEPTS

Many people who encounter an audit for the first time, in life or in professional activities, react about the same, whether one is asking for the audit or is being audited. Apparently, our culture has instilled the idea that an audit is an accusation or suspicion of fraud and dishonesty.

The financial audit often required in various aspects of the educational operation may offend many of the people who are to be audited. The same thing seems to occur with respect to audits related to aspects of the educational operation that are not financial. There is an inference in the word itself that seems built into our society and it must be changed. Persons asking for an audit are not necessarily seeking an opportunity to discipline. Those who seek the audit may have a noble purpose in mind, namely, to gain evidence that supports those engaged in the various tasks of the educational enterprise. A positive inference needs to displace the one based on suspicion of the quality and honesty of people's work.

Cultural suspicion in this case may be primarily the biases developed from personal experiences. One such bias is that an audit results in disciplinary action. Many people have had it happen to them, or know of people who have had it happen to them. It seems difficult for people to adjust their thinking habits about a reward and penalty system by perceiving it operating in many different ways. The audit becomes only one of the many aspects of that kind of system. There needs to be movement away from the sanction aspect of an audit and toward the recognition that an audit can achieve positive things. Support for additional opportunities to perform at a high level of expertise, thus improving the educational system, illustrates this point.

Rational definitions are needed for such words as *audit, evaluation,* and *report.* An audit, in this positive sense, is the process by which appropriate information is gathered, organized, and interpreted in order to determine how well the purposes of the agency are being achieved. Evaluate, in its positive sense, means to view evidence and information as the only rational bases for making decisions as to whether the present action is sufficient or whether changes need to be made. A report, in a positive sense, provides the appropriate people with the information and the proper interpretation of the soundest data that can be amassed.

An audit, in its most simplistic state, is a gathering of information about the operational aspects of an organization. It becomes more serviceable as the information is viewed in terms of its worth in the achievement of goals and purposes. This judgment of the information in terms of goal-related criteria constitutes evaluation. Thus, evaluation makes the audit more functional; reporting makes it an act of accountability.

The concepts of auditing, evaluating, and reporting must be viewed as a challenge to working adaptations. These adaptations seek to apply the format and principles of auditing, evaluating, and reporting to the task at hand that, presumably, has been identified and described. A part of the adaptation of any of these concepts requires continuous definition and interpretation. There must be a relationship between purpose and action. Some kind of evidence has to be viewed to make certain that the purpose is defined and that the action is appropriate.

The concepts of working adaptations of the audit and its associated activities perhaps can be realized through the development of alternative formats for the audit itself. There are different ways of identifying, collecting, and organizing data. No one format can be adapted to all of the activities characteristic of the school's operation. Alternative formats are referenced particularly to the audit pattern and not to the outcome of the audit. The outcome of the audit might stimulate the development of alternative plans of action and, in this way, the flexibility of arriving at a decision might increase the probability that appropriate evidence had been used in making the determinations.

A tempting action, when audit and evaluative data have been secured, is to begin predicting as though the audit and evaluation were made for that purpose. Making predictions, without developing alternative formats and plans, might mean that the audit data simply were used to reinforce a predetermined decision. Thus, the temptation to predict might look like an expeditious way to resolve a problem or to use the audit data.

The tendency to postpone prediction in order to review alternative plans for action is a wonderful way to accommodate the diversity that is found in the educational program. The diversity referred to here applies not only to the characteristics and abilities of people, but to the demands placed on the school by the variability of the students who seek to gain from the educational service.

Some of these concepts might lead to a worthwhile intermediate step, that is, raising the question of when *evidence is evidence*. This calls for a continuing desire to validate the information gained through the audit and evaluative processes. The validation of evidence, in itself, may help in the selection of alternative plans of action, the delay of predictions, and the arrival at a new plan of action on the most rational basis. Rationality is based on sound evidence and its careful review. In this way, judgment is reinforced and the probability of appropriate action is increased.

Examples of Strategy

1. *Offer staff members about six variations in the definitions of audit. Ask them to identify a preference or to give their own favorite definition.*

2. *Review previous audits and determine positive and negative aspects associated with them.*

3. *Involve staff in identifying support facilities, manpower, and environmental influences that could and should be included in the audit of instructional programs.*

EBB AND FLOW OF SENSITIVITIES

People react to each other in many different ways. This is one of the simplest types of conclusions that can be drawn about the interaction of people. Yet, it is recognized that the degree of sensitiveness that one person has for another varies greatly among people and with respect to environmental statuses at a particular time. Some of the built-in controls of the sensitivities that people have toward others, as those others seek to interact with them, will be discussed here. These are personalized concepts and inferences that people have about themselves and about others.

Certification is one of the requirements for those engaged in the educational service. Certification usually is determined specifically for the major type of service to be rendered. The person who has been certified often assumes that all requirements for practicing the profession have been met and that further review should not be necessary. No profession today enjoys that guarantee of freedom of action once the legal permission to practice has been granted. Every profession is constrained by legal requirements and public opinion. Sensitivities between the auditor and the audited may be tempered by the perception each has of the privileges guaranteed or presumably guaranteed in certification. The same view may be taken of the employment contract. When the contract has been consummated by the employer and the employee, a review under that contract is considered necessary or unnecessary, according to the personal concepts that the involved parties hold about themselves and about others.

Speculation and discussion of professionalization have been continuing phenomena of employment. There have been arguments over the years as to whether teaching is a profession or simply an employment area. There is little to be gained from debating this problem or definition, but there is much to be gained from a clear definition of what professionalization means to each person in each school assignment. Certainly, there must be some agreement on the expectations, constraints, and autonomy that are to be experienced and enjoyed under the professional certification, the employment contract, and the concept of the worth of the profession. All of these factors tend to cause an ebb and flow of the sensitivities that determine how people react to each other.

Observability increases when interaction involves auditing and evaluating processes. Parents have personalized concepts and inferences about their students, the school services, and their expectations of what that service should offer to their children. The sensitivities of parents, which control their associations with teachers, administrators, and the schools, depend very much on the kind of reports their children bring home from the school experience. The same thing can be said with respect to the professional educators. The kind of contact represented by their experiences with the student as a representative of the parents determines the ebb and flow of the sensitivities of teachers, supervisors, and administrators in their dealings with parents.

The taxpayer long has been recognized as having some rather unique personalized concepts about school personnel and school services. Perhaps taxpayer is an indefinable type of person or group with great variation. In general, however, almost everyone thinks from time to time as a taxpayer, more strongly than they think as a parent, as a board member, or even as an educator. Here again, the concepts held tend to bring about a variation in the sensitivities that describe the relationships between school personnel and those with whom they interact. The same type of problem can be seen with the religionists who have personalized concepts on which they base inferences of expectation with respect to what the schools should be doing. From time to time, as the situation changes, there is an ebb and flow of the sensitivity of the relationships between the religionist and the educator.

Quality may be defined as fitness for use as judged by the user. The community, as a collection of taxpayers, is the user of the school process and product and, as such, perceives a right to have input relating to quality control. The audit is perceived as an instrument of quality assurance.

The ebb and flow of sensitivities also may be influenced by the impact distance. An illustration of this is the idea that a person sitting across the desk in the classroom or the office is a more immediate threat or support than a telephone call from some distant point, no matter how violent the language may be on the telephone. This may be less threatening or less supportive than what takes place in the interaction in a face-to-face situation. Distance may have a great deal to do with the sensitivities that control the interaction between people in the profession and those outside the profession. The audit presents a situation in which this impact distance may be quite important. If the auditor is employed from the outside and unknown to the people being audited, chances are there will be increased reticence in response to the requests of the auditor. Within the school system, there is a lesson to be learned from impact distance. An auditor from the central office may seem more distant and less sensitive to an individual in the classroom or in a particular school building than an auditor who comes from within that school building. It is not always practical to put auditing on such a personal basis but, in planning the audit, the impact distance and its effect on the sensitivities of people should be a matter of careful consideration.

Sensitivities often are determined by the origin of an idea. The audit itself may seem to be a scrutiny of the action based on ideas. The person who originated the idea perhaps will be more sensitive about having that idea and its outcome tampered with than those who knew the origin but were not credited with it. In planning the audit system, some concern must be given to the efforts of trying to seem unchallenging to the idea originators. It is more important that the attitude prevail that the audit may provide an opportunity to validate the idea and its originator. Again, the positive connotation may add to the mutuality of the interaction between people.

Audits often are instituted when a crisis situation arises. There is discipline in crisis. But on the other hand, the initiation of crisis to gain discipline is a form of brinkmanship intolerable in the educational organization. When a crisis arises from outside, but focuses on the school, there may be a stimulus to establish effective understanding between the within—school auditors—and those audited. The crisis discipline is just the opposite from what might be called good times relaxation. Good times seem to result in little concern about what is going on or how it is going on, and there is a tendency to relax and say, "Anything goes." This, of course, can result in a new crisis situation, bringing back discipline that is undesirable and completely opposite from the good times relaxation.

Realism needs to be applied in all of these situations to promote clear thinking as to what controls the inclinations of people to work together effectively in an audit and evaluative situation. Prestige often is a factor in determining whether there will be good relationships between the audited and the auditor. Status perceptions do affect almost everyone and, when original ideas are challenged, status seems to be lost. In the good times situation, status is seldom recognized. In this case, instead of offense being generated by the person whose prestige is challenged, it is just as serious not to have prestige recognized.

Human beings are important to the concerns of auditing and sensitivities need to be recognized as the audit plans are developed. Every effort should be made to develop a stable mutuality among all people within the school system and, hopefully, with the people outside who constitute the school's environment. Unstable mutualities can lead to uncertainties, suspicion, and the defeat of an audit. Therefore, the concept of mutuality may be a key way of controlling the ebb and flow of sensitivities that exist between people.

Examples of Strategy

1. *Seek staff assistance in the early development of a procedure to implement changes that might be warranted by the audit.*

2. *Arrange for small group preaudit discussions to identify the audit scope as related to major controls and activities or an indepth review of a few functional areas or sections.*

3. *Identify with staff the most useful and acceptable sources of audit information.*
   a. *Observations — are there actual working conditions and procedures that should be observed?*
   b. *Interviews — should personnel be interviewed to determine their role in and their understanding of the inputs, processes, and outputs?*
   c. *Reviews — would important review information include publications, policy and procedure manuals, organization charts, budget records, minutes, memos, job descriptions?*

THE NEED TO KNOW[1]

The current period properly can be called the era of accountability. Cynics may claim that skill at avoiding accountability has been developed more rapidly and to a higher level of expertise than has acceptance of accountability. The contemporary social scene scarcely can be read without realizing, nevertheless, that people tend to hold *others* accountable. Employers are more likely to hold employees rigidly to predetermined expectations of the employment relationship than to accept rigid accountability systems for themselves. Public employees in all categories have been required increasingly to guarantee delivery of predetermined output.

Accountability, according to emerging practices, is the main demand agent for information that can be verified. Verified information is to be related to the objectives of the position and, in this sense, supports the recognition of quality achievement. An emerging concept related to accountability is that support provisions for those held accountable must be determined and verified. Support refers to the conditions that are essential to employee performance. It is realized now that expectations of responsibility cannot be levied against an individual who lacks control over conditions essential for success.

Attention turns to the conditions, factors, and facilities that support or thwart the individuals as they seek to accomplish their goals. Those persons who possess the capacity to support or thwart are part of the accountability observation. Negotiated relationships between the teaching group and the employer, namely the board of education, are receiving much attention. Administrative staffs normally are viewed by teachers as part of management, belonging to the board's

1. Glen G. Eye and Lanore A. Netzer. "Educational Auditing: From Issue to Principle," *New Directions for Education, Creating Appraisal and Accountability Systems*, No. 1, ed. Donald J. McCarty (San Francisco: Jossey-Bass, Inc., Spring, 1973) pp. 63–75. Reprinted with permission.

category of influence. Professional negotiations, therefore, focus increasingly on working conditions. They tend to identify those support elements that markedly influence the teacher's opportunity to fulfill the obligations of employment. The many and varied persons who have expectations about the outcomes of teaching and learning seldom are assessed as a part of the accountability system. Proof of efficiency should be derived from concurrent observations of environmental expectations, purposes, and behaviors, and of teaching and learning outcomes.

Slowly but surely, respect for objective judgment is growing. In other words, decisions not based on the intuitive inclinations of an individual but on evidence are being made more often in matters involving interactions of people. Identification and presentation of evidences long have been considered carefully by the courts, but only now are they beginning to enter the thinking of those charged with evaluating teaching support.

School personnel gradually are coming to the conclusion that they must know and tell, or an outsider may tell without knowing. It is much safer to have a systematic plan of educational auditing than to have ill-informed evaluators making judgments about the educational product.

Examples of Strategy

1. Select a recent public comment on education as reported in a newspaper. Ask staff members to list the kinds of data that the reporter should have had in order to draw the reported conclusions.

2. Seek staff assistance in developing a formal system for considering suggestions from employees. This activity can support the notion that disagreement can be dealt with in a positive, nonreprisal manner to strengthen the operation.

AUDITING AS SUPPORT

The preceding section dealt with the need to know and emphasized the premise that facts are supportive as well as destructive. It is hoped that, as increased awareness of the audit process becomes a part of the regular operation, more attention can be given to activities that render support rather than possess destructiveness.

The record of truth increases the amount of freedom that an individual can possess. It likewise increases the freedom that an organization can and should possess. The record of truth infers that the audit process must deal openly and frankly with all of the information that can be collected and construed as appropriate to the issue under review. As a total school organization gains respect for the auditing process and recognizes it as continuous evaluation, there can be an inclination to share responsibility as well as accountability. Perhaps our past is replete with too much inclination to assess individual responsibility and its accompanying individual accountability. People do work in an organization. People do contribute to an organizational goal in unique individual ways. Thus, an audit might tend to focus greater attention on unique responsibilities rather than on a global type of accountability expectation placed on the total school organization and each individual working within it. As the record of truth increases, suspicion tends to be reduced. Suspicion usually develops more from what people do not know than from what they do know. Thus, an audit might increase the opportunities for people involved in the educational process to see others as helping persons rather than to watch carefully for any derogatory movements or intentions on their part.

The bases for commendation should be fixed in the audit type of data. Commendation is not just an emotional type of response, although it can be embellished by it. Real commendation comes from careful observation of successes that individuals and groups achieve and, with the audit data available, the basis for commendation is bound to improve. An audit likewise is supportive in that it identifies the expertise that individuals or groups contribute to the educational process. It is discouraging for an individual, who has devoted time and expense to developing a unique expertise, to perform in that area without anyone noticing it. Here again, the audit can identify and recognize the expertise that is developed among the professional personnel.

Several references have been made to the fact that an audit tends to focus on all the variables pertinent to the outcomes of the individual and of the group as an organization. Far too often, the professionals have had to accept and offset the deficiencies in the non-people facilities. For instance, teachers who did not have adequate space, support, or appropriate load assignments have had to perform presumably at a high level without compensation for the burdens of inadequate facilities. The audit must focus not only on people but on support and, in this way, equalize distribution of the accountability load. The audit is a support that identifies and helps to control all of the variables involved in an operational purpose. In this way, the audit is positive, supportive, and beneficial and can be endorsed and supported by all members of the professional staff and the community.

Examples of Strategy
1. Ask teachers to list the support facilities essential to a specific teaching responsibility.

2. Identify the cost of maintaining support facilities at current levels or increasing support facilities to an optimal level, and relate this to observable effects on goal achievement.

3. Seek staff identification of unique or different styles of delivery systems employed that seem to provide effectiveness in achieving program results that can be identified and positively related to in an audit. The possibility of diffusing better ways of achieving goals into the system might be considered as an incentive for sharing and caring among staff members.

IMPROVEMENT BASES

References have been made in previous sections to the fact that auditing and evaluating procedures can provide support for the personnel in the organization and constitute a basis for designing alternative plans. The improvement bases can be found in information that comes from the auditing and evaluating processes. This guarantees some support for data-based planning systems. Planning should be initiated only with some specific information at hand. The auditing and evaluating processes can provide this information.

One type of improvement that can be gained from the auditing and evaluating experience is the development of analytic skills and strategies. People do not have innate approaches to the auditing and evaluating processes. But gradually, many people can be involved in those skills necessary to carry out these processes. After having gained the skills, they can be helpful in the operation and also more appreciative and supportive of the processes as worthwhile educational enterprises. As analytic skills and strategies are developed, there will be an increase in the precision of thinking and an inclination to look at the data to discover steps for the future.

A part of the analytic skill that leads to precision in thinking is the development of an inclination to break down any issue into its parts or categories. The process of categorization, in turn, adds to precision in thinking, and is essential to the auditing and evaluating demands. In this way, attention to the support facilities is almost guaranteed. Failure to categorize the elements of a problem or target will negate this probability. Two of the categories involved in precision thinking are identifying the support facilities and seeking to determine their amount of weight in the success of any particular part of the total enterprise.

Part of the auditing and evaluating system involves reporting responsibilities. There are feedback benefits for all who take part in the auditing process, as well as for those who provide the environmental supports for the educational system. With this concept of bases for improvement, there is no longer the problem of wondering to what extent the "quashables" (data concealments) are being quashed in the processes of auditing and evaluating. Gradually these quashables can be eliminated as a necessity for the so-called political benefits of administration and management. Feedback benefits make sure that more, if not all, people have access to the same set of facts, guaranteeing some agreement on the alternatives that will be identified and the criteria that will be used in selecting the best alternative for future action.

Examples of Strategy

1. Identify an improvement need and ask staff members to list the categories of desired information for the planning process.

2. Identify an assumed strength within a department or program and seek involvement among professional participants to identify parts or categories so that others, less proximate to the activity, might understand or identify the operating components. This could clarify to other staff, a school district board, or citizens, the support requirements necessary to achieve identified goals.

3. Identify, through the use of personnel records, professional staff who have had recent educational course work in evaluation, educational auditing, or educational accountability. A meeting among such staff members could shed light on a broad-based, in-service program to establish an understandable, acceptable working base within the school district.

CRITERION-OBJECTIVE LIAISON

Reference has been made numerous times to the fact that criteria need to be selected as a basis for making judgments. The objectives are held by those responsible for the performance. They may have originated in an all-school organization decision but individuals must accept them or develop adaptations that are more appropriate to their own abilities and assignment.

The criteria for evaluation of audit data must be closely related to the objectives of the people involved in the information audit. The liaison between the criteria and the objective is the people involved in the performance. The first step to an effective liaison is an effort to coordinate the individual educator and school objectives. Usually these are not far apart, but they must be brought increasingly closer together into a coordinated status, if not a common one, so that the ultimate outcome will not be a state of antagonism. It is a simple thing, although not often done, to relate the position description to the school objectives. Too many schools lack position descriptions, making it improbable that any such assessment or relationship can be made. One early step in bringing on the liaison between the criteria and objective is to make sure that there are accurate job descriptions for each position. Then, it is possible to relate school objectives to individual objectives.

Teacher competency is a word that has been used as though it can be determined precisely. Determination of competency is handicapped, more than anything else, by the fact that there is no clear statement of expectation at the time a teacher begins teaching or the supervisor or administrator assesses the responsibilities of a position.

It must be recognized, too, that there are different types of objectives. There are content objectives, process objectives, and outcome objectives. These need to be brought into focus to determine whether, at any point, the determination of competency or of evidences of satisfactory performance is related to one type of objective to the exclusion of another, or whether all have been considered.

The close relationship between the criteria and the objective for an individual in a group enterprise like the school requires each performer to take part in the establishment of criteria for auditing and evaluating. The liaison that can be provided by the individual performer is too valuable not to be used. The old idea that evaluation will take place without the subject knowing the criteria for evaluation is outdated and should not have been tolerated as long as it was. Many of the negotiations occurring at the present time focus on the evaluative process. There is great promise that performers will have sufficient input into the choice of criteria used in evaluation so that the process will be much more accurate in the future. When the criteria are known and are relevant to the objectives, there is a chance to achieve early patterns of evidence that can be used in the auditing and evaluating processes. It is much more likely that the individual being audited will make a valid contribution to the auditing and evaluating processes, and thus increase the services in the educational system.

The teacher, supervisor, and administrator are the chief liaison agents in the area of personal responsibilities to be assessed in terms of criterion related objectives and relevant performances.

Examples of Strategy

1. *Analyze the negotiated master contracts to identify the extent to which cooperative and coordinative efforts in criteria determination are fostered.*

2. *Organize a committee of professional staff members to suggest a common format or outline that can be used by each teacher to submit suggested job descriptions as well as individual objectives.*

3. *Assemble a group of professional staff members representing various grade levels to organize teacher suggested job descriptions in a manner that will permit a visible relationship between objectives and the job descriptions.*

DANGERS IN SNAPSHOT ARTISTRY

The past several sections of this chapter repeatedly have turned to the fact that continuing audit and evaluation processes are necessary. Continuousness is one guarantee that decisions will not be made until adequate evidence is available. This section is intended mainly as a warning against abandoning the more difficult and time-consuming procedures of continuous auditing and evaluating.

Decisions on the identity of categories take time. The standardization of the treatment of collected data takes time. Many people, unwilling to devote that kind of time to the professional obligations, simply take a snapshot of some particular phenomenon at some convenient period in time. There are, of course, many people who feel that evidence only deters the process of debate and decision. It is sad when facts are held at such a low value, namely, as impediments to decision and judgment.

The work pressure imposed on an individual in the school organization does encourage shortcuts. Perhaps those who are responsible for auditing and evaluating have not had sufficient time and facilities available to support the expectations placed on those processes and on them. Work pressure should be one of the first things audited to determine whether snapshot judgments are being made or shortcuts are being sought in the work process in the school organization. Speed is not better than accuracy. There may be occasions, particularly crisis ones, in which evidence is needed quickly for impending decisions. In this case, speed must be seen only as the last expedient available. It is hoped that the kinds of decisions that have to be made might be anticipated far enough in advance so that they would not have to be based on snapshot observations in order to fulfill the demands for judgment.

One look is not as good as many looks. Thus, the concept of an audit as continuous evaluation is still the soundest educational procedure. Those who seek to abandon this longer way only deceive themselves. They will destroy the concept of audits and of evaluation as vehicles of accountability if they continue to operate on the snapshot basis.

Examples of Strategy

1. *Keep a record of the time span between the identification and resolution of major problems.*

2. *Develop a list of auditing and evaluating areas that are longitudinal in scope. Review the objectives, stated or inferred, and determine whether they remained constant.*

3. *Determine, through an audit of attitudes, the staff perceived purposes of the audit in order to note and build on the positive purposes of continuous growth and development in staff performance.*

INTERPRETER DEPENDENCE

This section stresses a further caution, after seeking to establish a firm concept of auditing as continuous evaluation. Just as there must be a continuous search for evidence and relevant information, there must be a continuous pursuit of meaning. Once the data have been collected and the criteria determined, it is necessary to judge whether the two are relevant and what they actually tell. This means that the processes of auditing and evaluating depend a great deal on the expertise of an interpreter.

Some people must develop expertise in the interpretation of information, as well as in the development and organization of information. One element in interpretation that is hard to control is the variation in the perceptions of the people receiving the information. The variation may be in the receiver or in the presenter. It makes little difference as to which one takes that responsibility, but the outcome is one in which perception plays a great part. Perception is based, to a great extent, on the attitudes of the individual presenting or receiving. These attitudes must be recognized as influential factors in the interpretation of data, and the adequacy of the interpretation must be scrutinized at all times.

Data have never been self-interpreting and they are not going to become so. Thus, there must be an interpreter and a knowledgeable receiver of the interpretation before the communication about any audit or evaluative data can be considered adequate and complete. The tactics of interpretation need to be scrutinized at the time that information is presented. Tactics, such as, queries about the original intent of the audit, the choices of the format of the audit, and why a particular one was chosen are appropriate examples. These queries must be considered not only from the standpoint of the person reporting but also from the standpoint of the person receiving the report. The data producer, interpreter, and consumer responsibility are part of this total procedure of the presentation and interpretation of information that comes out of the educational audit as a continuous evaluative process.

Examples of Strategy

1. *Present a table of test scores to a group of professional educators and ask each one to list the meanings derived from it.*

2. *Review the present means of communicating test results to parents and check out the variations in parent interpretation.*

3. *Require a final meeting of the auditor and audited prior to the time that the final and interpretive report is given to "try on" the understandings and correct the misunderstood data.*

THE LOOK AHEAD

The individual holding an objective should be one of the best judges of what constitutes a relevant audit. That person holding the objective certainly ought to know the best kind of criteria that could be used. That person also could and should make a tremendous contribution to the choice of the kinds of information collected in the audit.

The person referred to here may not be the best judge of the audit process, but will be one of the best contributors to the design of the audit process since that person is involved in the actions that will generate the data sought, collected, and organized in the audit.

Harmony between the auditor and the audited is the main hope for accepted accountability and the assurance of self-realization. The purpose of chapter 13 is to present some thoughts and suggestions with respect to the multiple characteristics and responsibilities of accountability.

PROCESS OF CONTINUED READING

Blumberg, Arthur. *Supervisors and Teachers: A Private Cold War*. Berkeley, California: McCutchan Publishing Corp., 1974.

Bolden, John H. *Developing a Competency-Based Instructional Supervisory System*. Hicksville, New York: Exposition Press, 1974.

McCarty, Donald J. (ed.). *New Directions for Education: Creating Appraisal and Accountability Systems*, No. 1. San Francisco: Jossey-Bass, Inc., Spring, 1973.

Sciara, Frank J., and Richard K. Jantz. *Accountability in American Education*. Boston: Allyn & Bacon, 1972.

Sergiovanni, Thomas J. (ed.). *Professional Supervision for Professional Teachers*. Washington, D.C.: Association for Supervision and Curriculum Development, 1975.

Multifaceted Accountability

The previous chapter, "Auditing as Continuous Evaluation," dealt with auditing as a process of knowing. The process of knowing includes the purposes of evaluation. It must be recognized, however, that the audit as a system of gathering information does not establish automatically the quality of performance and outcome, nor does it point the way to the development of improvement programs. The audit, as a basis for improvement, provides useful data to those responsible for planning program design.

The emphasis in the previous chapter was on the increasing concern for involving the participants in the group action (the school operation) in the development of the audit process itself. The participants also should be involved in the selection of criteria used to relate the audit information to an evaluation of quality. Here again, the use of the audit in that chapter was focused primarily on improvement. The older concept of audit, that of finding out what is wrong, was not given much attention because it was irrelevant to the purposes of this publication and to the real purposes of an audit procedure.

This chapter extends the use of audit information to assure proper parties of the extent to which the expectations for the school's operation have been achieved. The audit information is directed to the members of the professional staff, the board of education, and to the citizens of the community. This identifies only some of the people who are properly entitled to evidences of accountability or responsibility in fulfilling the organizational purposes. The inference can be made here that, as the application of accountability is extended throughout the community, the basis for a positive approach to the concept of community education programs has been established. References will be made frequently in this chapter to the relationship of total community planning. This planning not only determines the accountability of the school for the educational enterprise but also of other agencies within a community that contribute to the educational opportunities of the youth.

Accountability is the application of the audit information that is related to the individual and group responsibilities in the achievement of the declared expectations. This means that not only is the educational influence of the school a concern of accountability, but other agencies also have contributions to make to the education of youth. The accountability, however, will be focused on each of the agencies as they go about the requirements that represent a unique assignment and contribution to the total educational program for the youths of the community.

SOME MISCONCEPTIONS OF ACCOUNTABILITY

The positive consideration of any phenomenon or activity usually is burdened with some false assumptions or misconceptions. The authors believe that, in order to clear the way for a positive treatment of the idea of accountability, some of the misconceptions need to be identified and hopefully eliminated. This would make it possible to establish the program firmly on the more positive aspects of accountability. There is no attempt here to catalog completely the misconceptions but rather to select some illustrative ones that can help to clear the mind for positive viewing.

One misconception that has been a burden to the development of accountability systems is that *self-judgment is always biased.* Certainly one of the trends, visible in many organizations at the present time, is to give some thought to the use of accountability systems that increase the participation of all who may be involved in the total activity. Each individual, nonetheless, can be looked at specifically for the unique contributions according to which assignments have been made. For instance, for many decades teachers were not permitted to enter into any part of the accountability process because there was a feeling that they would bias the information about the instructional program utilizing local norms.

The broadening of the concept of responsibility for a total education program to an entire community has done much to indicate the great need for teacher involvement in the development of the accountability system. Teachers certainly have given more specific help to the development of parent-teacher conferences than had ever been anticipated. We must recognize that the quality of the conference improved as the teachers increased their participation in its planning and development. The people in the community seldom have been burdened with the problem of deciding how well community enterprises were moving along. The real problem came when it focused on just one of the many groups in the community that had specific responsibility for instructing youth. So some progress has been made in eliminating the misconception that is related to the personal participation of those being subjected to the accountability system.

A current and long-held misconception is that *an outsider guarantees objectivity*. The long history of consulting work is evidence that school districts have been inclined to call in outsiders to review the operation of the local school and to make judgments as to whether it was acceptable. Problems can develop with respect to the outsider, and many of them are more disadvantageous than the so-called objectivity in the collection of information and rendering of judgments based on those data. Those consultants who simply help the people of a community and school district structure a system of evaluating progress and status of outcomes have been helpful. In this way, the involvement of local people stimulates their responsibility for collecting information and making judgments. The outsider is there only as a technician to help structure the attack.

The misconception that *accountability is a control device* has a solid base and a long history. True for many decades, people looked on the evaluation of local school systems and the development of an accountability program as a way of finding out what was wrong. The next step was to find out who was responsible. Thus, the whole process was a control and a penalty instrument.

The eternal desire to reduce things to their simplest form has led to a misconception of accountability that *educational expectations are universal*. The universality concept is rooted in the history of this country, particularly since education was seen as a basic requisite for citizen participation. The idea that national norms established for various types of tests describe the universality of educational expectations in this country has led to many unfortunate approaches to accountability.

One aspect of this unfortunate tendency is that the universal expectation has been applied to communities that did not have the so-called universal characteristics. The next step in this simplification of presumed universality is that any measurement or measuring device can determine a *rating on a common numerical scale*. The comparison of one figure at the local level to a national norm elicits some conclusions that do not account for the extreme complexity of education in any one community or school district. Recently, there has been a tendency to move away from the idea of universality and to find a better concept of the outcomes of teaching and learning efforts by utilizing local norms.

The simplification through universality and numerical scale points has negated the use of conditions affecting learning in the weighting of evaluations made in any particular community or for any particular person. The misconception evolving around the evaluation of teachers is that, since the support facilities were known at the time of the employment agreement, such factors need not affect the ratings of teaching outcomes. This certainly is a gross misconception of the real world, and has resulted in the administering of injustice, rather than justice, to many people and to many school programs and systems.

A continuance of the misconceptions listed here holds that *there has to be some sort of sanction system*. Rewards and punishments depend on the kinds of judgments that can be made. The processes of making these judgments often have been called an accountability system. They really are so far apart that it is difficult to detail how remnants of these misconceptions are thwarting many of today's wholesome efforts to develop a meritorious accountability system.

A renewed interest in accountability seemed to develop as the cost of education increased. Of course, the cost of everything else has increased as well, but it has brought about a new focus by the originators of funding on the accountability of local school systems. The role of the federal government is one of the prominent examples in recent years. The multitude of specific guidelines and required reports from recipients of federal funds sometimes take so much time from the local educational personnel that the original purpose of the school, for which the funding may have been designed, does not receive the proper amount of attention. As the state contribution to local education has increased, so has the desire for assurance of accountability. Unfortunately, the accountability placed on local school systems by federal and state governments has been developed almost independently by those governments. They have not used nearly enough of the concept that persons being held accountable should participate in the design of the accountability process. Perhaps more experience in using federal and state funds to support local school programs will increase the inclination to use local people, both professional and lay, in the development of the accountability system.

An awareness of what the misconceptions enumerated here are doing to the total educational program perhaps will hasten the day when more cooperative planning will be done. Eventually, community education programs, state education programs, or even federal education programs can be developed at the local levels. The scene of action is always the community, and that should be the focus of attention in eliminating the misconceptions about accountability systems.

Examples of Strategy

1. *Organize a series of small group roundtable discussions on the topic, "What is an accountability system?" Have leaders report group ideas. Direct the large group discussion to the differences in perceptions. Arrive at an acceptable definition.*

2. *Ask other employees to cite misconceptions regarding accountability. Use the examples referred to above and add others. Reach consensus regarding the misconceptions to develop confidence in the value of their participation in an accountability system.*

3. *Discuss the values of identifying what's right in terms of productivity within areas of instruction. Determine how data retrieved in the audit might be evaluated and disseminated to constituents to develop confidence and avoid destructive conclusions drawn from gossip or hearsay.*

4. *Review past accountability systems in your district and determine what misconceptions were contained in those systems.*

ORIGINS OF EXPECTATIONS

The consideration of the quality of expectations placed on the schools and the education programs is a proper activity. It is one, however, that requires a look into the extent to which our actions make that determination of quality. That is the point of the discussion here. In many ways, the expectations placed on schools represent a sort of *historical bondage*. For many decades, the public school particularly was expected to be responsible for the training of citizens to fit the existing concepts of government. A similar bondage applied to the parochial schools that were to nurture the particular pattern of belief characteristic of the sponsoring religious denomination. The most persistent bond from our past, however, is that in which the taxpayer presumes the prerogative of determining the quality and type of expectations placed on the education programs.

Other origins could be identified but they are not necessarily independent of each other. The people of this country long have had dreams of *equality and universality*. Usually, the concept of equality is that individuals should have what they perceive other people as having; the concept of universality is that whatever is good for one person also must be good for another. This is not to say that these concepts are ones of socialization of all society and its mechanisms. It does say rather that education somehow opens the gates to the future and provides the opportunity for people to march through into an equal competitive state.

Many of the expectations placed on the schools are to be found in *legislated action*. The reference in chapter 8 to the legislated mix of goals and processes contains many illustrations of the evolvement of these origins in legislated action. A few decades ago, legislated action seemed to point to a goal, whereas now it points not only to the goal but also to the processes by which the schools are to achieve this goal. One of the big problems of expectations established through legislated action is that they become rather immovable. If more leeway could be given to the procedures of achieving goals, perhaps the expectations might be more reasonable influences on local educational action.

Another origin of expectations is in *executive declarations*. These can be executive declarations of officials at the state or federal levels. They likewise can be declarations of the board of education or of the administrative bureaucracy within a local school district.

Judicial interpretations of the situations that can be analyzed and interpreted under established legislative action constitutes another origin of expectations. As the concept of jurisprudence seemingly evolves, more actions are taken at the judicial level that affect the local school operation than was true even in our immediate past. It is recognized, however, that only a few years ago the courts were referred to as black-robed school boards. Perhaps this is even more applicable at the present time when, just as the legislatures have tended to freeze the processes into bills establishing goals, the courts tend to deliver more edicts with respect to process than formerly. Perhaps the very fact of the legislated process has made it unavoidable for the courts to move in this direction. As these things increase, however, we have an ever increasing number of people and agencies, with varying purposes, who are establishing the expectations placed on education. Thus, in this chapter, multifaceted accountability is dealt with as one way of describing the ever increasing impact characteristics of the evolving list of educational expectations.

The references to legislated, executive, and judicial actions do not limit the concept of the origins of educational expectations beyond the boundaries of the local school district. *Bureaucratic agents* at the federal, state, and regional levels have great influence on the selection and establishment of educational expectations. These become the instruments by which accountability systems are established and operated.

Origins of expectations are found in the systems of funding education programs. References have been made several times to the inclination of federal and state governments to extend control over the process of education and, consequently, over the procedure of accountability for those funded programs. The priorities are not always easy for the local education agency to decipher. More, and sometimes conflicting, expectations are pressed on the local education programs when funding projects of foundations and other special interests are added to the federal and state contributions. Here again, when funds are granted there are usually conditions attached, and these conditions become a description of expectations and sometimes a system of accountability.

Apart from the legal and financial origins of expectations, there are others found in *the privilege of the people to petition*. Petition can be a personal presentation, a written list of names, or communication by whatever means. It is a vehicle by which "we the people" can make impacts on the agencies of education. There are origins of expectations to be found in the client and patron stated prerogatives. The client here is the student and the patrons are the parents and lay citizens of the community. Their prerogatives are communicated to the board of education and to the professional personnel in many ways.

The promising reappearance of community education programs seems to be moving along well at the present time. Here again there are fundings made possible. At the present time, however, the originators of these funds have not put particularly rigid controls over those invited to develop community education programs (CEP) throughout a given state and throughout the country. CEP provides people in the community excellent opportunities to contribute both to decisions of policy and to actual program requisites within the total education program. This means that special interest groups within a community may or may not join the community education approach. But whether or not they do, they still constitute an origin of expectation. It is a democratic privilege of special interest groups to indicate their expectations with respect to the outcomes of education programs.

Another source or origin of expectation is what might be called the *scriptural selectivities*. The past is replete with many expectations placed on the schools that originated in some religious beliefs and publications. From time to time, people have wanted to quote a particular bible to prove that a particular kind of expectation should be placed on the schools. The most recent concern along this line was related to values. Perhaps schools do drift one way or another as a result of the many expectations described in this section and elsewhere. Nevertheless, there is nothing wrong if people of a particular religious belief want to invoke their values on a total community. That community, then, has to make the choice as to whether those expectations will be accepted and pursued.

This final example of an origin of expectation is both frightening and distasteful. It is the *origin of greed, fear, and fraud*. There are some people who would influence an education program to create markets for particular items of merchandise. There are others who have generalized fears and want the schools to allay any probability that the horrible things envisioned might happen. Fraud, as an origin of expectation, occurs when individuals or special interest groups want to conceal true expectations in the guise of certain innocent types of expectations. A few types of origin have been listed here and, in all probability, the list could be extended; but, for the purpose of this discussion, these illustrations are sufficient.

Examples of Strategy

1. *Develop a list of contacts, requests, and pressures experienced by the board of education. Have these evaluated by a group of administrators, supervisors, department heads, and by teachers to determine feasibility and acceptability from the standpoint of educational principles.*

2. *Review, on the basis of newspaper releases during the past year, the printed public expressions of expectations that relate to the public schools. List various expressions by organized categories for review by staff during in-service meetings.*

3. *Use the categories referred to in this chapter and add your own to identify the sources and possible motivations for expressed concerns in your school district.*

4. *Review, through informal in-service discussion, expectations that staff have raised as concerns and encourage staff to discuss the basis or origins of their feelings regarding unmet expectations.*

THE URGE TO DO

The preceding section discussed the origins of expectations for education, primarily in terms of the people who wanted to impose their particular desires on an education program and, hence, on a total people. Those inclined to seek opportunities for impact on the education program are genuine in that they have an urge to do exactly what they are doing. People cannot be denied the privilege to pursue their particular proper desires. An important concern is to get some sense of the purpose for which people's urges are devised. Ego satisfaction may be the desire of the individual who attempts to influence the education program. Such individual desire, however, is not easily justified since public enterprises should not exist to satisfy the egos of selected individuals.

The urge to do also comes from rational decisions. Many people do survey their society and environment, they do collect information, they do organize the information, and they do come to conclusions. When people have an urge to influence education based on rational decisions, even though it might not be agreeable to everyone else, there is a wholesome reason for the urge. As long as the capacity for compromise can be retained, there can be positive outcomes from this type of urge.

Another urge grows out of genuine beneficence. There are many people who really want to do things for other people. One of the surest ways to make that perceived contribution contact is through the education program. There are many individuals with the urge to do something for the schools based on this noble reason or desire.

The urge to influence education may grow out of either assumed or ascribed responsibility. Individuals assigned to specific responsibilities within the school action, may have defined or assumed ways of making their own impact on the educational process. Many people are recognized as having unique abilities to do certain things and they have responsibilities ascribed by others. In either instance, there is a way to analyze the type and quality of the influence on the education program.

Reference often is made to the bureaucratic or hierarchical organization within any group action. Schools prove to be no exception to this. Within the school structure there are positions that often have job descriptions that detail many of the specific tasks and responsibilities placed on the individuals who occupy the positions. This is true for boards of education, central office administrators, supervisors and directors, and department heads, as well as teachers. There are expectations unique to these positions and they seem to change slowly. This does provide a way, however, of analyzing the urges that move people to try to influence the instructional programs. The well-stated goals and facilities of the school operation often stimulate people to go about their own tasks more successfully or even to alter them or add or shift to other responsibilities. It is perfectly proper for people to react in this way, and it provides a way of looking at the urges that they have to influence education.

Schools always have been a ready target for influence efforts, whether within the school organization or the environmental community. In the first place, schools have a high level of visibility—*they are there*. It is easy to walk in and the people who walk in from the community feel that they have some qualifications for inquiring or for suggesting. Perhaps the basis for this idea of their right qualification comes from the fact that most people who walk into the schools once were students there. This gives first hand knowledge and an increased confidence that the right to suggest or influence is theirs. This has been a long held concept of local control. It has eroded substantially in recent years with the increased fundings from federal and state governments. Local control is still an ideal and a much talked about one. Local control does make the school accessible through orderly means, such as, meetings with or petitions to the board of education and school staff, as well as other means of communicating wishes. There is a proximity to action on the part of the people in the local community. It seems to increase their efforts to influence education, as opposed to people at a great distance from the local school who seem to feel that the only thing they can do is to give money and requirements. Proximity certainly encourages people to influence education and must be recognized as one of the more orderly ways of discussing the problems and hopes by achieving some adaptation.

Taxpayer syndromes have always existed and perhaps always will. Taxpayer organizations often tend to influence local education through analyses and publication of financial support and expenditures. These are not misplaced influences and the schools are logical targets of such influence. It is proper, nonetheless, to analyze the reasons why these interests wish to exercise this influence.

A cultural-based confidence exists in the all-purpose potency of education. Perhaps education has been unworthy at times. On the other hand, it has fulfilled many times the expectations that people have for its curative powers, as well as for its progressive developmental potential. It is hoped that urges to influence schools will never lose this basis of confidence, but perhaps the perception will be modified just a bit by recognizing that the potency is not as all-purpose as we would like to believe.

Examples of Strategy

1. Develop a five or six item data-gathering instrument that will provide a quick analysis of the reasons for specific efforts to influence. Give wide publicity to the instrument. Tell where it is available.

2. Select administrative or supervisory job descriptions for positions currently vacant and distribute to the school board and to another group of interested constituents. For example, a local vocational education coordinator (L.V.E.C.) job description might be presented to a lay vocational advisory board for review. Seek a written response identifying areas the board feels are strongly supportable. Suggest that the advisory group add areas that may be important and that were overlooked in the job description.

3. Add a tear-out section to your school district regular mailer (to be returned to the central office) that queries residents as to their reactions regarding operational aspects of their school district. Use the returns to form the basis of in-service discussion with the school district board and staff. Follow up with evidence-based responses in subsequent mailers. This will provide a vehicle for knowing and relating to "urgings" as the community interprets to the school and the school interprets to the community.

4. Review your recent administrative or supervisory behavior regarding a decision issue to determine whether you made sufficient effort to help the individual having an "urge to do" in saving face or in receiving positive rewards for being open and communicative, whether or not their feelings were well founded and accurate.

WHEN WINNING IS LOSING

A concept analyzed here is to discover, if possible, the results of the urge to influence schools in terms of whether achieving that influence is always good. There can be positive and negative aspects of almost every pressure or influence directed at the school. These positive and negative influences are thought of in relation to the person doing the influencing. A few instances might help to clarify the kinds of problems that are involved in the accountability system, when it is pursued vigorously and without enough concern for some of the attendant happenings.

Many campaigns for project funds are successful and many references are made to the fact that the federal government has been a mammoth source of funds for local education enterprises. Many enterprises have been sought and funded in terms of projects. The success of campaigns to secure funding for projects must be viewed also in terms of the loss of the local control of projects. There is no doubt that many people would like to have the freeloading potential of unlimited funding in which there would be no question as to how funds would be used. This does not mean that fraud would ensue necessarily, but it would be difficult to determine when public funds should be increased or decreased for a specific purpose.

Many times there are local efforts to win the support of local organizations in the passage of a bond election for some new educational facility. Those who seek to win support may feel the effects of the winning circle when the bond election succeeds. Often, however, the local organizations may feel that, because of their efforts in helping to carry the bond issue, they deserve some space for a noneducational project related to their own organizational purposes. This could mean the loss of educational space in order to accommodate the persons who helped in the winning. Thus, winning may be losing for certain aspects of the school system.

Professional educators often seek to stimulate parent groups to study the needs of a local district. When these needs are evaluated, the school can consider the extent to which accomplishment can be achieved, thus, using the grass-roots approach. One thing that might happen, when a parent group needs-evaluation has been completed, is that those same parents might demand immediate delivery of a need satisfaction remedial package. The school might not be able to deliver according to the expectations of the parent group; thus, winning the group action constitutes an unbearable burden on the school because it may not have the facilities or the staff to deliver the needs with the speed desired.

Many educational workers, teachers particularly, have responded to developmental encouragement beyond the contract requirements, and have gone on for advanced study. Often this advanced study brings some recognition for unique expertise. One thing that might result from this increased expertise is that the individual may be assigned to duties displacing those that had been chosen originally and that caused the person to seek the increased professional competence

One of the often recounted experiences in developing accountability systems is to increase the participation of staff members in the development of evaluational instruments. Certainly the teachers, supervisors, and administrators in the local school system need to be involved in expressing the things to be included in an evaluation instrument. The instrument is almost certainly better and, in all probability, it will be accepted for use by all personnel with a greater sense of confidence. On the other hand, experience indicates that, when the instrument is applied, some of the individuals who contributed to the development may find that the results violate their self-images. A sense of distress may result. It must be recognized that whatever use is made of evaluative data, there may be some problems for individuals as a result of that use. This is not the purpose of the instrument as a part of the accountability procedures.

Some of the positive and negative aspects have been described here as winning or losing. It is recognized, however, that there are some win situations and some lose-win situations. In the win situation, people get what they attempt to get and, perhaps, the results are entirely positive and everybody is happy. On the other hand, it is possible to put forth effort to influence the education program and to fail in achieving the change or impact that was sought. It may prove later that, had it succeeded, the impact might have been most unfortunate even for the persons doing the influencing. So it is possible to have the lose-win situation, as well as the win-lose and the win-win. A new kind of insurance is needed, however, as we move into further consideration of accountability systems. Attention must be given to possible negative effects of what is planned, at the time the plans are being developed. This might be the kind of insurance that would guarantee against some of the negative results that have been indicated in this section.

Examples of Strategy

1. *Analyze the reasons given by staff members when requesting materials and equipment. Does the request of one member for an item result in other requests for the same thing? Are the requests filled for all, for one, for none?*

2. *School construction bond issues are often sold on the basis of using the new facilities as a community center. Review the areas of interest and the impact on keeping the teaching stations in repair and supplied for regular daily classroom activity. If an interest, for instance, is expressed by the adults to build projects in a shop or laboratory, where will they be stored by day?*

3. Review past changes in the local educational program where the school system "lost" and the influencing group "won." List specific examples in the win and loss columns.

4. In a panel discussion, review the possible "wins" and "losses" of educational principles resulting from the negotiated agreement between the professional teachers and the board of education.

EXTENSIONS OF COMPLETIONS

The idea of accountability has evolved in many ways over the past decades but there is still one burden being carried forward, namely, that accountability infers completion. True, an accountability system wants to know whether a goal has been achieved. But the achievement of a goal is an ongoing responsibility, just as the education of youth can not be seen as a series of completions.

Continuity is the concept prominently associated with community education programs. The basic concept is that learning never ends and even the completion of the unit, or of the diploma or degree program, does not signal the completion of the educative process. The reason why the inference of completion is a burden to the accountability system is the popular notion that "When finished why keep on doing it." People assume that when accountability tests have been made, the job is completed and it is time to go on to something else. The urge to find something else has supported the enormous body of literature on change. It is unfortunate that change has become a goal. Change is appropriate when improvement is needed, but change for the sake of change has been nourished by the concept of completion involved in the idea of accountability.

The posture that completion must be followed by change destroys the concept and the obligation of maintenance. When a developmental or improvement program has been instituted, the planning should have some longevity so far as the operational processes are concerned. When something is good, it ought to be maintained. Adaptations can be made while it is being maintained, but to feel that change is a dominant requisite simply may mean the loss of some of the best achievements. Another support for this idea of completion-then-change is that things that are new seem to draw the premiums. The payoff to people involved in developing something new often is better than the payoff to those who have maintained something deemed good. A balance needs to be struck between maintaining what is good and seeking what is new. The operational pattern relating to personnel rewards should not have undue influence on educational programs through the system of payoffs to personnel.

Another unfortunate characteristic of the idea of completion-then-change is that choppy program planning evolves. The idea that, when a task is completed, something new must be found and implemented disrupts continuity. It would be much better to develop what has been established than to scrap and start anew. As programs are developed, many of the participants may have developed expertise that was a requisite of the program. With the idea of completion and change, much of the expertise that has been developed is lost because the program is discontinued. New expertise must be sought and, consequently, time and talent is lost.

The people in the school environment often want to solve all problems by changing or by having something new, and so the concept is nurtured by the environmental values. We need to keep evaluating what is new versus what is worth keeping. If more thinking along this line is developed, perhaps the idea of completion will shift to the idea of goal accomplishment, and then proceed with adaptations and extensions. The completion of one task or program is a rewarding launching base for planning new programs or extensions of programs. Thus, if one considers the idea of extending completions rather than creating something new, an economy of expertise will be visible and a solid base for the continuing development of programs will be maintained. Accountability is for continuity, rather than for completion and discontinuance.

Examples of Strategy

1. Make an inventory of the status of present innovations. Include (1) date of introduction, (2) time projection, (3) evaluation procedures, (4) staff time allotment, (5) etc. In your analysis find out what is happening to the remainder of the involved staff member's time obligations. Are other staff members being used or abused for those duties with or without recognition? Is the time spent on the innovation out of proportion to the initial request? Add others.

2. Review existing job descriptions of aides and other classroom support staff. Identify performance expectations and unique abilities that have been nourished in existing programs. Recognize levels of talent that could continue to have impact on the program when considering new programs. Use this inventory as an assurance of continuing use of the talent bank assembled in prevailing programs.

3. Identify programs that have successfully fulfilled particular educational goals in your school district. Encourage continuation and improvement of "the stepping stones" that exist by recognizing the continuing nature of the program and its relationship to the larger body of knowledge in the particular discipline. Reveal student progress at intervals each year by inviting media representatives to visit the school and preparing written materials for release. In each instance, reveal the programs directed at higher levels of achievement in this area and the coordination that prevails to assure the continuing nature of the identified point of recognized achievement.

4. Do you have any specific examples of projects that were ended just because the accountablity system had been completed? Attempt to determine if the projects were actually completed or should have been continued for educational improvements.

5. Review past innovative projects (new for your district) and relate each project to a stated goal of your district. Is this possible or have past projects been developed without direction? Discuss your outcomes with other staff members.

THE WILL OF WHICH PEOPLE?

A previous section of this chapter indicated a wide variety of people who seek to make an impact on the school and the education program. This in large part accounts for the multifaceted accountability phenomenon that is the topic of this entire chapter. The problem encountered by those responsible for the immediate management of a local school system, and for the teaching in each classroom, is to determine who, of the many seeking to influence the school, are to be permitted to influence it. It was indicated earlier that, under no circumstance, should there be an effort to avoid any types of confrontation. But it is also true that those who manage the instructional programs must be somewhat selective in their response to those who would influence. We must distinguish between the origin of expectations and the obligation to respond while, at the same time, maintaining quality in the education program.

The decision as to who will be permitted to influence the instructional program and the educational design may be determined largely by certain legal priorities that must be recognized. Certainly a legislated requirement at either the federal or state level has higher priority than the wishes of some citizens who do not like a particular program or want something else. Those responsible parties in the instructional program must know what these legal prerogatives are and must set them into a priority arrangement.

Another determinant of who will be permitted to influence the instructional program may come from the structural formalities of an organization. There are hierarchies, not for control only, but for communication and for support facilities. These cannot be ignored if any source of rational relationships between people and between programs and accomplishments is to be maintained in the school system.

Judicial precedence at one time seemed to be a keynote that gave stability to the anticipation of clear interpretaions of the laws and of challenged situations. In recent years, the first amendment to the constitution has been getting an amazing amount of attention compared to a few decades ago. Judicial actions now seem to use the first amendment to set aside many of the legal priorities and structural formalities that formerly gave stability to an educational operation. This means that the influence on instructional programs has taken on many facets that were not experienced only a few years ago. This also means that the open-field runners abound and they now have ready access to legal assistance that can increase the potency of their influences on the schools. Here again, there is need for some stable base to make a decision as to who shall meet the response to influence efforts insofar as the professional personnel are concerned.

Eventually, an ethic will develop to help in the interpretation of the response privileges and obligations of those working in the instructional program. There are some guiding factors that might help at the present time as a search is made for a plan for controlling the response to those who would influence. There are certain contractual agreements between professional workers in the school and representatives of the community, namely, a board of education. These contractual agreements must be respected and often provide help in making response determinations.

Educational principles long have been one way of giving stability to action, in the administrative and supervisory areas as well as in the specific teaching responsibilities. A principle gives stability because it can be defined as a persisting relationship between two phenomena. If these phenomena can be identified and the persisting relationship determined, it will assist in deciding which people will gain responses to their expressed will about education programs. It is fair to raise the question whether the people who seek to influence have a rationale with respect to the influence they wish to exert. There must be a reason supported by as much evidence as can be gained.

Another factor that might help in guiding the decisions of when and how to respond is to determine the school's ability to deliver. There is no sense in maintaining that schools must continue all efforts on any occasion to deliver whatever it is that the petitioner is asking. An assessment of the ability to deliver and the information given out on that point perhaps can help in this dilemma.

Another thing that must be studied and openly discussed is that a petitioner's attempt to influence the instructional program may represent the potential displacement of other aspects of the program. In recent years, many demands have been put on the school and often this has meant that, in order to accommodate some new demand, some aspects of the existing program have had to be eliminated. The Title Program provided funds for local education agencies, but administrators have not always dealt frankly and helpfully with the things that were given up in order to have the things that were funded. A study of human and social needs is another guiding factor that might help in determining the kinds of impacts on the schools that will be recognized, honored, and subjected to response and action.

Examples of Strategy

1. When a committee is appointed and the tasks assigned, have ready for the group a list of federal, state, and local regulations that will have impact on the assignment. Ask the committee to review these and to add any others that need consideration in their deliberations.

2. Review the recommendations of past committees, task forces, informal groups, petitioners, etc., and determine if the guidelines presented in these sections were adhered to and were deliverable by the school district.

3. Review the impact of new legislation such as federal requirements for new program opportunities for the handicapped. Study prevailing constraints, such as state imposed cost controls or spending limitations, to identify the impact of other influences on identified groups of students, such as, the gifted and talented.

4. Any school district can count on a community of advocates of a narrowly defined list of three R's. Discuss with staff the impact of increased funding on those areas and on the practical arts and fine arts, including performing arts. Also, review the level of district support for athletics to determine the impact of funding for "reading, writing, and arithmetic." This review of potential program displacement should be made only after certain assumptions are agreed to concerning future levels of funding at federal, state, and local levels, as well as demographic data regarding projected enrollments.

CAN SUBJECTS CONTROL VERBS?

The great complexity of our society and the great variability of the values and wants of the people who constitute that society make it difficult to determine who shall influence the school and how much influence they shall have. The question indicated in the heading for this section is "Can the professionals in the school organization control those who would register their impact on the education program?" It is not a pleasant thought, but it might as well be recognized that assassins do not send invitations to a shooting. It is likewise true that many people who want to change or discontinue an education program, do not send an announcement to the board of education, or to the professional administrative, supervisory, and teaching staff, indicating when they are going to attack the target, namely, education.

Third party negotiators might be introduced into this complex scene. This sounds like an arbitration in labor negotiations but it is not meant in quite that context. It is more in the spirit of an ombudsman who might be able to receive the impacts from the environment, analyze them, and interpret them to the people responsible for the education program. In this sense, it might allow the professionals in the local educational agency to attend to the main responsibility, the development and maintenance of a good instructional program. This would be more rewarding than having to deflect time and talent to the sincere person or crackpot who may want to influence the school. Certainly the third party negotiator offers a legitimate way for open confrontation. A series of successful negotiations may support increased confidence that influence of the education program can be achieved without using massive legal, judicial, and pressure tactics.

The education program recipients of influence efforts must not seek to avoid confrontation. When target avoidance becomes the purpose, initiators are stimulated because it becomes a game beyond the educational issue perceived. Just as school personnel should not avoid the impacts of influencers, the initiators of the influence must be able and willing to discuss their motivations in seeking to influence the schools. If the initiators are unwilling, it is just as well for the targets of the influence to indicate that, until motivations are declared, no response will be forthcoming. The targets, or educational personnel, must be able to analyze the operational pattern and program outcomes in order to provide a base for the confrontations between those who would influence and those targeted for that influence. This might influence, in turn, the initiators to offer more assistance in explaining the motivation that stimulates them to seek an impact on the school. Either side, namely, the professional educators and those outside the school who would influence, must recognize that control for control's sake is a bad purpose. The relationship of interaction has more positive rewards than does control. The desire to control, however, sometimes becomes the goal of the influencer and the opportunity for interaction becomes much more difficult to achieve. Perhaps it is a responsibility of professional workers to establish an interaction procedure. If such procedures are established and widely communicated to people in the community then, in all probability, the interaction can be orderly and the influence of the education program based on a rationale that is defensible.

Cooperation is always more productive than a contest. Deciding who shall control, the targets within the program or the initiators outside the program, may be the origin of a contest. And the contest will not result in as many positive and developmental results as will cooperative approaches.

Examples of Strategy

1. In conference with your committee chairpersons, arrive at a consensus on the meaning of these words: coordinate, cooperate, compromise, confrontation, conciliation, *and* accommodation. *Ask your chairpersons to do the same with members of their committees. Stress the positive and operational aspects of these terms.*

2. *Analyze the organizational structure in your school system. Determine if a position exists related to the concept of an ombudsman. If so, cite specific examples of situations where this position has been used and list positive and negative outcomes.*

3. *It may be more interesting and productive to take an offensive position rather than the customary defensive approach to a registered concern or issue. Develop a cooperative and tactful opportunity for the influencer to meet with you to hear and discover the origin of the expressed concerns.*

4. *Provide private thinking time in recognizing that every effect has a cause. List the underlying premises that might assure accurate conclusions as you assess the motivations of those registering their impact on a program.*

5. *Develop a data bank supporting at least two expressed points of view. Summarize your findings and test your evidence with trusted colleagues. If the influencer is amenable to a follow-up meeting, it may be possible to work out differences at your level, assuming the motivations of both parties are sincere and not directed at the mere desire to control.*

EXPOSURE VERSUS EXPLOSIONS

Several statements have been made in previous sections of this chapter indicating that confrontation should be open and should be based on rational consideration. It was indicated that confrontation avoidance stimulates those who want to exercise an impact on the school and the education program.

Unmet personal expectations usually stimulate a sense of frustration. Those in the environment or within the school organization, who prefer some goals and procedures not presently a part of the program, may feel a growing sense of frustration because their expectations are not receiving attention and action. Frustrations often lead to an attack that may or may not be a rational process or result in a desired outcome. Frustration has to be worked off in some way. It is not very effective simply to say, "Forget it." People do not forget it. The work-off targets usually are those persons or things perceived as the cause of the unfulfilled expectation. This means that the frustration being worked off will have some target in order to relieve the sense of frustration. People in the professional organizations must give some thought as to how frustrations can be disarmed. One recommended approach to disarmament would be evidence and action. If the unfulfilled expectations can be defined, a means can be worked out to collect the available evidence. Then, you can interpret the evidence and act. This can be a positive way of disarming those who have frustrations due to unfulfilled expectation.

Administrators, supervisors, and teachers also can help those in the school's environment by presenting information on the bad along with the good. Somehow, when this is done, people are convinced that a straightforward operation is taking place and they have more patience to wait for the resolution of the problems that result in their unfulfilled expectations. Many reports, scheduled and delivered, can help the people in the community as well as the people within the professional organization to maintain more balance in viewing and attacking those things that need development and remediation. Exposure is the recommended, positive way of preventing frustrations that lead to explosions. Cooperation becomes the possibility and rewarding interaction the probability.

Examples of Strategy

1. *Make a list of your own frustrations. Select one and find the cause for it. Analyze the evidence and develop a plan of action to dissolve or reduce the amount of frustration.*

2. *Ask department heads or chairpersons to have their groups list their frustrations, analyze them either as a group or individually, and develop plans for action to dissolve or reduce the amount of the frustration.*

3. *Attempt to define the frustrations of small minority groups within your educational community who want to influence the educational program, but have been unsuccessful. List alternatives to their strategies that may make them more successful in the future.*

4. *Identify individual colleagues whom you believe may not be supportive of your program specialty or approach to teaching or supervising. Develop a plan for providing support of that other person's area of interest. Volunteer help at that person's activities through classroom cooperative efforts or working at student public performance activities may provide an opportunity for developing a mutual feeling of respect. Once the initial barriers are removed it may be possible to develop a caring and sharing relationship.*

5. *Develop a department or course "sunshine approach" to teaching. Invite other professionals to attend special student achievement or performance sessions. Make a special effort to share with them the revealed weaknesses of the work as well as the strengths. Treat visitors as "experts in residence" and seek their reactions or inputs that might strengthen your work. Offer your services to reciprocate.*

BUT ACCOUNTABILITY MUST BE

The discussions throughout this chapter on the multifaceted phenomena related to accountability might lead some readers to view accountability systems as a hopeless enterprise. Such is not the intent of the authors. The intent of the chapter is to analyze many of these facets so that they will be considered as people approach the responsibilities of achieving accountability programs.

Accountability has always existed in some form. As indicated earlier, it was a management control instrument and perhaps that caused accountability to gain a rather unsavory implication. On the other hand, when accountability systems were used primarily as sanction systems, reward and penalty were the dominant characteristics of the action. This has been shifting over the past decades and accountability systems are now becoming instruments by which improvement programs are instituted and carried forward. Accountability in this sense has a positive purpose and even though many of the facets discussed earlier still exist, they now can be resolved by more humanistic approaches. Certainly the accountability systems of recent years have been much more humanistic in purpose and in operation.

The support variables indicated earlier have not entered accountability considerations nearly as much as they should. The working conditions and the requisite materials for successful operation of an education program are now being viewed and to some extent weighted as the results are recorded, reported, and interpreted.

The responsibilities of the professional staff are being subjected to more careful definition and these descriptions are being communicated to people who would alter or direct their own efforts to influence on the basis of those descriptions. At any rate, it is much easier for positive confrontation to lead to cooperation between members of the professional staff and between the professional staff and the community.

Ways have not been found to reach those who are operating at a far distance from the scene of instructional effort, such as in the national or state capitol. A substitute is needed for the proximity that makes more interaction possible and leads to better accountability practices. In summary, we should be spending time defining the process of accountability rather than distorting or destroying it with the burdens of the past that are not sufficiently sound to merit continuance. An accountability system must be developed based on knowledge and skills.

This chapter, of necessity, included many references to and examples of the negative aspects of contact in the accountability system. Although these alerts seemed essential, it is pleasant to turn now to the delightfully positive aspects of inter-relationships. Chapter 14, Direction Through Indirection, provides these positive outlooks.

MORE READING FACETS

Bell, Terrel H. *A Performance Accountability System for School Administrators.* West Nyack, New York: Parker Publishing Company, Inc., 1974.

Browder, Lesley H., Jr. *Emerging Patterns of Administrative Accountability.* Berkeley: McCutchan Publishing Corporation, 1971.

House, Ernest R., ed. *School Evaluation: The Politics and Process.* Berkeley: McCutchan Publishing Corporation, 1973.

Sciara, Frank J., and Richard K. Jantz. *Accountability in American Education.* Boston: Allyn & Bacon, Inc., 1972.

The Report of the President's Commission on National Goals. *Goals for Americans.* Administered by The American Assembly, Columbia University, 1960.

Direction Through Indirection

The closing paragraphs of the preceding chapter, "Multifaceted Accountability," focused on the tension potential of direct expectation pressures from many sources. Inferences were made that the accountability system should be modeled more in the pattern of a research laboratory and less like a shooting gallery. This implies a softening of the hard directiveness of power, command, one-way communication, and control by reward and punishment. It implies increased use of the indirectiveness of joint inquiry, analysis, exploration of alternatives, and collaboration as the dominant work motif. The discussion of many potentials for greater productivity are presented here as Direction Through Indirection.

The new systems procedures assure more efficient methods for evidencing accountability and visibility to those inside and outside the ongoing daily activities of the classroom. The procedures also assist as a continuous reminder of the cause-effect relationships and the need to establish goals or targets. The ingrained goals of past decades have acquired different dimensions as society and institutions interpret to each other their perceived needs. The fears induced by a computer mechanized age or imaged robotry are being deferred, if not overcome, by those in this age who are devoting needed attention to the needs of the individual. The industrial model of cutting from the same pattern is being replaced by the laser model where unique differences are nurtured and developed at a more efficient rate than in previous industrial years. The innumerable methods that might be deployed for the achievement of goals, and the incumbent indirection, requires a new mode of operation that ultimately will assure that targets are identified and hit. The social science developments that cause a renewed concern for the individual will not stand alone as the assurance of goal attainment. Nourishing human relationships may do little more than raise the happiness quotient among role incumbents unless direction can be achieved through what may be termed operational indirection. Shakespeare's Hamlet declared, "By indirections find directions out" (act 2, scene 1).

The purpose of this chapter is to reduce the fog level that exists in complex organizations such as school districts in order to assure the achievement of desired goals. School district citizens, including board members, often assume that through the use of delegation the administrator is in a position to control the school district completely, even to the last detail of classroom activity. Many facets of delegation were discussed in chapter 9. It is not enough, however, to delegate with clarity and to exercise the power of the delegated office to impose influence, restrictions, or conditions of performance on delegatees. The way that the delegation is accomplished is a greater determiner of the quality of outcomes than the evidence and use of power.

History reveals a time when the direction or focus of the educational mission was determined by those at the top of the formal organizational chart. The determination of the course, and the modes for arriving at predetermined points, were dictated in a direct and presumably efficient manner. In more recent times, social observers have learned substantively about the nature of the human being and the positive influence that each individual can have on the achievement of organizational direction, if permitted and motivated to do so. With this backdrop in mind, the authors are suggesting a process of finding direction through indirection. The historic reliance on formal power structure to achieve administrator conceived missions is tempered and redirected through the strategy of indirection.

Direction can be defined as the point toward which a district faces or the line along which actions move. Direction is the thread of continuity that influences the way in which decisions are made, the quality of decisions rendered, and the targets to be met.

Indirection can be defined as a strategy of positive influences that is evidence based, tapping the human resources wherever they may exist, and that bears on the actions, resolution of issues, and the achievement of district missions (directions). It is the cultivation of interaction leading to staff congruence of direction, without undue reliance on the organizational hierarchy. It is based on the ability to motivate action through persuasion of or coalition with others.

Implementing the system of indirection as explored in this chapter becomes increasingly paramount as we view the age in which we live. The era of authoritative leadership and tight bureaucratic patterns has been replaced through political influence and the evolution of collective bargaining. Goal creation and achievement often have become obfuscated by state and federal legislation. This has increased over the years to permit, if not require, school boards to negotiate with employees for increased salaries and improved working conditions. Recent rulings by employment commissions and state departments of education have clarified, with broad interpretation, the areas that are negotiable. Policy issues that were heretofore left to school boards and administrators to establish are, in many instances, codetermined with the employee groups. It is amid these political realities that every school district must create a system of assurances that will guarantee the direction necessary to achieve goals and fulfill essential missions.

ENGINEERING FOR RESULTS

Engineering the orderly growth and development of any system requires that all parties to the institutional activity possess uniformly accepted goals. There can be no accountability unless some consensus is reached regarding goals and goal priorities. When the superintendent declares that the primary function of department heads is to supervise instruction, and the department heads believe the primary function is to teach, it may mean the pursuance of a collision course. One useful activity that can prevent incongruencies between administrators and staff in determining work priorities is the auditing of a specified number of goals and their placement in terms of priorities. The goal clarity that evolves from discussions among peers regarding work priorities can be particularly beneficial to the system. Department heads could review their mission and establish priorities to determine whether goal congruence exists among staff members. A partial list of missions to be reviewed for goal congruence could include some or all of the following: (1) supervising instruction, (2) teaching, (3) budgeting responsibilities, (4) developing curriculum materials, and (5) coordinating the curriculum within the department. The auditing of goals and their priorities may have a direct bearing on the management of the individual staff member's day. The establishment of meaningful priorities in terms of urgency and triviality should form the mission and goal analyses. This holistic focus will superimpose a directional compass on subsequent day-to-day activity, where the complexity of issues at times transcends understanding. An identification of employee priorities to achieve mission congruence will assist in building an undergirding of purpose that will expose complex intersystem relationships and the hazards of linear, single focus answers or direction. The identification of priorities may serve effectively and indirectly to direct thought to the essentiality of goal agreements among staff members.

Most administrators who engineer for positive results will recognize the importance of rapport and the need for loyalty. Perhaps all leaders believe that they possess some degree of charisma that causes others to be positively influenced and directed. It is well recognized that legitimizing, by sensitivity to the needs and interests of others, provides an indirect route to a deference for authority. The ability to detect the level of deference to authority that may exist in people is a task for the administrator. A high sensitivity to the personal and professional contingencies among coworkers can influence whether mutual goal acceptance will evolve and whether these goals will be met. Patience and understanding must prevail to avoid the temptation of using the power of position for the purpose of controlling others. The temptation prevails to give advice and "lay it on" rather than induce suggestions and "pull it out" of the other persons.

Militancy among people in diverse assignments may be symptomatic of prevailing conditions that produce dissatisfaction. The overt contingencies for which people work, such as, salary and fringe benefits, now appear to be hygienic items that are not necessarily related to job satisfaction. The more covert contingencies related to working conditions, such as, the assurance of identity, that affect one's sense of fulfillment and job satisfaction in the education profession, appear to merge as staples for the future. Certain controls or assurances of continuity may enhance the personal and professional relationships between members of the organizational groups. Administrative operational systems can influence the extent and maintenance of personal and professional identity. It is important that every staff member feels personal as well as professional worth and dignity. The objective is to have all educators feel that they are a part of the decision-making team and capable of identifying with ongoing organizational goals and objectives of the school system. The superordinate-subordinate, parent-child relationship is no longer, if it ever was, an acceptable base for leadership. Nor is such a relationship acceptable between school boards and professional employees.

Direction is given by initiating action on a task that needs to be accomplished. Instead of giving the answers, you cause the staff to seek the solutions. The administrator's role in indirection is to see to it that time is allotted and necessary funds, materials, and facilities provided to carry out the task. Staff members should be helped to feel their part in decision making.

Examples of Strategy

1. *Invite the staff to review or develop position descriptions and determine areas of priority that will lead to goal/objective accomplishment.*

2. *Select a smaller group to study the position descriptions and priorities as an outgrowth of the above strategy. Assign this group the tasks of finding the overlaps and omissions and preparing a report for the total staff involved in this activity.*

3. *Ask an administrative group and a teacher group to review past issues in collective bargaining, as presented by either teachers or mid-management groups. What issues are oriented toward personal fulfillment that are congruent, and can be classified as impetus for needed direction, with the goals/objectives of the school district.*

AUTHORITY RELATIONSHIPS

The people who are part of an organization and who are expected to influence the organizational action must have a clear view of authority relationships, powers, and influences. Duncan defined an authority relationship as an interpersonal relationship in which one person is given the right to make selected decisions that affect another person's behavior.[1] Written and unwritten authority is given and assumed by role incumbents. A principal or assistant principal may, for example, exercise the authority to establish a duty roster for other building employees. The limits of that authority may be determined formally and legally in a negotiated master contract identifying the type of duty to be performed, a plan for the division of labor that could identify those qualifying for such deployment, and the minimum and/or maximum duty to be performed. Regular nonemotional channels could be used to submit a duty roster at preestablished intervals. This could be referred to as maintaining a low level of interpersonal tension. The use of general and impersonal rules keeps the power relations visibility low, avoiding personal employee confrontation.[2] If, on the other hand, the authority figure waited until the week, day, or hour of the duty and informally approached the employee and ordered the person to perform, it could be interpreted as an authoritarian action, which is decidedly different from the normal, prudent exercise of authority. Timing of assignments, then, is related to the indirectness and directness of action.

Some people spend much time pursuing the outer limits of their authority, like those members of the animal kingdom who would rather fight for an expansion of territory than spend time using the previously claimed area. There are those who use their power indiscrimin-

1. James K. Duncan, "The Curriculum Director in Curriculum Change," *The Educational Forum*, vol. 27, no. 1, November 1973, p. 62.

2. Lawrence W. Downey and Frederick Enns, *The Social Sciences and Educational Administration* (The Division of Educational Administration, The University of Alberta, Edmonton, Canada, 1963), p. 17.

ately, rather than assume that authority is given to provide an orderly vehicle for decision making and operational efficiency and effectiveness. This misuse or abuse of power, in some cases, often has given rise to a redistribution of power in many areas with guarantees of due process, grievance procedures, and other legal or formal and informal agreements. The responsibility of the administrator to assign duties can be accomplished with little use of direct power. If the decision is made to assign a teacher to a duty relating to an activity that is controlled by certification requirements, the administrator has no power to violate the certification code. The formal power limits are prescribed and the administrator has authority to exercise only that power given in such a case. There also may be informal power limitations influenced by the physiological or psychological needs of the employees affected by certain duty assignments. The proper exercise of power takes into account these employee needs so that power and authority are in complementary relationships.

Few decisions are made that can occur in isolation from other related issues and their consequences. The art of compromise and the necessity for group consensus should be assessed regularly. Skills in two-way communication, coping calmly with conflict, and surveying individual and group feelings or actions are vital to legitimate helmsmanship at all levels within an organization. The ability to discern similarity of positive underlying feelings and to paraphrase consensing notions can bring individuals together to achieve common purposes within the organization. The indirect channels of creative returns can optimize effective decision making where others feel that they are making important contributions to the system and the management can be assured that issues are resolved. This does not presume that preconceived answers are patently established by the administrator, who seeks subsequent acceptance for a precast point of view or personal bias. It does mean that the leader brings together issues so that others can view a pattern for decision making that is clearly, simply, and briefly conceived.

Cases can be cited where some group members have assumed control over others that extended beyond the needs of the organization. New social models and the perpetuation of collective bargaining, however, have come to the forefront in recent decades to reverse the condition and obfuscate the whole issue of management control as though it were unnecessary. It is necessary that the pendulum return to the center point in order to focus on meeting both the needs of the organization and the needs of the individual. Control is not to be construed as a tight, inflexible programmed system of tying down everything that might come loose. Confidence in those around the administrator cannot be blind faith, but one that is rational and based on reason. The teacher may know a given subject far better than the supervisor or administrator. It is to be remembered that the controls must reflect the fact that superordinate, peer, and subordinate relationships are, at all times, realized and assumed by each. The alternating roles can be filled while recognizing the need for interaction and self-stimulated creative responsibility on the part of all parties to the educational process.

Examples of Strategy

1. Identify for your staff the legislation and other regulations that affect each position. Include local, regional, state, and federal levels. Ask all staff members to study their position descriptions in light of your statements and to make the necessary modifications. Discuss changes in a staff meeting.

2. Ask a small group to review the negotiated contract and determine operational management rights and the extent to which they prevail. Make the results a topic of discussion for a staff meeting.

INFLUENCE AND INFLUENCED

Persons have been influenced in their thinking and behavior by people who used neither power nor authority to affect the behavior, just as everyone has at some time influenced the thought and behavior of others when they had neither the authority nor the power to do so. Most persons derive personal satisfaction from the exercise of influence and participation in mutual influence relationships. The development of influence relationships, as discussed in detail in chapter 5, takes time; time to develop the mutual trust and respect that are essential to effective influence. The position of superintendent or principal carries with it some degree of authority and power, but an undetermined margin of influence. Administrators must realize that they start from where the group is. When a group has been accustomed to rigid control, with no opportunity for initiative or responsibility, giving complete responsibility in the beginning would only result in a laissez-faire situation. In such cases, responsibility must be extended gradually with careful encouragement and opportunities for leadership given to the group members. Only insofar as leaders are responsive to the influence of the people being led, can they expect employees to submit productively to the exercise of authority and power. The greater the degree to which mutual influence exists, the greater the probability that the leader's exercise of power and authority will be effective in changing the behavior of the people with whom the leader works.

Power and authority usually are viewed together. The right to make decisions usually is accompanied by the power to force others to act according to the decision. It is the presence of significant amounts of influence that makes the exercise of power and authority tolerable. Influence is a mutual and reciprocal relationship; one of the surest measures of this relationship is to assess the degree to which the leader has been influenced by members of the staff. A leader must be sensitive, both emotionally and rationally, to interpersonal relationships. Influence is a potent skill of indirection in the administrative process.

Examples of Strategy

1. *Identify the subpublics of your school district that have major influence in policy formulation. Select groups within the district and ask each group to study one subpublic and note the means it uses to influence school policy. Use the staff meeting to analyze results.*

2. *Identify informal leaders who have developed mutual trust and respect from peers and identify the origin of that respect. Recommend these leaders to various groups working on problems significant to them.*

LEADERSHIP AND AUTHORITY

Research has been accomplished that identifies various types of leadership styles. It is assumed that the self-identification of leadership styles employed by a role incumbent is a healthy and potentially constructive venture. There seems little reason to assume that the administrator will improve in performance unless that person is cognizant of the leadership styles employed and at times audits the extent of success or failure.

This chapter is not intended to review the literature related to leadership theory and what is known about leadership today. We recognize that every leader identifies acts to be accomplished and chooses, consciously or unconsciously, the behavior to be employed. Theoretical background and practical skill will arm the leader but provides no assurance of control or guarantees of influence in the ongoing operation. The feelings and attitudes in personal relationships are covert requisites to be dealt with in influencing behavior. The potential for acts of indirection prevail and may serve as control elements. Many unidentified influences bring about change and affect control and direction. Predetermined conditions and relationships can influence decisions and thus control. The acceptance of the influence can be affected by whether freedom in decision making prevails, even if minutely related to the ultimate decision. The assumption is that direction must be accomplished by recognizing basic human needs, such as, worth, respect, dignity, autonomy, and security. It is then assumed that control success is influenced by the expertise the administrator has gained through formal education or experience; but variables within each unique school district will call for a sensitivity to the potential for control through indirection.

Authority role incumbents must permit task/role exchanges so that, depending on the direction of the problematic wind, the seeds of resolution will be sown by those individuals in the best position to contribute professional strength, thus causing the notions to germinate and grow to fruition. An authority relationship can be established without resorting to authoritarianism. Adults working within organizational structures are, all too frequently, treated like children. As a result, their overall growth potential is either overlooked or only partially realized. The parent-child relationship referred to earlier, which at one time prevailed between teachers and administrators, is being dissipated perhaps due to the expansion of unionism and the collective bargaining process. The gentility of indirection, nonetheless, remains an active element in administrator-teacher relationships.

Others can be influenced when administrators proceed through logic and truth. Administrators must avoid the temptation to dabble with interesting programmatic seeds that have begun to germinate and develop a useful root structure. To step in at unannounced times, or to pursue the resolution of issues in areas delegated to someone else, may result in plowing under rather than cultivating. It takes time to develop consistent working relationships that build the trust, confidence, and respect so essential in terms of control effectiveness.

Ways to delegate with systematically designed reporting schedules that continually provide feedback will provide necessary progress information. The administrator in the higher authority role often may not exhibit proper confidence or may tamper with the decision-making process to reap personal reward. There are some who just want to bask in other peoples' successes. This close proximity to the action, if exerted with spontaneous direction, can be destructive to the ongoing processes. It could be said in paraphrasing that, if you "smell the rose of classroom activity" too extensively, it may be killed for lack of oxygen.

Administrator confidence in employees is necessary but not blind. People tend to fulfill expectations of them. When people are made to feel they need to be pushed or watched over, they incline toward dependency and lack of individual initiative. The feeling that others have extended confidence in them, and expect important contributory production, promotes independent personal and potentially collective positive contributions.

Griffiths said that, "Good human relations in administration are (sic) built upon a firm foundation of mutual respect, good will, and faith in the dignity and worth of human beings as individual personalities. It is further necessary for the administrator to develop skills in relating himself and others to the social situation in which they are placed."[3] Leadership styles will vary among and between administrators, but should be employed in all instances to influence behavior through logic or truth.

Examples of Strategy

1. Analyze in-service programs for administrators to determine the various leadership styles in which the methods of indirection can be identified.

2. Trace the development and rationale of midmanagement collective bargaining processes throughout the country since 1950. What are the motivations for this development?

3. Circulate to professional staff members a copy of a matrix listing an array of alternatives based on facts available to assure intended consequences in an operational decision. Seek reactions from staff to suggest, on the basis of evidence, the optimum answers in the decision.

POSITIVE AND NEGATIVE INDIRECTION

The assumption should not be made that control through indirection will bring about positive results. The attitude and motivation behind the individual employing the system will make a great difference. Control through indirection can be negative and bring about tight, inflexible, fearful, and sterile behavior. The identifying signs of negative indirection are the sowing of seeds of fear and despair with self-imposed, contrived, or real emergencies. Crisis management should be reserved for the unavoidable crisis. The creation of dependency and immobilization can bring about decisions that are controlled by the instigator. The instigator of negative indirection could emerge at any level within the school organization. The person using this condition of chaotic hopelessness probably seeks some self-perception as being the master mind of the organization.

The method of negative indirection to bring about control could be further identified by the type of questions asked or responses given by the individual. The induced dependency is obvious in questions or responses such as:

"If it were me, here's how I'd do it."

"Do you understand?"

"You don't have to take this suggestion, but—"

---

3. Daniel E. Griffiths, *Human Relations in School Administration* (New York: Appleton-Century-Crofts, Inc., 1956), p. 17.

"If you were to ask me —"

"My experience tells me —"

"If I were to do it —"

The importance of the above telltale signs as indicators of induced dependency is obvious. Many basic physiological and hygienic needs have been provided for and are nurtured in a continuing fashion through the collective bargaining process. Human contingencies that are now emerging include esteem, love, appreciation, and belongingness. These human needs are not always nourished by leaders representing the interests of employers or employees. The seeds of mistrust can be sown by anyone. Leaders in the negotiation process, on either side of the table, can and in cases have created a following of employees motivated by fear and seeking a feeling of esteem and belongingness. The power or "clout" that certain individuals might have because of their election or appointment to the negotiations team can be misused in an effort to gain allegiances and alliances that encourage adversary relationships and counter-splinter groups.

The use of indirection should be understood and nourished for positive use if administrators are seeking truth and a higher level of humaneness. Cultivating the unique qualities of the individual and nourishing positive contributions can add to the fulfillment of personal and professional aspirations and especially to the good health of the institution. The method of positive indirection can be nourished with control assurances permitted in evidence-based questions such as the following:

"What is the history of —?"

"What are some ways listed in priority order for achieving the goal?"

"What are the short- and long-range effects of this decision?"

"Is it possible to cross-reference the variables on a matrix in order to view and weigh alternatives?"

The questions people ask are endemic telltale signs of whether positive or negative controls might be instituted in the process of indirection. Administrators should undergird their daily operating practices with the notion that they learn more by asking questions than giving answers. Platonic questioning is a valuable tool in "pulling out" the thoughts prevailing within the human mind.

Cultivating our sensitivity to the beauty in life and the need for humane feelings is basic. The philosopher Whitehead recognized this in his aphorism, "Culture is activity of thought and receptiveness to beauty and humane feelings." Search for the good and the beautiful — lift our eyes from the gutters and cast them on the gardens. Positive, optimistic, and high expectation attitudes are contagious, as are negative, pessimistic, low level attitudes of expectation. The sincere smile and the bleak frown are seeds that will grow and determine the crop nurtured in the institutions. There is a continuous need to "accentuate the positive," as the old song said. The power of positive influence will go far in the pursuit of organizational goals.

Control is an implicit constant at work in the lives of people, and it begins very early in life. There is no way to absent manipulation of people/people intervention in our lives. Developments in media in the past decade clearly show that large numbers of people can be and are being influenced and, in a sense, controlled. Behavior control is inevitable.

Complete freedom of choice rarely exists, although some freedom of choice must exist for an individual to maintain human dignity. The realities of control are dynamic and the danger of self-righteousness must be recognized. Control must be exercised to assure rationality. When instituting the process of indirection, it is assumed that what is best for the individual and/or institution may very well be identified by anyone inside or outside the formal organization. It is necessary to recognize that the incumbent leader exercises product control while working within the organization, as discussed in chapter 9. If the controls foster the achievement of the process contingencies that teachers, administrators, and supervisory personnel are seeking, they can be justified. Good ideas come from people in all organizational categories. The administrator must not suffer from what Dale called, "hardening of the categories."[4]

Developing human relation skills implies the use of skills to influence positively the organization in which one works. If employees at all levels feel that they and the organization (school district) are one, it is reasonable to conclude that each will feel responsible for monitoring and improving the system. The scientific listener, who audits and records the concerns and priorities of those who are part of the school district and the respective publics, must have the integrity to manage the system honestly, without voicing what people want to hear while accomplishing a separate list of self-conceived purposes. The fear exists for some social scientists that the knowledge they are providing about influencing and controlling people may be used for more effective manipulation of human behavior.

Identifiable behaviors exist within every organization that will inhibit goal attainment. There is no better way to suppress behaviors that interfere with goal attainment than to reinforce opposite behaviors. Negative direction is normally met with negative reactions and

---

4. Edgar Dale, *The Humane Leader,* The Phi Delta Kappa Educational Foundation (Bloomington, Indiana, 1974), p. 17.

actions. Indirectly, positive reinforcement will motivate desired behaviors and prevent actions counter to the best interests of the school. Do not overlook the fact that persons other than the appointed authority may indirectly fulfill the control function. Loyal employees, understanding the accepted policies, will fulfill control functions, particularly if they were a party to the creation of processes to fulfill the missions. This mode of indirectly controlling the operation will permit the administrator to retain a reserve power, or another level of control, for use at more critical times. The overuse of direct control can weaken the system. Complex relationships become all too obvious as the incumbents in intermediate positions exercise their individual attitudes and characteristic operational differences.

The control function will rest with different members and different areas of staff members. System adjustments will occur as individuals and groups generate the knowledge and competence to fulfill the control function. Every individual has specific assigned tasks. Although they are not often reviewed and overtly identified, job expectations vary greatly even among teachers in any given school system. Co-opting the sources of strength in the system, namely those incumbents in their individual positions, can provide a framework for an indirect control mechanism. A basic understanding of system evidence-based, decision-making procedures will enhance the willingness to support and control at all levels. It will form a base from which the employee can carve out "a portion of the kingdom" and, in a sense, "be somebody" when given the authority and identified responsibility for controlling. The subliminal teaching of "we, our" attitudes replaces "I, me, mine" attitudes when control and the power to bring it about are not personalized.

Perhaps it is natural for those anticipating leadership positions to identify with discernible levels of influence or control. No one brings about lack of influence and control more quickly than the person who internalizes situations by behavior revealed in an overt-broadcast "I, me" approach to colleagues. The tendency to collect regular dividends for the successful resolution of issues endangers the continued good health of the control agent and, potentially, the enterprise or school district. The individual, therefore, runs the risk of being included in society's list of endangered species. The administrative willingness to distribute positive dividends to others who were part of successful experiences will gain the respect and support of employees. The administrator will gain power from those who have received fair and rewarding treatment.

Open, well-communicated signs of objectivity in decision making must be conveyed to those affected. The suspicion among subordinates of an administrator's personal motivations in decision making is stilled by a high confidence atmosphere, nourished by well-communicated objectivity in decision making. Needless to say, counter forces are always at work to raise questions and possibly suspicions regarding the motivations of leadership to make certain decisions. Dispelling idle gossip and potentially damaging rumors can be accomplished best by factual and unquestionable revelation of the variables involved, and the positive and negative effects that influenced the final decision. Productive and contributing working relations depend on acceptance of the notion of standing on each others' shoulders to enhance the organization's view or overall vision. This enables the tapping of individual resources within the organization to maximize efficiency and effectiveness.

Examples of Strategy

1. *Review with selected staff members examples of negative indirection and develop strategies to correct and make them positive direction modes of action.*

2. *Create good news informal meetings in order to share and support positive contributions.*

3. *Identify a position taken on a current issue by subpublics and identify the strategies of negative indirection employed. Determine what conversions would be necessary to bring about a mode of positive indirection.*

CLIMATE FOR CONTROL

Any workable or acceptable educational program thrust should reflect the following considerations:

Need—does it exist?

Substance—does it address the need?

Process—will it facilitate the implementation of the substance?

Staff—who is going to do what?

Clientele—who is going to be affected by the action?

Each school district, as well as each attendance center and individual classroom, will contain specific and diverse needs. Controls must relate to the self-perceived needs of those who are role incumbents in each setting. The administrative capability of identifying perceived needs will help determine whether satisfactory resolutions will be obtained through the custom-devised control mechanisms.

The relationships between district and staff needs must be brought into proximity in order to satisfy the needs of each. Improved personal and district images must be a part of all plans to be implemented. Controls should be flexible or discreet enough to deal adequately with broad issues, as well as special problems that may arise.

A common system of sharing information should be cultivated initially to find a direction that is properly influenced by the parties affecting the decision. This type of procedure, coupled with broad use of staff members in ad hoc functions, will assist in identifying specific competencies people can bring to bear on problem resolution. This also will prevent the continuation of outdated policy and assure a live, dynamic, future-oriented operation.

Drawing information from a base of individual strength will assure the district of better decision making since it reflects a system of competency-based professional input. The total saturation of staff involvement will assure the continual and fearless sifting and winnowing that results in truth and commonly accepted results. It is within this climate that the process of indirection can best serve individuals and organizations.

Examples of Strategy

1. *List the formal organizational assignments made to individual teachers and invite each to estimate the relationships between assignment demands and their perceptions of their related expertise.*

2. *Review an item in the negotiated teacher contract and identify the obstacles and the benefits to the tasks to be accomplished by midmanagement.*

SOME PRACTICAL THOUGHTS

People at times naturally have feelings of failure, insecurity, hopelessness, uncertainty, resentment, and frustration. All people should develop a sense of direction, understanding, courage, charity, self-esteem, and self-confidence.

Someone once said, "No one plans to be dependent, but yet no one becomes independent without a plan." There must be a feeling of human independence in the organization, not only for personal happiness but for organizational enhancement.

Administrators can no longer be reluctant to know well the individuals with whom they work. Social distance should not necessarily be a requirement among superordinate role incumbents. Administrators must examine and ameliorate the ways in which they can develop productive relationships. The notion that friendships will hinder working relationships, or that praise will end productivity, must be seriously questioned.

Administrators must examine and in some cases restructure concepts of control. The inspectorial know-it-all, authority image must be replaced by systematic operating practices that call for mutual goal focusing and discernible targeting where objectives are visibly met.

All staff members must agree to differentiated treatment based on diagnostic reviews. Prognosticating is required continually to perceive long-range goals that are based on policy expectations.

A consistent administrative behavior should prevail, sprinkled with the ingredient of humility, which reveals at all levels in the hierarchy a willingness to be subservient to issues and evidence-based answers to achieve common goals. Everyone optimally should be able to feel powerful and contributory to the daily operation. Every human being can unleash valuable thoughts, words, and deeds if permitted and encouraged to do so. Each must be responsive to the issues and controls, which they had a part in developing, rather than to an artificial responsibility to someone. Administrators must recognize the relevancy of complex individual and organizational matters that transcend administrative understanding. This means that in large organizations it is not functionally possible to control all essential matters in the ongoing operation through a direct line-staff hierarchy and linear, single focus answers. Personality and unique patterns of behavior are underlying strengths to be harnessed by clarity of goals and shared responsibility for developing and implementing the processes that achieve the missions. Administrators must recognize that there are more similarities than differences among professional educators, and that evidence-based decision making promotes respect and trust. Open and honest systems of communication can keep alive the channels of understanding and the levels of interest in promoting and improving the system. This open communication system may promote more secure, cooperative, and helpful members. The administrator, of necessity, must know how the total system operates and be able to predict the effects of changes in subsystems on the total system. Providing incentives or contingencies that promote the worth, respect, dignity, autonomy, and security of individuals will encourage and stimulate indirect action by employees to fulfill the missions of the institution and those of the individual—that of being human.

Direction can best be achieved through indirection—the strategy of positive influence, which is evidence based and cognizant of human resources wherever they exist, brought to bear on the actions, the resolution of issues, and the achievement of missions. The process of indirection requires the cultivation of interaction, leading to employee congruence of direction without undue reliance on the organizational hierarchy. The system of indirection can be a key to success as one cultivates the ability to motivate action through persuasion or coalition with others.

Many characteristics of interaction between persons and within groups have been explored in this chapter. These characteristics can help chart the way to more productive outcomes of individual and group effort only if individuals develop the capacity to remake themselves as they fulfill the evolving expectations of the educational programs. The next chapter, "Directed Self-Management," takes up this challenge.

SOME DIRECTED READING

Dale, Edgar. *The Humane Leader.* The Phi Delta Kappa Educational Foundation, Bloomington, Indiana, 1974.

Downey, Lawrence, and Fredrick Enns. *The Social Sciences and Educational Administration.* The Division of Educational Administration, The University of Alberta, Edmonton, Canada, 1963.

Duncan, James K. "The Curriculum Director in Cirruculum Change," *The Educational Forum,* vol. 27, no. 1. November 1973.

Griffiths, Daniel E. *Human Relations in School Administration.* New York: Appleton-Century-Crofts, 1956.

Directed Self-Management

Direction points toward the goals that have been chosen for achievement. The procedures used in the selection of behaviors may be direct or indirect, as was discussed in the preceding chapter. The origins of those procedures may be identified in others, in self, or in a combination of the two. It seems desirable to increase the origin in self to the maximum. The central theme of this chapter is to explore some of the ways in which the individual might achieve more direction through self-management.

The members of a school organization are participants in an action. The action of concern here relates primarily to the development and maintenance of an instructional program that will yield the results that the sponsors of the school organization envisioned. These sponsors are the people of the community, the state, and the nation. It must be recognized that all participants in the school action constitute a focal point of concern, observation, and influence on the part of those within the organization as well as those who constitute the environment of the school.

The proprietors of the action within the organization constitute all personnel who have made a commitment to serve in that organization. It is unrealistic to regard the sole proprietor of action as a superordinate in the old bureaucratic sense. Bureaucratic relationships that prescribed a flow of authority, communication, and controls are no longer dominant and perhaps never were essential to the successful enterprise of education. Individuals in the action are proprietors of their own responsibilities and unique functions committed to and expected by the school organization. Anyone who hopes to live in isolation in a complex organization such as a school ought never to have accepted the responsibility and should immediately set about getting a clear picture of what the individual's purpose is in a group enterprise.

The involvement of many people requires that interaction occur between these people. As a matter of fact, interaction is essential to the success of the individual and of the group constituting the personnel of the organization. Simply stated, interaction calls for each person to share and to be shared. This does not indicate a loss of freedom and autonomy. It does not indicate that the individuals have to subdue themselves and be submissive to the group or group leaders. It does mean that each one contributes a unique function. This unique function is a sharing of individual expertise with the organization, and all those who are recipients of that sharing claim a part of each person in the interaction.

Each person must have had some unique talent to contribute to the purpose of organization or that person would not have been put under contract. Talent is like skill; if it is not used, it diminishes. Action in the pursuit of talent realization builds strength for the contributing individual and for the total organizational effort.

Each person must be aware of an employment ethic that is an obligation that must be met. The most basic ethic is the acceptance of a contract with the intention of going to work. People should not accept a contract expecting not to work at all or to work under self-chosen conditions that may not have been explicit at the time of the contract commitment. The disposition to work needs to become a part of the concern. Another concern is to work as an individual for the purposes of the organization. Anything short of this means that self-management has been directed as antagonistic to the organizational effort and the individual contribution to it. This is not the purpose of this chapter and it certainly is not the purpose of a contractual relationship.

Helping structures exist within the organization that support an individual's obligation to self-management. The first direction of self-management is found beyond the individual and in the structure of the organization . This structure usually is designed to support maximum self-management by every participant in the organization. A position name is a structural help. A description of the function related to that position is a structural help. The communication system is a structural help. The policies agreed on by the total organization constitute a part of the structure that helps individuals direct their self-management in terms of their responsibilities in the organization.

Directed self-management, in its simplest form, is self-help with a navigator. It simply means that individuals must accept the need for some direction from others. These directions need not be constrictive.

They probably are constrictive, more because of their rejection by an individual than by their intent to be directive in a positive way. Guides are useful in every activity. This chapter will explore some of the ways in which self-management is an acceptance of direction from others supplementing the direction given by oneself.

SOURCES OF DIRECTION

The laws, governmental regulations, and the courts are prime sources for the definition of the direction that each member of the school organization should go in order to fulfill the obligations of a contract. It is foolishly simplistic, however, to say that each individual under contract is responsible for knowing all of these legal obligations. Self-management requires some effort to gain such legal information but, at the same time, each person is entitled to help from specialized sources in the review and interpretation of these legal obligations. Directed self-management calls for the school organization to provide such specialized sources of information to clarify in meaningful terms to all participants what these legal directions are. At the same time, each participant in the organization must be willing to make some effort to understand what this specialized information constitutes.

Each person in the organization has a contracted commitment. This commitment is a source of direction. The individual's contract or the negotiated master contract involves many of the controls and directions by which management takes place. As each individual becomes a party to this understanding, each one has had the benefit of directed self-management. A contract should not be signed unless the signature is regarded as a moral and ethical bond to accept the contract as a source of direction in fulfilling obligations and commitments.

Another source of direction might be called advice and advisory pressures. Advice and advisory pressures can come from all quarters. Each individual's personal perceptions of the work obligation make a difference as to which advice and advisors are accepted and which are used to support the concept of self-management. Many who offer advice can be called "influential others." These influential others usually maintain that relationship to the individual not because of their positions but because the individual chooses to accept that influence. The people that you like can get to you. The people that you dislike need some assistance, other than personal likes, to register influence. Influential others, as a source of direction, can be a source of bias that makes for imbalance within an organization. A part of self-management should be the frequent evaluation of whether the individual is inclined to select a choice group of people who are able to direct the self-management efforts of that individual.

Another important source of direction is that of personal knowledge. It might be said, hopefully, that it is the chief resource for self-management. Personal knowledge, as inferred in an earlier statement in this chapter, may be a matter of the individual's effort to accept the information, direction, and advice that comes from others. As advice is received and information is contributed, the person's inclination to add this to their own stock of knowledge constitutes one of the more productive and certainly one of the safest sources of direction for self-management.

A source of direction can be found in the efforts to identify and evaluate alternative ways of doing things. This can be considered the essence of freedom and autonomy. There is little freedom and autonomy if individuals make a commitment to a predetermined posture and impose that posture on all tasks that are confronted. Direction thus becomes embalmed into one-wayism, making it impossible even to identify and to explore the value of alternatives.

Freedom and autonomy can be linked closely to the sources of direction that are accepted in the activities of self-management. The goals that are accepted as the individual enters into work obligations constitute a source of direction for self-management. These accepted goals become the individual's goals. It is less important to determine the source of the goals than to determine the acceptability of those goals. When the acceptability is satisfactory and the goals become the individual's own, the source of direction has been positively determined and progressively used. The nature of the directions chosen, as the ways of self-management are explored, constitutes one of the very interesting but complex sources of direction. The personal, organizational, and environmental purposes espoused by those who create and maintain the school as an organization are brought into positive relationships. These sources, and many more, need to be kept in mind as we continue to explore directed self-management as a resourceful way of bringing about the individual's maximum contribution to the organizational purposes. Conversely, the organizational structure and operational procedures are strong supports for the realization of individual participant's personal and professional purposes and goals.

Examples of Strategy

1. *Invite each staff member to list the legal constraints that are the most difficult to understand.*

2. *Investigate the administrative ramifications of a school district issuing individual teacher contracts when all teachers are included in a negotiated master contract.*

3. *Seek suggestions from the classified and unclassified staff of existing conditions that do not stand their tests of reasonableness in terms of personal management of some aspect of their job.*

4. Consider the employment of an informal reward system for staff who earnestly seek out input advice from a broad spectrum of sources to influence decision making. This system might encourage the facilitating, cohesing, evidence-based, decision-making habit to replace the "I-me" self-limiting system employed by those who believe it is unnecessary to stand on the shoulders of others to gain vision.

CONCEPT OF SELF-STATUS

Inferences and direct statements have been made in earlier sections of this chapter to the effect that much of the direction for self-management does and should come from the individual involved. The individual has some internal controls of this direction that need to be explored.

The concept of self-status is based on many factors, and these factors vary from individual to individual. Perhaps each person is concerned about the personal competency level expected in the work accepted. Each person wants to be competent and to be recognized as such. Each person also wants this competency to be at a high level of performance and outcome.

Much personal concern by individuals is directed to self-status, as it relates to the amount of goal control that is retained. Self-management is less challenging to those who believe they have no control over the goals they are supposed to pursue. The imposition of goals is not enough. The acceptance of goals is an absolute requirement if any freedom is realized and support through a certain degree of self-control over the goals established and against which competency levels are determined.

Each individual has a self-status concern in the perception and reality of acceptance as a group participant. The acceptance may be a matter of how others react, but it also is a matter of how individuals perceive others reacting to their contributions to the organizational effort. Close to this perception of the individual's participatory stature in the group is the peer respect that is gained and held. Peer respect can result from individual performances within the group, from the contribution as an individual occupied in a unique assignment, and from the overt interactions that occur between the individual and others in the group.

A part of the concept of self-status is found in the way persons see themselves as influencing goal determination and selection of alternative patterns of action. Self-status is tempered by the experiences of reinforcing associates in the organization, whether they are in the same work category or in some other discipline, such as, a teacher, supervisor, principal, or superintendent.

Another aspect of the concept of self-status is the way people see themselves as being influenced. Few people are happy when they realize that they have been influenced by somebody whom they do not respect. To say that it cannot happen is to ignore the characteristics of human nature. If an individual yields to the influence of another, because of the power presumed in a position or the prospect of advantage at some later time, self-respect and self-status have not been supported. Another facet of the concept of self-status is the proneness to fear what is not absolutely secured at any particular time. The proneness to fear undermines each individual's concept of self-status and consequently thwarts the ability to engage in self-management.

The vision of the future is another determiner of self-status concepts. Images of success and recognition are more acceptable than nightmares of failure and embarrassment. These images give much direction to the processes of self-management. Persisting images of the pleasing variety support a vigorous and enlightened type of self-management.

Examples of Strategy

1. *Ask staff members to identify one major area of work responsibility and to describe two aspects of it that they would like to have given recognition.*

2. *Survey the staff to determine understanding of goal direction, job description, and organizational format as a means to increase self-status.*

3. *Seek goal clarification recommendations from staff that relate an area of existing concern and the performance of present duties. Recognize by immediate feedback the receipt and/or acceptance of the recommendations.*

GOAL BALANCE

The trite and aged wheeze that, "You can't eat your cake and have it too," was worn out many generations ago. Once in awhile, it might be well to look at some of these trite statements to see whether there is a message for us in the present day. Many instances can be found in which people want too many things for themselves or want too many things from someone else. At the present time, one of the great global debates is whether there will be ample food to feed the people while the birthrate remains under natural controls. It is not our purpose to debate such issues. Rather, when trite or global concepts are related to the individual's own responsibility, the question can be raised in our day-to-day work whether there is an effort to secure more things than the individual's capacity can support or more things than the environ-ment is willing to see individuals possess.

Real problems are encountered in scrutinizing the goals that each person holds, as well as the goals held by an organizational entity. The habit of maintaining the concept of continuous growth is coming under careful scrutiny at the present time and seems to come as a great surprise to many educators. The declining enrollment demands skills, concepts, and values that are new and forces a new look at the things needed to be accomplished by individuals and organizations. There are constraint factors that properly can be con-sidered, such as, ethics, peer tolerance, institutional commitments, and limited expertise. It is not a waste of effort to consider these con-straint factors. It is the traditional defiance of no progress and no growth that causes most individuals to regard current situations as constraints that limit individual freedom and autonomy.

The concept of freedom and autonomy as a goal has led to some goal imbalances that need scrutiny at the present time. Ethics can help each individual to balance goals. Peers are going to be present as long as work progresses in a group situation. Institutional commitments will remain if the institution continues as a contractual agent for ser-vices of professionals. The matter of goal balance can be seen as a matter of negotiability. Individuals can negotiate in terms of their own strength versus their own desires. They can negotiate between the goals of an institution and the working comfort of the individual. Negotiability, in order to serve these purposes, must be seen as a pro-cess and not as a game. Negotiation at the present time, has become a goal in itself for many people. Their aim is to keep the negotiations open rather than to seek an acceptable end to them. In this case, nego-tiability does not serve to balance goals but rather serves as a game in which individuals on both sides of the table allow personal goals to dominate educational goals.

Goal balance can be served extremely well if the people involved have a certain amount of "yieldability." It is not possible to maintain an interactive group when certain members have no ability to yield, either to the privileged expression of other people or to the work-ability of their suggestions in their personal and professional life. Yieldability is basic to the process of association, association not in the sense of an organization but of people working together—people who can respect others enough to yield occasionally to their wishes and their advice. At all times, yielding to the possible resolution of dif-ferences allows the work of an organization to progress.

Goal balance is affected by the personality of the people involved, their individual goals, habits, skills, and sense of acceptable working conditions. Contracts, likewise, can have much to do with the balance of goals. If negotiated contracts have resulted from intelligent compromise and yieldability, it is possible to develop goal balance not only within the organization but also between the individuals and the organization. This means that the goals of the individuals and the institution can and must be related if goal balance is to be achieved with any degree of satisfaction and reward.

Personal purposes and goals envision a future and ways of accomplishing them. Nonetheless, as the individual seeks to accomplish personal goals, the action does not completely thwart or block the purposes and goals of other individuals or of the institution. The same kind of thought must be applied to institutional purposes and goals. It is just as unreasonable for an institution to place its own purposes and goals above those of the individuals working in that institution as it is for individuals to insist on their own particular brand of priorities with respect to goals.

Goal balance raises the issue of singularity and plurality. Isolation may be desired by some people, but isolation should not be sought in a group enterprise such as a school organization. Having chosen to work as professionals in a school organization, all members of that organization must recognize the plurality of goals when balance is sought. Morality, in this sense, means that modifications must be made by some and new potentials developed by others. Singularity can be applied only when one person with a single goal, which may have reached a balance with the organization, becomes an individual responsible for accomplishment of and contribution to the basic purpose of the institution.

Balance is multiple-ordered. There are many involvements as seen from the suggestions above. The most important thing is that a sense of good-for-all must be maintained at every level and in every aspect of the organizational enterprise and structure. The concept of good-for-all builds strength and satisfaction and, in this way, goal balance is more readily and satisfactorily achieved.

Examples of Strategy

1. *Offer illustrations of conflicting goals to the staff and invite suggestions for the resolution of such conflicts.*

2. *List the suggestions or expressions of others revealed during the most recent staff meeting that caused you to yield or compromise your position or action. Were there other expressions or suggestions that could or should have been compromised to some degree?*

3. *What first principles could be identified as being held in common, by individuals as well as by the institution, that might serve as a basis for reaching resolution of some recognized goal conflict.*

SELF-AUDITING

The concerns expressed about goal balance in the preceding section can be applied to the consideration of how people can be mutually helpful with respect to self-management that is supported by self- and alter-auditing. Auditing does take some specific expertise that must be available to all members of a staff. It should not be imposed entirely by the upper levels of hierarchy of the organization. Rather, it should involve the cooperative efforts of the expert person and the person seeking to do some self-auditing leading to self-management.

An auditor, when applying expertise, teaches other people how to self-audit. Moreover, the auditor, with the expertise in auditing, can apply the same skills to the self as are applied to others who are being audited. It becomes even more confusing (although simple in concept) to realize that an auditor can assist in the evaluation or auditing of the self-audits of others. If a skilled auditor can perform an audit independently, can help others to develop a self-audit, or can apply personal skills to a self-auditing process, then an audit of the self-audits of others becomes quite feasible. If the attitudes reflect a wholesome acceptance of auditing and self-auditing as the basis for self-management, there can be an extension of the expertise of the professional auditor. Above all, the professional auditor must not seek to maintain a high self-regard and an unreachable level of personal expertise by withholding that expertise and information from others. The mutuality of the tasks of auditing and self-auditing must be part of the concept of management in every possible aspect of individual and organizational effort.

Audit effectiveness depends on the maintenance of esteem while gathering data. Reference was made above to the professional auditor who might maintain self-esteem by withholding expertise from others. This defeats the effectiveness of an audit; it cannot maintain the esteem of those who are not expert in auditing and who ought to be encouraged to self-audit, something that cannot be done without the assurance of self-esteem. The discussion regarding the mutuality of the auditor and the audited, and the need to share auditing expertise with others, does not deny the fact that there are differing levels of skills. These skills must be recognized in a professional auditor and in a self-audit, regardless of the post within the school organization. It is hoped that these differences in skill levels can become a strength of mutuality, rather than something that divides people into contesting sections or warring camps. The whole point of this discussion is that auditing and self-auditing must be rewarding interactions between people on the staff. Those with auditing expertise must be accepted as people who can help. Those who have that expertise must share it with others so that the process of self-auditing can proceed. No one needs to worry that the expertise of auditing will become unnecessary eventually because the expertise has been transferred to the individual professionals in the organization.

Examples of Strategy

1. *Conduct a series of small group meetings in which an auditor could explain procedures and open opportunities for discussion.*
2. *Review professional workshops, seminars, and conferences for programs emphasizing auditing procedures.*
3. *Create "good news" sessions to share sucessful audit experiences of staff. The "care enough to share" sessions can provide a support mechanism that will filter through the informal organization.*

WORK PROCESSES

An extended discussion of work processes is found in chapter 7. These processes were identified as Managing, Influencing, Evaluating, and Planning. The concern here is that all of the supports to directed self-management must recognize these differing categories of work process. Each one has a different focus demanding a different set of skills, applications, and acceptances. So, do not regard self-management as one element of operation that is generally applicable to all responsibilities and behaviors within the school organizational activities.

Each of the work processes must be related to the position expectations. Thus, it means one thing for a teacher, quite another for a principal, another for a supervisor, still another for the central office administrators, and certainly another for the board of education and the people they represent. The analysis for directed self-management has many different facets, not only in process but also in focus, and these foci are identified in the categories of work process. A generalized concept at this point is that concern must be given to managing the process of management. This is part of the responsibility of every member of the professional staff. Each person, even though involved in the total management of the organization, performs further management in the unique responsibilities and expectations placed on the position held.

There needs to be some influence of the process of Influencing. Conversely, there must be influencing in the process of Influencing. The impact that one person makes on another, or one group on others, is part of the level of acceptance, the level of possible adaptation that is related to the power in the process of Influencing.

Evaluating the process of Evaluating is perhaps more extant in the total activities of evaluation than comparable relationships in the other categories of work process. Evaluating the process of Evaluating becomes one of the most important concerns in the direction of self-management.

Another responsibility is that of planning the process of Planning. Too often the process of Planning is started as an isolated action, even without considering the goal or the products that are intended and that make the planning worthwhile. And so the skills of planning, which becomes one of the work processes, must be planned with exactly the same care.

A concluding thought for this section is the recognition that process at times can be a product. As we look at the work processes in this section, we see a process that, when refined, becomes the product of directed effort. This, perhaps, can help to maintain a steady view of the kinds of responsibilities involved in directed self-management.

Examples of Strategy

1. *Ask an auditor to make a presentation of a specific support service, such as supply management. Explain how efficiency can be monitored in each work process.*
2. *Identify times when every member of the professional staff has a primary managing role in their day-to-day work.*

AUTONOMY AS PROCESS AND PRODUCT

Autonomy long has been perceived as a state of being that relieves the person of constraints imposed by others or by organizations. It has been considered synonymous by many with the evidence of freedom. Others may have seen the extremes of autonomy as a catastrophic type of anarchy. Perhaps it is time to look anew at the positive side of autonomy.

Few people would want to deny some degree of autonomy to all people. When an individual's autonomy conflicts with that of another, certainly that person feels that autonomy has been lost because of its possession by another. Autonomy should be looked at not as a state of being but as a process and a product. It is a process in that it supports the freeing of creativity and ingenuity of individuals. It is a product in that an awareness of it gives the individual possessing it a feeling of accomplishment. It might be helpful to look at some of the situations in which it is both process and product.

Those administrators, and other leaders who attempt to build a recognition of assurance in others, are using autonomy as a process. The recognition of assured security, consistency, and support releases others to accomplish some of the things of which they are capable. In this sense, the person who attempts to build this recognition of assurance and to give support to it uses autonomy as a process. Those who react to the efforts of one person or many, in building a sense of assurance in individuals in a group, may achieve a sense of belonging to the group. The sense of belonging is characteristic of a good working group in which all individuals are happy being a member of the group. The defense of people's rights to react to things they encounter is an act of preserving autonomy for that person. Defending the right of all people to act and react is a basic process in the development of an interactive relationship between members of an organization. In this sense, autonomy becomes a process and one that characterizes effective leadership.

Those who have had their rights to react defended will probably be inclined willingly to compromise when differences of opinions and policy are involved. The autonomy of defending the right to react results in the encouragement of compromise that expedites rewarding relationships to people in an organization. In this sense, autonomy is a product. When those in leadership positions in an organization seek the participation of organization members in modifying organizational goals, the result gives greater autonomy to individuals because of their participation in the choice of goals. The modification of organizational goals encourages autonomy and autonomy becomes a process. As individuals gain a sense of confidence in the fact that organizational leaders have accepted participation in the modification of organizational goals, those individuals are more likely to make a commitment to the modified goals of the organization. Here again, autonomy has been realized in the modification of organizational goals, and the increasing inclination of individual commitment to those goals becomes a product of autonomy.

The evaluating and auditing functions of an organization, which seek to match the evaluative criteria to the goals of the organization, constitute a process of preserving autonomy for individuals. This process, in all probability, will build an acceptance as well as a supportive stance on the part of members of the organization who may be objects of evaluation. The fact that the evaluative criteria are related to goals that each one in the organization had an opportunity to influence makes it possible to get a sense of autonomy from this process. The acceptance of an audit system by all members of an organization is more likely to result when there is a matching of evaluative criteria with organizational goals. This means that increased autonomy is realized and the acceptance of an audit system becomes a very desirable product.

Examples of Strategy

1. Invite staff members to list the sources of constraints they perceive as affecting the functions of their positions.

2. Seek oral and/or written suggestions from staff relating to ways of improving the mesh of evaluative criteria with the established goals of the system.

3. Critically analyze job descriptions to determine if the process or product of autonomy is lost.

STRUCTURING SELF-REALIZATION

Self-realization has been considered primarily a matter of individualized achievement. Self-realization too often has been regarded as the sole responsibility of the individual who seeks that state. There are many elements beyond the individual, however, that can affect it. Some of these are presented in this section.

Consistency in decision procedures, on the part of those who have leadership positions within the organization, gives people a sense of security in that they can anticipate future interaction. This consistency in the decision procedures results from policies developed as a result of the interaction of all members of the organization. Once the decision procedures have been accepted and have been pursued, in all decision situations, people gradually feel a sense of security in knowing what the future holds, at least with respect to how it will be confronted. Consistency is a structural part of the organizational operation and can encourage the self-realization of individuals within that organization.

A clear statement of position function can add to the security of individuals who enter into contracts with the school district. Knowing what the job is, in some detail, provides an opportunity to identify those expectations that may be assessed in an audit process. The knowledge of these expectations, in advance of individualized objectives and goals, can provide another avenue to self-realization.

Another structural aspect in the organization is the equality in the support benefits. Support benefits here go far beyond the equalization of monetary remuneration. Support benefits include the providing of adequate space, materials, time, and opportunities for planning and review. Commendation for work well done is a matter of equality when it is extended to all members of the organization. When support benefits appear based on a crony system of simple neglect on the part of some members of the organization, the structure destroys the concept of equality in support. Equality is a structural aspect of the organization that can lead to self-realization and, consequently, to self-management.

Full, accurate, and accessible information, on all occasions, about all aspects of organizational activity and purpose is a structural aspect of the organization that encourages self-realization. People who have to imagine the true state often will be deprived of the full, accurate, and accessible information that can be structured in an organization and that encourages self-realization. Each organization probably has a sanction system of some type. Sanction systems include both rewards and penalties that may become part of the structure of the organization. When the participants have an opportunity for input into the nature and application of the sanction system, they find it much more palatable. As participation in the sanction system is made available to all, is implemented for the total organization, and is applied consistently in the operation of the school, the sanction system will be supported and will accomplish what it is designed to do. The individual responsibility for organizational accomplishment may become a vital factor in directing individual effort. Then all of these structured elements of self-realization are brought to bear on the awareness of all individuals in the organization. A sense of responsibility is not something that can be imposed on people. It is a result of experience with the organizational operation. The self-realization achieved by individuals in the organization becomes the main support for the individual's sense of responsibility to organizational goals and processes.

Many variables are seen in the successful operation, or even the unsuccessful operation, of an organization. These variables go far beyond the individual employees and internal resources of the institution. Entirely too often, teachers have been asked to take sole responsibility for the success of the learning enterprise. Too often, administrators and supervisors have been solely responsible for providing an environment of friendly and supportive people for the school program. None of these things can be brought about in equal amounts. The variables differ from time to time and have different impacts on individuals and organizations at various times. It is important, then, that these variables be weighted in some manner as the accountability system is developed and carried forward. If the building is in an area in which disruptive noises continue through the day, location becomes a variable that needs to be weighted heavily in estimating the fulfillment of the purposes of the institution, and each individual's contribution to it. The accountability system must involve something more than people and their behaviors. It must involve many variables so that, once the weighting occurs, the structuring of the organization again provides good support for the self-realization and self-management of the individuals within that organization.

Examples of Strategy

1. *Institute small group discussions on, "What would help me most to become what I think I can be?"*

2. Initiate discussions with teachers individually or in small groups to determine what the system can provide to assist individual actualization. This discussion may follow the question, "How do you hope to teach, different from the ways in which you have been taught?"

3. Audit the consistency of administrative reward sanctions to fulfill the goal of providing some positive support to some aspect of each professional employee's work. This can accentuate the positive nature of developing and improving in one's work, rather than continuously auditing from points of weakness.

MANAGEMENT ACCEPTABILITY

The case for management, hopefully, has been achieved in this publication. At no point has there been the inclination to see management as the top priority of all kinds of activities that take place. As self-management increases, management becomes more effective and less of an imposition on the members of the organization. Previous sections of this chapter identified some of the elements that make management palatable and acceptable, as well as effective in accomplishing the purposes of the school organization.

The maintaining of unknowns at a minimum certainly is the first requirement for management acceptability. The current thrust to eliminate secret and undercover meetings is one element that can achieve greater citizen confidence in this country's government and its accomplishments. Just as this is true for people and their government, so it is true for employees of a school district and those who are responsible for the leadership-management of that school organization. Openness is a key to achieving management acceptability.

Reference has been made in this book to the opportunities for participants to become involved in many of the controls that bring about coordination of differing individuals within the school organization. The rule of mutuality is one way in which management acceptability can be achieved. If people understand how the organization operates and that there is mutuality of understanding and support, there will be a steady increase in respect for orderliness in the organization. Orderliness makes it possible for each individual to support the autonomy and participatory opportunities of others; orderliness makes it possible to establish the accountability of the organization as an organization.

The support services referred to earlier are means to achieve management acceptability. The adequacy and equality of support are essential to the administration of services that support the individual staff member's efforts to accomplish the position purposes within the organization.

The strength of organizational purpose is another means of achieving management acceptability. Poorly stated purposes, unknown purposes, day-to-day living, and getting by with whatever needs to be done at any moment do not constitute a strong organizational purpose. Purposes need to be clearly stated, well interpreted, and reviewed from time to time to determine whether they are adequate to the present and the anticipated future.

The individuals in an organization who exhibit logical thinking rather than expedient rationalization, when anything occurs or is to be sponsored, become a base for management acceptability. Logic calls for information and evidence. Rationalization is expediency that simply tries to find a reason for what already has been done or what has already been determined to do. Logic must replace rationalization if management is to establish acceptability.

Adversarity must no longer be the favorite game. There will be more opportunity for people to participate on an equal basis as intelligent beings when adversarity is no longer a natural state. The nursing of adversarity, either by management or by employees within an organization, cannot be a sound base for accomplishing organizational purposes. Adversarity has been used both by leaders and followers to achieve personal desires, resulting in a lack of confidence in both the leadership and management functions. Adversarity is not a leadership tool nor a device by which people can gain their own wishes at the expense of others. Through the elimination of adversarity and the substitution of some of the most positive types of relationships indicated in this chapter, possibly management no longer will be seen as the ogre of the organization. Rather, it will be thought of as an essential ingredient for a successful organizational effort, as well as for satisfaction among the individuals in that organization.

Examples of Strategy

1. *Release occasionally a personal concept of management philosophy that will help others to understand why you do what you do.*

2. *Identify an adversary relationship existing in your school system and isolate, by fact and logic, the differences of position and how they came about. Determine whether clarification of differences on the basis of fact and logic might ameliorate the condition of adversarity.*

3. *Provide, through a consistent sense of fairness, rewards for objectivity so that employees can deal comfortably and confidently with failure. It is necessary to avoid the positive results syndrome, where everything has to be worked out successfully as new ideas or thoughts are tested. A scientific, evidence-based form of management can go a long way toward removing community feelings that educators are pollyannaish stereotypes swimming around in a "goldfish bowl." It*

> can, in fact, improve on the confidence level and elevate the general dignity that people give the educational system. Isolate specific goals to be performed by staff and relate this procedure to creating an open reporting system that might be employed in a fair and consistent manner throughout the school district.

Hopefully, the discussion presented in this chapter and the examples of strategies may give some direction to the self-management of choice of direction for personal and professional behavior. It takes as much or more finesse to direct self than it does to direct others. Yet, it is a refreshing goal when one chooses to harmonize the contradictions with self and master the strategies of self-direction. The final chapter brings into focus the internal and external interactions between strategies and strategists.

MORE READING TO MANAGE

Bell, Terrel H. *A Performance Accountability System for School Administrators.* West Nyack, New York: Parker Publishing Co., 1974.

Bogue, E. G., and Robert L. Saunders. *The Educational Manager: Artist and Practitioner.* Worthington, Ohio: Charles A. Jones Publishing Co., 1976.

Mager, Robert R. *Goal Analysis.* Belmont, California: Fearon Publishers, 1972.

_____, and Peter Pipe. *Analyzing Performance Problems.* Belmont, California: Fearon Publishers, 1970.

Sciara, Frank J., and Richard K. Jantz. *Accountability in American Education.* Boston: Allyn & Bacon, 1972.

chapter

16

Strategies and the Strategists

The opening chapter in this book dealt with management acceptability. A number of reasons were given for placing such high importance on the acceptability of management by those involved in
organizational activity. The strong belief is expressed often that it is as
impossible to manage people who do not accept management as it is
to exercise authority over someone who does not recognize that
authority. Such phenomena appear often in human interaction. There
also was an enumeration of a number of states and actions that make
management effective and acceptable. While the focus of this book
is on the strategies of instructional management, the relationship
between management and those categorized as staff members or
unclassified employees makes the difference between successful or
unsuccessful management.

The kinds of actions that characterize those responsible for
initiating management relationships constitute an important concern
throughout many of the chapters. The thrust of the intervening chapters, that is, between 1 and 16, is to explore many of the more
pertinent areas involved in the behaviors of management and in the
interactions that result from responses to management impacts. In
those fifteen chapters there are many definitions, designations of
administrative purpose, identification of administrative involvements,
broad participation of all people involved in the organizational effort,
and key behavioral characteristics that support the concept of
management acceptability. In most sections of those chapters, there
are administrative strategies. The strategies are not to be used as a

manual for selecting or designing strategies; they are intended to stimulate thinking along the lines of custom-built strategy development within each school system.

Chapter 16 brings into focus many different items discussed in the previous chapters. It attempts to relate the quality of the person (strategist) to the managing styles (strategies) that result in an influence impact on all people involved in the organizational effort. There are numerous places in which these managing styles are explored with respect to the responses of the recipients of the management impact. There are many occasions where earlier chapters are brought into focus so that the suggested strategy delivery systems become a compact summary of the other discussions.

The authors wish to show that strategy patterns are reflections of the individual strategist. It is important that the focus be kept not only on the strategies but also on the strategists.

THE CASE AGAINST POWER DOMINANCE

The long held concept of the leader, administrator, or manager as a possessor of great power has been difficult to infiltrate with more humanistic thoughts and actions. Human beings have a great capacity to build an ego image on power that is felt and exhibited in the administrative position. When the power of the administrator becomes the leadership goal, power itself becomes an obsession. When power becomes an obsession, it negates the opportunity for interaction that should occur among all people involved in the organizational endeavor.

Power, as a dominant characteristic of the administrator, violates the basic concept of desired interaction between people in all positions in the organization. Power, when it shuts off the opportunity for increased interaction among staff members, puts authority in the position of flowing downward from a supercontroller. Authority that originates from the staff is more effective than authority from power-crazed administrators.

Part of the power concept of the management process has been the use of rewards and penalties as a means of control. During the age of dominance by the so-called highest administrative position, the concept of power practically always existed and many devices for "keeping people in line" were developed and used. Society in recent years has become more enlightened. Most people now meet a higher educational requirement, controlled by certification, than was true a few decades ago. As the level of required education increased in order to work in educational programs and organizations, the enlightened state of the staff made it more difficult for a strong and dominant leader to bring into submission those in the so-called lower levels of the hierarchical arrangement.

Recent years have produced a much more legally protective society than experienced earlier. There are many more opportunities for people at any level of an organization to use the facilities of the law and the court in order to gain what they perceive as their own just dues. Certainly the legal protectiveness extends to people who feel that they have been aggrieved by someone in the so-called upper levels of management.

Management by power alone is antithetical to the increased dispersal of responsibilities. As the drive for accountability extends, there is the need to attach specific responsibilities to practically all of the assigned tasks and positions. This dispersal would not be effectively possible if management by power was the sole concept. In recent years, lower level hierarchy representatives began to use the powers of organization and negotiation. Many early attempts found that people high in the professional organization were as inclined to be power managers and administrators as were the school administrators and managers. The representatives of these organizations only now are beginning to see the limits of their own power over the members and to seek some other means of achieving the benefits that can come from organized efforts.

Leadership strategies must place increased emphases on total group power to achieve goals, rather than on personal power over other persons. There are better strategies of management than those that depend alone on power dominance.

SELFLESSNESS MAY NOT BE A VIRTUE

The idea of selflessness is used here to gain a concept of the opposite state of power dominance. In the case of power dominance, the individual sees self as a person who knows best and who, because of this state, has the unique prerogative to impose the perceived superiority on others. Really, the concept here goes from power madness to zero influence; the individual seeks to minimize the unique personal characteristics possessed and to conceal acknowledgement as a contributor. In this case, it is completely antithetical to the management concept in which leadership must be exercised and can be observed.

The urge to refrain from exposing personal unique expertise by organizing the efforts of all people involved in the education program means that an individual seeks only to identify the self of others, not to influence them. It is somewhat characteristic of a vacuum—a vacuum has nothing to give. It is unfortunate when the individual seeks to create this kind of restraint over self so that whatever unique expertise is possessed will not be identified with the person or the self. It has the appearance of nobility to be so gracious to other people. On the other hand, some ego-awareness is essential to the analysis of any problem and to the identification of the true characteristics of any task to be performed. This ego-awareness does not have to exhibit power dominance, but it can be much more aggressive in structuring an environment in which others can exercise their unique expertise. In this way, a much more wholesome concept of management emerges. The emphasis should be on what to do, rather than on what not to do. Those who seek a high degree of selflessness eventually achieve it only by studying what not to do for fear that what is done might deprive someone else of displaying their own expertise and contributions to a total effort.

An earlier indication was that management cannot exist unless people accept management efforts. It indicated also that authority does not exist just because a person wants to exercise it, but rather because others are willing to accept it. Any major efforts toward selflessness as a status will result in a loss of status, as well as the respect of those whom the individual should be able to influence. This also means that a loss of status is a loss of resources needed to maintain stimulus in group action. This was discussed at some length in chapter 4, "Reciprocities As Building Blocks." Reciprocity means reciprocation between people who observe an equal right to participate. This is impossible when one person blocks out others or blocks out oneself as a contributor to the group enterprise.

The loss of interest in the self may lead to lost insight into the self of another. This is a major misfortune for those who try not to impose their own dominant power on others but, in the process, lose the capacity for sensitivity to the self of another, necessary to any person in a management position. This is equally true for the position of assisting peers. The belittling or negation of self places a great burden not only on the person's creativity but on the creativity that might be generated by equal interaction opportunities with many others. A response practically always follows an impact and, if the leadership impact is reduced to zero, there can be no response on the part of others. This concept is discussed at considerable length in chapter 2, "Instructional Impact-Response Areas." It does not apply just to instructional areas, but is a way of describing the interaction that occurs between two or more people.

Selflessness also may be a strategy for noncommittance. If this is true, it certainly introduces a weakness into the performance of the person who becomes selfless, as well as into the contribution that ought to be made to the entire activity in association with others. Realistically, while people do not want an individual to be exceedingly dominant over them, they do want other people to be themselves. It is important to have a sound concept of what the individual can be and to let other people help be just that.

ETHICS SUPPORT STABILITY

The previous section of this chapter indicated some of the unfortunate things that can happen when a person tends to reduce self to a non-influence stature. People simply must stand for something. If they do not, it will affect the kinds of activities and the vigor with which they pursue those activities until they have some known goals to pursue. There can be no known goals and no direction when we seek to be nothing.

The relationships between purpose and effort were presented in chapter 3. The emphasis was on the synthesis of purpose and effort; the individual knows what the goals are and puts forth effort to pursue those goals. All of the people in the school situation have a fairly common understanding of what the goals are for the institution. They understand the mutual obligations that must exist if all the varied things to be done in educational programs are to be accomplished. There must be substance to the relationship among people and the recognition of common goals—the acceptance of mutual obligation is the substance of that relationship.

A mutually supportive relationship between members of the instructional staff invites continuity of shared responsibilities. This gives greater strength to the goals that are established, the objectives that are set, and the activities or processes that are chosen to reach the goals. Shared responsibility must occur not only at the process level but also at the goal selection level. The substance of the relationships inferred here can displace unrecognized personal assumptions. In other sections of the book, references have been made to the fact that assumptions sometimes prove the basis for action. Assumptions serve as guidelines for chosen behaviors as a person goes about the assigned tasks. If these personal assumptions remain unrecognized, they must be displaced by the shared responsibilities and the recognized substances of interaction among the people in the organization. In such instances, gains are made.

Ethics tend to guide value priority determinations. Stability is gained from the value system that does so much to make people behave as they do. There is no way to seek avoidance through neutrality when one recognizes that there are ethical responsibilities involved in the acceptance of a position in the educational organization. To be neutral with respect to ethics is to have no ethics. To be neutral with respect to value priorities is to lack those values that guide actions.

This results in a haphazard pattern of behavior as the individual goes about the professional task of education.

The individuality of people involved in any group enterprise often carries conflict potential. If there is much opportunity, as indicated above, to seek a mutuality of understanding and of relationships, a rational view of conflict potentials probably will result. Here again, ethical standards tend to incline people toward those whose rational views provide a way of resolving conflict, if not eliminating conflict potentials.

Ethics outlast management decisions on guidelines and regulations. It is important, as ethical standards of behavior are chosen by professionals, that thought be given to their general application to the great variety of activities that occur within the organization. Ethics provide stability because they provide a stimulant to people-oriented types of strategies of action and management. People orientation, as opposed to power orientation or material orientation, can be the most creative structure for the interaction of people as they share their responsibilities in the total demands of the instructional program.

PARTICIPATION NEEDS PURPOSE

Reference was made earlier in the chapter to the inclination of people in leadership or administrative positions to use power dominance as the primary mode of accomplishing the task presumed unique to the position. Reference has been made at numerous points in the book to the participation of all people involved in the operation. Those who are the objects of management are involved in the activity and should have the opportunity to participate in the determination of the management design.

Participation in any activity cannot avoid increasing the interaction among people. Interaction among people is much more likely to increase creativity rather than to stifle that creativity. The chief purpose of management should be the increased participation of all involved, so that positive results ensue and the unique contributions of each person are not stifled. People have reasons for acting the way they do. Participation in goal determination, in process selection, in evaluation procedures, and in all other activities involved in the support of an education program gives people reasons for acting. One reason was discussed specifically in chapter 5, "Loyalties and Influences." It is not enough for people to have loyalty as the only reason for acting. The participation and the increased interaction can provide many more ideational bases for acting that do not destroy the stimulants of loyalty.

People tend to display their own expertise best. They might appreciate the unique things that others can do, but they probably could not adopt or adapt effectively what somebody else does as their own mode of behavior. Their own talent is unique, but that does not signify contradictive, competitive, or conflictive behaviors with the uniqueness of others. This was explored in considerably more detail in chapter 6, "Talent and Decisions." Reference was made earlier to the fact that individuals acting as individuals tend to possess potential conflict sources. Here, participation and increased interaction can provide opportunities for resolving individual differences prior to the generation of a destructive conflict.

Many individuals are engaged in tasks of their own selection. But almost every individual, at the same time, is involved in some task that has been delegated, either by the leader in any particular segment of the organization or by mutual consent with peers. Delegation means a dispersal of assignments. Coordination becomes the key requisite. Delegation and coordination were discussed in chapters 9 and 10 in much greater detail than summarized here. At this point, they need to be brought into the picture again as the matter of strategies and strategists is discussed. Coordination can be achieved by many different ways. One thing basic to all situations, however, is that coordination assumes a commonality of purpose. Until the goals have been determined and commonly accepted, they will not serve as the focal point by which the many individualized contributions to the educational program can be brought into a coordinated relationship.

The common purpose or goal requires a clear identification and definition if it is to serve as a common target for all. If participation increases in the determination of goals and purposes, it is more likely that individuals working in the organization will find ways to coordinate their postures. It is essential to maintain an effective two-way communication system if participation is to occur. There is no better way for the commonality of goals and purposes to be known and held than through the free exchange of thoughts about action. Participation begins with the goal determination rather than with the selection of alternative work processes. This was discussed in chapter 8 and is only alluded to here as one of the essentials in the purposes that bring about increased and effective participation. This kind of interaction can result in a satisfying experience for individuals. As this satisfaction is maintained, it is extended into a more productive group effort.

HARMONIZING INDIVIDUAL AND GROUP PURPOSES

Goals and objectives are not the same. This was discussed at length in chapter 3, "Synthesis of Purpose and Effort." The goals are the general targets that must be held by all involved in a group enterprise. Objectives are the more immediate targets, but they must be related to the general goals. The objectives have the capacity to organize the individual and group processes so that they can be harmonized in a coordinated attack.

Goals provide the vehicle by which the many unique objectives can be related rather than conflicting. The multitude of tasks that must be accommodated in the school organization require a wide range of abilities, skills, and understandings on the part of the professional staff. The assigned tasks may not always be the first choice of the individual recipient. It is recognized, however, someone must accommodate those tasks. If harmony is to be achieved between the individuals receiving assignments with the total group enterprise composed of the supportive relationship of the many individuals, there must be a rationale for the assignment. If a rationale is established prior to or at the time of the assignment, there is much less probability that conflict or resentment will develop as a result of the assignment. People are rational persons, as a rule, and do respond to the logic behind task assignments.

The unique objectives that go with each task do not require that they be done by only one person. Tasks may be alternated between several people or they may require the input of more than one person at any one time. The objective for each task is unique to that task and, were this not so, there would be no way of knowing when the common goals were being served. With many immediate objectives serving a major goal, there are certain to be a multitude of unique behaviors and actions related to that common goal. Here again, if the rationale is well established at the time the tasks are allocated to individuals or groups, consensus can be achieved. Once consensus has been achieved, acceptance has occurred and the individuals can proceed with the unique assignments for each of the task objectives.

The judgment as to whether harmony between the individual and group purposes has been achieved may be tested by the criteria that are used to judge the contribution of individuals to the group effort. At the same time, criteria must be selected to judge the effectiveness of that group effort. Well-established criteria involve participants in their selection and in the determination of evidences to be used in making judgments with respect to those criteria. This provides the harmonizing of effort for individuals working on separate tasks within the total group effort.

The strategy to keep in mind while working toward harmony of individual and group purposes is the recognition of the need to control change speed. It is very probable that there will be many occasions when change must occur even though it is a minor adaptation of things that are being done presently. The speed of the change effort must be considered in light of the harmony that has been achieved within the group—harmony achieved is harmony to be maintained. Strategies must build not only toward harmonizing individual and group purposes but also toward harmonizing the change of individual and group purposes that may become necessary with the change decisions.

STRATEGY DELIVERY SYSTEMS

Some benchmarks of good strategy delivery systems can be identified here as giving direction to a way of thinking about the total responsibility for strategy. The leadership style might best be characterized by an invitation to success. This was the main thrust of chapter 14, "Direction through Indirection." The whole point was to develop a leadership style that did not rely on power dominance but rather on gentility in working through assistance, suggestion, and collaboration. This is the pattern of leadership that emphasizes the success of the individual, rather than the success of the leader who might command that things be done a certain way and at a certain level.

Goal achievement is another means of judging whether the delivery system has been working. If goal achievement can be the dominant point of observation, rather than power realization, there is more likelihood that all participants will have a good experience in the group enterprise and will be much more amenable to continuing and improving that process. The previous section mentioned that a rationale would help to establish harmony among individuals within the group. This means that every action has a reason. The individual need not develop that reason but certainly those involved in the total enterprise must see a reason for each action. A satisfactory delivery system never judges action that has been established only for action's sake.

Developing action readiness is another benchmark for the delivery system and a basic part of the strategy of stimulation. Developing action readiness depends on the clear understanding of all involved as to what the purposes are, what goals are to be achieved, and some agreements on the alternatives that might be chosen for the appropriate behaviors. Those responsible for the stimulation of others must be sensitive to the individual actor temperament. In other words, it is better to have people happy in their work than to walk through it as though it were a dull experience. The variations in the attitudes and dispositions of people need to be sensed so that others working in the organization and particularly in the so-called leadership roles, will quickly recognize the temperament of people and try to keep them disposed toward creative activity.

Those who give careful thought to strategy delivery systems will be as aware of the environment as of the individuals working in the environment. A strategy of stimulating creative and enthusiastic actions can result from favorable working conditions. This then becomes a part of the strategy delivery system.

Along with a keen sensitivity to the individuals working within the group, recognize both the contributors and the contributions. Earlier in the book, mention was made several times of the art of commendation. Commendation can develop bonds between individuals within the group, and between individuals and the organizational activity. It is more than perfunctory congratulations to the individual who has produced some excellent outcomes in the educational effort. A telephone call is not nearly as personal as a face-to-face exchange between the achiever and the person recognizing the achievement. To make it even more stimulating, it might be well to establish a pattern of written commendations to individual staff members or groups, when outstanding contributions have been made to the institutional efforts. This is stimulating because individuals appreciate visual evidence of the commendation. Further, there is statisfaction in being able to share that commendation and this is possible when it is written rather than spoken.

Another benchmark of the delivery system that was referenced in a previous chapter is that of controlling the action pace. This gives each individual an opportunity to devote thinking time to the responsibility and to the manner in which the responsibility will be met. If the action pace is kept in mind, perhaps the changes in processes and purposes will be slow enough so that interaction through communication can maintain the rewarding relationships within the group. In this way, there will be more mutual supportiveness than would occur if people felt pressed for speed, especially when they would like to approach their tasks much more deliberately.

A delivery system must have the capacity to register the fact that, when you have attained a goal, you know that the attainment occurred. Many times, the sense of achievement settles on process and people feel that, if the process continues, they are contributing. But, when the task is completed, it is not necessary to drop it but rather to know that it has been achieved and to take rational action from that point on.

The final benchmark to the strategy delivery system is the quality of feedback. If the people engaged in the activity can report in some form to those who encourage them or even assign them to the task, participant reaction to the assignment and to its outcomes will be evidenced. Good feedback improves with known utilization of the processes available in the total enterprise. Feedback becomes the material by which judgments can be made to determine next steps.

EVALUATION OF STRATEGIES

Many references have been made throughout the book to the necessity for selecting the right criteria and choosing the right kind of data in order to have an evidence-based judgment when evaluations take place. In the discussion of evaluation of strategies in this section, the authors have chosen to raise one question with respect to each chapter in the book. Thus, the answering of these questions becomes not only a pattern of the evaluation of strategies but an evaluation of the authors' strategies in choosing the particular organization for discussion of strategies for instructional management. These follow in numbered form with the chapter referenced.

1. Is management acceptance management effectiveness? (Chapter 1) It is important, as has been established, that management be accepted if it is to gain its established purposes. The importance here, however, is to make further assessment as to whether the acceptance really did lead to outcomes that could be identified with the organizational purposes. Acceptance is a vehicle to effectiveness and must not be considered an end in itself.

2. Do impacts and responses include all of instructional management? (Chapter 2) The point of this question is to make certain that all of the most relevant variables that can be identified in impact and response have been viewed. In all probability, this will not include all of instructional management. There may be individualized variables that cannot be identified as management influence in the form of impact and response. The important thing, however, is to determine whether enough impacts and responses have been identified and controlled so that instructional management can be achieved at the level desired.

3. Is purpose and effort real or synthetic? (Chapter 3) The answer to this question must be found in the feedback from individuals at the delivery end of the planning and action. Here again, effective purpose and effort will produce the achievement of goals. In this case, it is real when the goals have not been modified for the purpose of evaluation. The relationship between purpose and effort, however, could be a synthetic type of rationalization.

4. Can reciprocities be identified in program development? (Chapter 4) The idea of reciprocities as building blocks for group action and accomplishment has been stated. The important thing now is to determine whether the program development, if the assessment starts there, would at the same time identify the processes by which it was developed and whether the reciprocities established between people were a force in the program development.

5. To what extent do loyalties influence? (Chapter 5) A case was made for the influence of loyalties on the behaviors chosen by people in the organization. It was never declared that other influence sources did not exist; rather, loyalties seem to be a major influence factor and were explored as such. Now the problem in evaluation is whether other influences can be identified. If they can be, a determination must be made of the extent to which they influenced the behavior of others.

6. *What percent of decisions utilized talent? (Chapter 6)*   Decisions can be made off-the-cuff or after careful deliberations by many people, by individuals, and by many other means. The important thing here is to determine the extent to which available staff talent has been used in the decision process.

7. *Do the categories of work process include all instructional management tasks? (Chapter 7)*   The categories of work process were arbitrarily selected but based on the rationale that comes out of many different analyses of the instructional program. The important thing now is to analyze the instructional program, to identify the kinds of management tasks that are needed, and then to determine whether each of those management tasks can be assigned to an established work process area.

8. *How many work processes have identifiable goals? (Chapter 8)*   The question is whether an instructional or educational goal is related more to one work process than to another. It is not to infer that it makes any particular difference, but rather that the analysis ought to have a system so that the processes can be viewed in terms of the institutional goals that are to be achieved. It is possible to evaluate each category of work process to determine whether it has made an expected and appropriate contribution to goal achievement.

9. *Are delegations defined clearly and supported appropriately? (Chapter 9)*   Delegation has been held as much more important than perfunctory action. Delegation should join the required work processes with the best abilities and talent available within the staff. It is not particularly difficult to assess whether the delegations have been defined. Those who have received the delegations could very quickly indicate the extent to which they had been informed prior to initiating action on the tasks. The support referred to here is what would come from the established rationale that we could use to justify the delegation.

10. *Are tasks coordinated by both goal and process? (Chapter 10)*   The tendency to categorize things sometimes raises a question as to whether categories become so important that cooperation is thwarted. That question is raised here to indicate that information might well be gathered to determine the procedures by which coordination took place, and the extent to which the process was chosen to best suit the task activities leading to the chosen goal.

11. Do the preparations for action include all relevant variables? (Chapter 11) Antecedents to action are extremely important in the minds of these authors. It is not satisfactory simply to start action as though a switch had been closed, a button pushed, or a whistle blown. It takes time and planning to make sure that the expectations that go with an assignment have the proper time arrangements, material arrangements, and abilities available to those who accept the responsibility. These are the relevant types of variables that must be viewed to determine whether appropriate preparatory action has been observed.

12. Does continuing evaluation satisfy all audit requirements? (Chapter 12) The drive for an audit of outcomes is prevalent and perhaps lasting. It is important, then, to question whether continuing evaluation will produce all the evidence that an audit would require. It could be held, with some logic, that the audit plan should be drafted so that all continuing evaluative data might be used in the audit and, to that extent, it would satisfy the audit requirements.

13. Have too many people, conditions, and expectations been included in the accountability system? (Chapter 13) The multifaceted characteristics of accountability are almost frightening, primarily because, so many times, it seems that people in education programs are being tossed this way and that by other people of widely varying and possibly conflicting purposes. It is better, however, to identify these characteristics and to know that they are there, rather than have them spring up unexpectedly. So the question is whether there should be an attempt to limit or curtail the number of different pressures that can be brought on those in the educational activities, to make sure that an accountability system has been established and is satisfying.

14. Is gentility an inappropriate antidote for powerful aggression? (Chapter 14) There is always the danger of being labeled as soft unless power is displayed. It may be a contest between the sensitivity of one person to another and the dominance of one person over another. The real test is whether gentility will accomplish as much as power dominance or aggression in relation to the amount of work done and the quality of the outcomes. With the conflicting attitudes toward management itself, it is well to raise this question to determine the strategy delivery systems that might be most appropriate.

15. Is self-management evidence of an avoidance device for efficiency? (Chapter 15) Self-management might appear to be a way of avoiding submission to the management of those in command post positions. It is well to gather some evidence as to whether increases in self-management cause the efficiency and effectiveness of outcome to deteriorate. The major answer here must be in the outcomes, and not in the management incidence or arrangement.

16. Can strategies be developed by unskilled strategists? (Chapter 16) The whole point of this chapter was to relate the strategies to the strategists. These authors believe that the strategy must be developed by skilled strategists. The skills envisioned are the capabilities to develop strategies of management that will stimulate those talents that assure success in the instructional program.

STRATEGIES MAKE THE STRATEGISTS

People are much affected by what they do. Perhaps this seems inconsistent with the matter of selecting goals and planning processes as though each individual had an ability or expertise apart from the substance of the planning and action. All of that can occur, but it must be recognized that those experienced in teaching tend to think like a teacher when analyzing those phenomena unrelated to teaching responsibilities. The same thing can be said about those in management positions. They become more like the things that they do and, in that sense, the strategies do make the strategists.

Actions have proven time and again to be stronger than position. Holding the title to a position that infers leadership and control does not mean necessarily that the persons in such positions automatically behave as might be expected. The actions of those people, however, are observable and are much more likely to determine any judgment about the effectiveness of the persons than the description of the position expectations.

Open strategies are made by open-minded people—people who profit from interaction with others and who are inclined to view alternatives in the process of making decisions. It is much better to have open-minded people working with open strategies than to have obscured strategies dominated by devious people. Confidence in the individual and group purposes and processes can be affected mightily by the open or obscure nature of the developed strategies or the strategy development processes.

People can make creative strategists of themselves primarily by developing creative strategies. The strategies that prove to be creative are the ones that not only accomplish the group goals and purposes but that, in the process of achieving, develop the creativity in other people. There is no limit to the amount of creativity that can be generated, providing the strategies are developed in a creative manner.

Management is orderliness in operational patterns, and strategies are the quintessence of management.

STRATEGIZED READING

Bowles, Harold W., and James A. Davenport. *Introduction to Educational Leadership.* New York: Harper and Row, Publishers, 1975.

Bureau of Business Practice, Inc. *The Magic Meeting Minimizer.* Waterford, Connecticut: Croft-NEI Publications, 1975.

DeBruyn, Robert L. *Causing Others to Want Your Leadership.* Manhattan, Kansas: R. L. DeBruyn and Associates, Publisher, 1976.

Hamilton, Norman K. *New Techniques for Effective Administration.* West Nyack, New York: Parker Publishing Company, 1975.

Hyman, Ronald T. *School Administrator's Handbook of Teacher Supervision and Evaluation Methods.* Englewood Cliffs: Prentice-Hall, Inc., 1975.

Jensen, Gale Edward. *Problems and Principles of Human Organization in Educational Systems.* Ann Arbor: Ann Arbor Publishers, 1969.

Wadia, Maneck S. *Management and the Behavioral Sciences.* Boston: Allyn & Bacon, Inc., 1968.

Index